ASPECTS OF LEEDS

RO   1/2

ASPECTS *of* LEEDS

1

Discovering Local History

Edited by
Lynne Stevenson Tate

Series Editor
Brian Elliot

Wharncliffe Publishing Limited

First Published in 1998 by
Wharncliffe Publishing
an imprint of
Pen and Sword Books,
47 Church Street, Barnsley,
South Yorkshire. S70 2AS

Copyright © Wharncliffe Publishing 1998

*For up-to-date information on other titles produced under the
Wharncliffe imprint, please telephone or write to:*

Wharncliffe Publishing
FREEPOST
47 Church Street
Barnsley
South Yorkshire S70 2BR
Telephone (24 hours): 01226 - 734555

ISBN: 1-871647-38-X

A CIP catalogue record of this book is available from the
British Library

Cover photograph: Crowds queuing for *The Thing* outside
the Tower cinema. *From the collection of Mr R H Whincup*

Printed in Great Britain by
Redwood Books, Trowbridge, Wiltshire

CONTENTS

INTRODUCTION..................................*Lynne M Stevenson Tate*   **6**

1. BRIGGATE AND ITS PUBS..................................*Barrie Pepper*   **9**

2. AT THE FLICKS..................................*Robert Preedy*   **23**

3. A VISIT TO THE PALACE..................................*June Walton Pearce*   **35**

4. A LETTER TO THE EDITOR: READERS' LETTERS TO THE LEEDS   **37**
   PRESS, 1795–1850..................................*David Thornton*

5. THE HEATONS OF *CLAREMONT*..................................*Dorothy Payne*   **57**

6. ST CHAD'S, A HOME FOR WAIFS AND STRAYS: A HISTORY OF   **77**
   HOLLIN HALL, 1894–1996..................................*Samantha J Fisher*

7. NOTHING BETTER: A SHORT HISTORY OF THE CITY SCHOOL OF   **93**
   COMMERCE..................................*Lynne M Stevenson Tate*

8. WOODHOUSE MOOR..................................*Edna Bews*   **109**

9. THE MOSAICS OF ST AIDAN'S..................................*Barrie Pepper*   **119**

10. BRAMLEY TAKES OFF..................................*Anthony Silson*   **125**

11. THE BEGINNINGS OF GOTT'S MILL
    IN LEEDS..................................*John Goodchild*   **143**

12. LOOKING BACK: MEMORIES OF
    MILL WORK..................................*June Walton Pearce*   **155**

13. THE LEEDS JEWISH COMMUNITY: A SKETCH OF ITS HISTORY
    AND DEVELOPMENT..................................*Murray Freedman*   **161**

14. GYPSIES IN LEEDS LOCAL HISTORY..................................*Freda Matthews*   **175**

CONTRIBUTORS..................................**191**

INDEX..................................**205**

INTRODUCTION

by Lynne M Stevenson Tate

The last decade has seen an ever increasing number of books appearing on the history of Leeds. These have ranged from hardback, fully illustrated histories, through to short pamphlets produced by some of the many local history societies and privately published family histories. The growing interest in local and family history in the city is well served as Leeds has an excellent local and family history library based at the Central Library which is manned by knowledgeable and helpful staff. Local and family history courses are run at many of the city's Further Education Colleges, and both Leeds University and the Leeds Metropolitan University offer post-graduate courses in local and regional history.

Aspects of Leeds is the latest venture of Wharncliffe Publishing Limited in the field of local history. They have previously published *Aspects of Barnsley*, which has currently reached volume five, *Aspects of Rotherham* 1 and 2, *Aspects of Doncaster* and *Aspects of Sheffield*. These serve to offer writers, local history groups, local and family historians, opportunities to have their work published and made available to a wider readership. The authors who have contributed to this volume of *Aspects of Leeds* are drawn from across the city and the surrounding areas. Some are 'old-hands' at writing and publishing articles and books whereas others are 'first-timers'. The range and subject of their articles are equally as varied, and there should be much of interest to the general reader and the academic alike.

Although unplanned, when collected together the subjects of the articles began to suggest a number of common themes. In particular leisure, industry, society and immigrant and migrant communities. Such categorisations however are to be regarded as a general guide only, as many of the articles address more than one of these themes.

The inns and pubs of Briggate have long been a feature of the city and Barrie Pepper takes the reader on a short walk through their long and varied history while introducing some famous and infamous visitors. Public houses were places of much social activity, be it business or commercial lunches, mutual aid societies, political meetings or pure socializing. They have not been places where 'respectable' women were to be found until recently.

It was not until the advent of cinema houses that women and children, as well as courting couples, found congenial places of entertainment outside the home and church. Robert Preedy lifts the lid on the culture of cinema-going in Leeds. The inevitable decline in cinema audiences with the advent of television resulted in a large number of cinema closures, which are charted here in the article with real regret. The article ends on a more positive note of the advent of the new multiplex cinemas. June Walton Pearce was one of the thousands of children who attended the matinees, and shared one of the 'courting seats' when older. She casts a humorous eye back to those days when visits to the cinema had a certain magical quality all of their own.

Leeds has been a place which has had a long tradition of top quality journalism, and it has been the home of newspapers from the *Leeds Intelligencer* to the *Leeds Mercury* in the early eighteenth century to the *Yorkshire Post* and the *Yorkshire Evening Post* of today. Leeds residents have written letters to the editors of these papers throughout all this time. David Thornton introduces a thoughtful and well-chosen selection of readers' letters between 1795 and 1850 that reflect the social concerns of the times; from Oastler on factory reform, to chimney sweeping and the ever-present problem of smoke and pollution!

A one-time resident of Leeds, Samuel Smiles wrote a bestselling book on self-improvement called *Self Help*. One feels that he would have been in favour of all the 'improving' activities undertaken by the Heaton family and their friends which are so ably chronicled by Dorothy Payne. Dr Heaton lived in the Little Woodhouse area of Leeds in a house called *Claremont*, which today is the home of the Thoresby Society, the Victorian Society and Yorkshire Archaeological Society. Along with the ethos of self-improvement, a strong philanthropic movement existed in Victorian society. The late nineteenth century saw the birth of many charities and societies that are still active today. Samantha Fisher has traced the history of *Hollin Hall*, in Far Headingley back to it's beginnings as one of the first Church of England's homes for waifs and strays. Here in this home girls who suffered some form of physical disability were placed and trained in knitting and laundry skills that would enable them to lead useful and productive lives. The parishoners of St Chad's Church and many local worthies were active supporters and benefactors of this home.

Edna Bews was brought up in the area of Leeds known as Woodhouse Moor, and her reminiscences of the events that were held on the moor, such as brass band concerts, the Woodhouse Feast and various touring exhibitions, will strike a chord with many a Leeds resident. Past and present students at Leeds University might find it interesting to read something of the varied history of the area in which they have lived and studied.

In earlier years Leeds' expanding commercial and industrial sector depended on privately run commercial colleges and schools to provide them with the fully trained staff they required. Lynne Stevenson Tate charts the history of one of these schools, the City School of Commerce.

It is a well-know saying that you can't judge a book by its cover, so neither can you tell what's inside a building until you enter. St Aidan's Church in Harehills is home to the hidden treasure of a mosaic created by Sir Frank Brangwyn which represents the life of the saint in Britain. Barrie Pepper knows these mosaics well and has produced a short article to introduce the gem to a wider audience.

The presence of the woollen textile industry has been one of the major driving forces behind the continued growth and prosperity of Leeds. Three articles deal with some aspects of this growth. Anthony Silson takes a look at Bramley and shows how the rapid growth in population was closely tied to the number of available jobs in the newly developing industrial base in the township. John Goodchild's article concentrates on one of the early entrepreneurs, Benjamin Gott, and the building of his integrated mill complex at Bean Ing. Gott was not an easy man to do business with as his mill architect found out to his cost. His letter of resignation to Gott, setting out his exact reasons for resigning is a masterpiece of 'gentlemanly' invective. For many children leaving school until the late 1960s, the mills were the only possible employers. June Walton Pearce remembers starting work in the mills, and her subsequent career as a 'burler and mender'.

Murray Freedman and Freda Matthews provide articles on Leeds' migrant and immigrant communities. Murray gives a brief overview of Leeds Jewish history from the fifteenth century to the present day. Freda's article on the gypsy community is a welcome addition on a people whose history is very rarely a matter of public record.

My thanks are due to all those at Wharncliffe who have initiated me gently into the complexities of the world of publishing, after I have spent so many years selling the finished product: to Brian Elliott, the series editor, Charles Hewitt, Roni Wilkinson, Paula Brennan, Mike Parsons and Barbara Bramall. Finally, to Alan Twiddle who first thought that I could do it; to Roz Radmore who said I should do it; and to Michael who gave me confidence to do it, and then supported me through all the stages of its gestation; my thanks and gratitude to you all.

1. BRIGGATE AND ITS PUBS

by Barrie Pepper

BRIGGATE IS THE FOCAL POINT of Leeds and its present day buildings and character reflect its historic past. In the alleyways and yards off this main thoroughfare were many of the early inns and taverns of the city and at one time the area teemed with over-crowded and unsanitary housing. The Moot Hall which served as town hall and courthouse stood in the middle of Briggate for more than two centuries; the markets were nearby along with the cloth halls, the corn exchange, the parish church and other buildings that have made Leeds for centuries the most important city in Yorkshire.[1]

Leeds Bridge, the bridge from which Briggate got its name, was the site of the ancient cloth market until 1684 when it moved into Briggate itself. Ralph Thoresby, the city's most famous historian, wrote of a practice called the Brig end shots:

> . . . *where the clothier may, together with his Pot o' Ale, have a Noggin o' Porridge, and a trencher of either Boiled or Roast Meat for Twopence.*

Defoe wrote favourably of this practice in 1724 in his *A Tour Through the Whole Island of Great Britain.*

> *Leeds is a large, wealthy and populous town. It stands on both sides of the river AIRE . . . and the whole is joined by a stately and prodigiously strong Stone Bridge, so large and wide, that formerly the Cloth Market was kept . . . on the very bridge itself; and therefore the refreshment given the Clothiers by the Inn-keepers is called the BRIGG-SHOTT to this Day.*[2]

But another and earlier traveller, Celia Fiennes was not so compli-mentary when she came to Leeds in 1698:

> . . . *here if one calls for a tankard of ale which is always a groat – it is the only dear thing all over Yorkshire, their ale is very strong – but for paying this groat for your ale you may have a slice of meat either hot or cold according to the time of day you call, or else butter and cheese gratis into the bargain . . . there is still this custom on a market day at Leeds the sign of Ye Bush just by the bridge, a custom called the Bridge End Club* (Figure 1).[3]

The Inns and Pubs of Briggate, Leeds, around 1850

Where pubs are marked in **bold** it indicates that there is still a pub on the site though not necessarily with the same name.

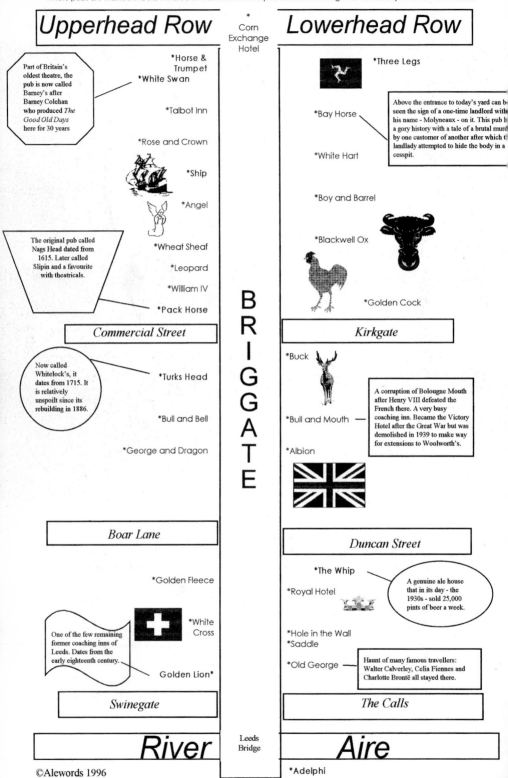

Upperhead Row

* Corn Exchange Hotel

Part of Britain's oldest theatre, the pub is now called Barney's after Barney Colehan who produced *The Good Old Days* here for 30 years

*Horse & Trumpet
*White Swan

*Talbot Inn

*Rose and Crown

*Ship

*Angel

The original pub called Nags Head dated from 1615. Later called Slipin and a favourite with theatricals.

*Wheat Sheaf

*Leopard

*William IV

*Pack Horse

Commercial Street

Now called Whitelock's, it dates from 1715. It is relatively unspoilt since its rebuilding in 1886.

*Turks Head

*Bull and Bell

*George and Dragon

Boar Lane

*Golden Fleece

*White Cross

One of the few remaining former coaching inns of Leeds. Dates from the early eighteenth century.

Golden Lion*

Swinegate

River

©Alewords 1996

Lowerhead Row

*Three Legs

*Bay Horse

Above the entrance to today's yard can be seen the sign of a one-time landlord with his name - Molyneaux - on it. This pub h a gory history with a tale of a brutal murd by one customer of another after which t landlady attempted to hide the body in a cesspit.

*White Hart

*Boy and Barrel

*Blackwell Ox

*Golden Cock

Kirkgate

*Buck

A corruption of Bolougne Mouth after Henry VIII defeated the French there. A very busy coaching inn. Became the Victory Hotel after the Great War but was demolished in 1939 to make way for extensions to Woolworth's.

*Bull and Mouth

*Albion

Duncan Street

*The Whip

*Royal Hotel

A genuine ale house that in its day - the 1930s - sold 25,000 pints of beer a week.

*Hole in the Wall
*Saddle

*Old George

Haunt of many famous travellers: Walter Calverley, Celia Fiennes and Charlotte Brontë all stayed there.

The Calls

Aire

B
R
I
G
G
A
T
E

Leeds Bridge

*Adelphi

Figure 1. Locational map of Briggate and its Inns and Pubs

Figure 2. The Adelphi. *Author's Collection*

In recent years the fine late Victorian pub the *Adelphi* has been used
to recreate the brig end shot. Whilst not actually being on Briggate it
is a good starting point for a visit to the inns, pubs and taverns of the
area. Early records are vague but it seems that there was a pub on the
site before 1839 although the present building dates from the turn of
the century. The original pub was bought by Alfred Bellhouse in 1889
and at that time it stood thirty feet back from the present line. The
council, anxious to improve conditions in the streets, conveyed 200
square yards of land to Bellhouse for £1,300. It called upon him to
re-site the *Adelphi* in its present position on Hunslet Road and
declared that it should be: 'not more than three stories in height above

Figure 3. Interior of the Adelphi. *Author's Collection*

the level of the adjoining footpaths' (Figure 2).

Bellhouse stayed at the pub until 1920 when he sold it for £20,000 to Frederick Myers. He stayed five years and in that time he conveyed, reconveyed, mortgaged and sub-mortgaged it eight times. The eventual purchaser was The Leeds and Wakefield Breweries Company, better known as the Melbourne Brewery. The brewery, and the *Adelphi*, became part of the Tetley company, then called Allied Breweries, in 1962.

The name *Adelphi* is probably a corruption of the Greek word for brothers, but as to why it was used as the name for a pub is uncertain. It may be that it represents the comradeship of brothers who use an inn – a brotherhood of drinkers. Signs on the pub have shown portraits of John Adam and his three brothers the architects who built the area of London known as Adelphi. Above the main entrance door of the pub the landlord is noted as being 'licensed to brew' although it is many years since this was the case (Figure 3).

The *Adelphi* is in a group of fine buildings on the south side of Leeds Bridge which also includes the *Old Red Lion* which dates from late Georgian days. There is a carved and painted lion above the front door which may possibly be original. The stained glass windows however only date from the turn of the century. This pub was once owned by a company called McQuat's which had a brewery nearby in Meadow Lane. In 1947 the Samuel Smith brewery of Tadcaster paid £178,940 for the company with its estate of nine pubs including the *Old Red Lion* and the *Eagle Tavern* in North Street.

On the north side of Leeds Bridge is one of the few remaining former coaching inns in the centre of the city – the *Golden Lion* which is now a residential hotel. *The Griffin* in Boar Lane has similar credentials. But the most historic of Leeds's coaching inns was the *Old King's Arms* located close to what is now the corner of Briggate and Duncan Street. It was first a private house, then shops and in the seventeenth century it became the *Kings Arms Tavern*. Cock fighting was popular there in the early eighteenth century and it was the city's first coaching inn and the northern terminus of a service to the *Swan with Two Necks* in London. The coaches which were described in a contemporary advertisement as 'flying machines on steel springs' originally took three days but later this was extended to four to avoid the late arrivals and early departures at the overnight stops. The fare was £2.5s. and each passenger was allowed fourteen pounds weight of luggage. In 1750 Sir Arthur Young recorded in his diary that he stayed at the *King's Arms*. The cook, he said, was 'disagreeable and dirty'. For supper he had veal cutlets, tarts and cheese which cost eighteen pence but to his obvious surprise there was no charge for ale or what he called 'malt liquor'.[4]

The *Old King's Arms* was also the home of the magistrates' courts and the turnpike commissioners held their meetings there. It was the scene in 1753 of a terrible riot when objectors to turnpike charges stormed the inn breaking many windows in an attempt to secure the release of three men imprisoned there charged with refusing to pay the toll at Beeston. One man was released but then a troop of dragoons stationed at Harewood was called and the Mayor read the Riot Act. The mob was not intimidated by the soldiers rather it became more incensed and refused to move. A round of powder was fired which only served to make things worse. The order to open fire was then given and eight men were killed immediately; another thirty were injured some of whom died later. A guard was kept on the houses of the mayor and the recorder for several weeks afterwards. The turnpike riots which had been particularly prevalent in the Bradford area gradually died away after the Leeds incident.

On 29 September 1762 William Wilson was elected Mayor of Leeds. The practice of the day was that he was presented with a half guinea and the old mayor one guinea. It was recorded in the *Leeds Mercury* that:

As is customary the court adjourned to Mr Thos. Moxon's at the Old King's Arms where, as usual, the old mayor spends his guinea and the new mayor his half guinea.

Six days later Mr Wilson was sworn into office and another party at the same inn cost the princely sum of £2.10.6d. The *Old Kings Arms* closed in 1813 when it was converted to shops.

Another coaching inn was the *White Horse* in Boar Lane. In the heydays of coaching the *Blue Diligence* ran from here to London in less than two days with an overnight stay at the *Angel* in Sheffield. It left there at four in the morning arriving at the *Swan with two Necks* in Lad Lane, London in the early evening. The fare was £2.8s.0d.

The names of the coaches running from Leeds were as picturesque as those of the pubs that serviced them: the *True Briton* ran to Kendal, the *Pevril of the Peak* to Buxton, the *Highflyer* and the *Duke of Leeds* to Bradford and Manchester, the *True Blue* to Wakefield and the *Red Rover* to Halifax. At the high point of 1838 coaches arriving and departing from Leeds totalled 130 each day.

Coaching started at the *Bull and Mouth* in 1800 and it was noted as one of the busiest houses in Leeds. The name is probably a corruption of 'Boulogne mouth' after Henry VIII defeated the French in the harbour of that town. A most unusual event occurred there in 1831. A box was deposited at the inn from the *Duke of Leeds* coach from Manchester marked: 'To the Rev'd Mr. Geneste, Hull per Selby packet. To be left until called for. Glass and keep this side up.' A curious servant opened the box to find to his great surprise two corpses in it. This was during the high period of body snatching with Edinburgh surgeons prepared to pay high sums for freshly interred corpses.[5]

During the early nineteenth century the horses of the Leeds City Fire Brigade were stabled there and brought up to Park Row where the fire engines were housed. When the new station in Park Street was built in 1883 stabling was provided on the site. The nearby *George Inn* was linked to the station by a bell to warn firemen drinking there that a fire call had been received and to return immediately. In 1903 the *Bull and Mouth* changed its name to the *Grand Central Hotel* and again, after the Great War, to the *Victory Hotel*. It was demolished in 1939 to make way for extensions to Woolworth's store.

There are still memories of the *Royal Hotel* on the east side of Lower Briggate for high above a development of flats built in 1983, the first in the city for many years, is a stone showing that the original building on the site dated from 1692. It started life as the *New King's Arms* distinguishing it from its neighbour the *King's Arms Tavern* which later added the prefix 'Old'. It had several other names; in 1773 it was recorded as the *New Inn* when it was said to be 'a house used by common carriers' from where slow coaches took freight from Leeds to London in four days at six shillings for a hundredweight. In the nineteenth century it was called the *Hotel Inn* for a period and immediately behind it in Call Lane was a separate pub named the *Hotel Tap Room*.

A neighbour of the *Royal* was the *Old George Hotel* which was one of the most popular houses in Leeds. At one time, in the early seventeenth century, it was probably the last inn in the city on the roads to Hunslet, Rothwell, Pontefract and Wakefield. It stood on the east side just below where the railway bridge now is. In its early days it was called *Ye Bush* but contemporary diarists have left some confusion. In 1694 Sir Walter Calverley wrote: 'I met Sir Walter Ramsden at the George in Leeds . . .'[6] Yet four years on that intrepid traveller Celia Fiennes chronicled her visit to Leeds where she dined at *Ye Bush*.[7]

Further uncertainty about Calverley's record stems from the fact that pubs often changed their names on the accession of a monarch. The first of the Georges came to the throne in 1714 and this may have been the date on which *Ye Bush* became the *George*. Additions like the prefix 'Old' were commonplace and usually followed the opening of another inn of a similar name in the vicinity. There was an inn called the *George and Dragon* in a yard to the west of Briggate shown on a map of 1815.

On the other hand Charlotte Brontë in *Jane Eyre* which was published in 1847 draws us an excellent picture of the early nineteenth century inn:

*A new chapter in a novel is something like a new scene in a play; and
when I draw the curtain this time, reader, you must fancy you see a
room in the* George Inn *at Millcote* [being Leeds], *with such large-
figured papering on the walls as inn rooms have; such a carpet, such
furniture, such ornaments on the mantle-piece, such prints; including
a portrait of George the Third, and another of the Prince of Wales, and
a representation of the death of Wolfe. All this is visible to you by the
light of an oil lamp, and by that of an excellent fire, near which I sit in
my cloak and bonnet; my muff and umbrella lie on the table . . .*[8]

George III came to the throne in 1760 and it is possible that
Calverley's reference was edited at some stage so as not to confuse
the contemporary reader, an act which has ended up doing just the
opposite.

The details of the closure of the *Old George* are not in dispute but
they are curious. Sometime around the turn of the last century the will
of John William Cudworth the owner of the inn was published. He left
it to his cousin William J Cudworth of York a Quaker, a member of
the Society of Friends, and opposed to
the drinking of alcohol. The bequest
left him in an invidious position. But it
was resolved for despite his views on
drink he had genuine concern for his
fellows. Closing down the inn would
have put people out of work. He therefore decided that whilst the tenant – a
widow, Mrs Simpson – remained at the
inn the licence must stay. When she
died in 1919 the licence was not
renewed. Later, the *Old George*, close to
three centuries old, was demolished.

The *Rose and Crown*, also known as
Binks's Hotel was very old and was in
the forefront of coaching. Many
coaches operated from there, the first
being the *Defiance* which from 1783
ran between Leeds and Hull. Strolling
players performed on platforms in the
yard of the pub although later a
concert hall was built. However it was
not licensed for plays therefore no
payment was allowed. Patrons were

Figure 4. The ornamental stone of the *Bay
Horse Hotel* showing the name of the
proprietor. *Author's Collection*

asked to pay for singing which took place between the plays. This did not last long with the advent of theatres in Leeds, the first being the *New Theatre* in Hunslet Lane in 1771 (Figure 7).

The *Rose and Crown* stood in a yard of the same name that was demolished in 1889 to make way for what is now the Queens Arcade. Leeds was way in front of most other cities in providing pedestrian foot streets or arcades, the first of which was Thornton's Arcade built on the site of the *Talbot Inn* in 1875. In its heyday this pub was the place from which horses and jockeys were weighed in before progressing to the fashionable Leeds races on Chapeltown Moor. In earlier days the *Talbot* was a favourite of Ralph Thoresby the Leeds historian. He described a room there painted rather curiously in fresco

Figures 5 and 6. Interior of Whitelocks. *Author's Collection*

with the arms of the nobility and gentry of the West Riding as they were in Elizabeth's time. Originally the inn fronted onto Briggate but later a part of it was converted into shops and like most other inns in Briggate it was virtually up a yard.

Opposite is a yard that once housed the *Bay Horse* and above the entrance can be seen the sign of a one-time landlord with his name – Molineaux – on it. The pub had a gory history with a tale of a brutal murder by one customer of another after which the landlady attempted to hide the body in a cesspit. In the next yard was the *White Hart* which was described in the 1889 *Jackson's Guide to Leeds* as being the oldest existing hostelry in Leeds. It was then more than two centuries old and had sometimes been known as the *Broad Yate* with perhaps the meaning of wide street although, like the *Talbot*, it finished up in a yard (Figure 4).

McConnell's, more properly known as the *Alliance Vaults* stood close to Market Street. It was one of Leeds's most popular pubs even though there was little seating except for a few old barrels. This was not a beer house and two thirds of its trade was in spirits. But it sold a strong beer – Ind Coope's Old No 2 Ale – which could only be bought in half pints. And despite the strong spirit connections more than 3,000 pints of beer were sold each week during the 1930s.

Briggate in Victorian days had its yards, alleys and fashionable Victorian arcades each of which had a pub in it, but has few left today. The best known of those remaining ones and the best loved pub in Leeds is *Whitelock's* in Turk's Head Yard with its location reflecting its former name. There has been an inn on the site since 1715 but the *Turk's Head* name came about around 1784. The change of name was in 1880 when the Whitelock family bought it. Six years later it was rebuilt to its present style and since then little has changed. It advertises itself as 'The First City Luncheon Bar' a function that continues (Figures 5 and 6).

John Betjeman enjoyed the atmosphere of *Whitelock's* describing it as:

> . . . *the Leeds equivalent of Fleet Street's Old Cheshire Cheese and far less self-conscious, and does a roaring trade. It is the very heart of Leeds.*[9]

Turk's Head Yard which can be entered from either end is long and narrow and this is reflected inside the pub with its long marble topped bar. Long gone breweries and their beers are remembered here and advertisements on etched mirrors offer soup and bread on sale for one penny. The original trade mirrors are just one element of this grand

Figure 7. Drawing of *The Rose and Crown*

Figure 8. The Whip. *Author's Collection*

pub with its art nouveau glasswork, polished brass, cast iron tables,
settles and the general ambience of the Edwardian era. Its closeness
before 1964 to the offices of the city's three daily newspapers made it
a newsworthy place too.

The pub had its idiosyncrasies – for a period only dwarfs were
employed as waiters. *Whitelock's* always held an attraction for the
artistic community. The Leeds Savage Club met there; a group of
writers, artists and musicians founded by the eccentric Edmund Bogg,
a Leeds picture framer. He was known as 't'owd chief' because of his
idiosyncrasy for wearing a Red Indian chief's head dress. It was one
of the first places in Leeds to have electric lighting and an electric
clock. Ironically at that time Charles Francis Tetley, a grandson of
Joshua Tetley and a Lord Mayor of Leeds, was offered a free trial

of electricity in his house at Headingley and refused it.

A pub that has claimed to be the city's oldest is the *Pack Horse* in a yard of the same name. Business started there in 1615 although there is some evidence that the original building dated from the middle of the sixteenth century. It started life as the *Nags Head* and was part of the estate of the Manor of Whitkirk which belonged to the Order of St John of Jerusalem, successors to the Knights Templar. A Templar cross, high on the original building, indicated this. During the eighteenth century it became known as the *Slipin*, a nickname often used for popular pubs. Maps of Leeds in the early nineteenth century showed Slipin Yard as the only access from Briggate to Lands Lane.

In 1750 Mr Baker of London opened a dancing academy at the pub and later it became a favourite with theatricals because of its location close to four of Leeds's theatres. This continued for many years. The journalist and author, Keith Waterhouse, relates how he met a mind reader who was staying there who told him how he got off jury service because he claimed that he might know what the accused was thinking.[10]

In 1987 the *Pack Horse* closed down for some months for alterations and despite promises that part of the old building would be retained the subsequent rebuilding was on a different, albeit adjacent, site and this does not reflect the historic character of the original pub which was demolished. All that remains is the Templar cross. Another pub with a Templar cross was the *Harrison Arms* in Harrison Street. When it was demolished the stone cross was bought by Mr Lakeland Whinkcup for a half-crown and presented to the Thoresby Society.

In the next yard to the *Pack Horse* is the *Ship*, a Georgian pub that was also popular with actors and musicians. But the *White Swan*, now called *Barney's*, in Swan Street, has the most tangible and lasting links with the theatre. It was built in the early eighteenth century as a coaching inn and from around 1765 there was a singing room attached to the pub. A century later Thornton's New Music Hall and fashionable Lounge was built above it. In 1897 Charlie Chaplin, then aged only eight, trod the boards in a clog dancing team known as the Eight Lancashire Lads. It became established and better known as the City Palace of Varieties often shortened to the City Varieties or even the 'Verts'. Fifty years after Chaplin a young man from Liverpool who was studying at Leeds College of Art had his first professional engagement in the name of Frankie Abelson. He moved to fame and fortune as Frankie Vaughan.

In 1953 filming of the BBC programme *The Good Old Days* started there under the producer Barney Colehan after whom the pub now takes its name. The television programme continued for thirty years and today occasional performances of the show take place in the theatre which is now established as not only Britain's oldest music hall but Britain's oldest theatre. The pub still provides a necessary essential for the theatre although it has its own rather splendid circle bar

The Wrens in Upper Briggate still retains a theatrical ambience particularly with the members of Opera North. Its connection with the nearby Grand Theatre – where the opera company is based – started when it was opened as a hotel and restaurant in 1880 by Mr Alfred Wren. At times the pub's sign has had birds on it but it actually takes its name from the first owner and is a rare survivor of the once common method of naming pubs and hotels (Figure 8).

The Whip, which is tucked away in an alley off Duncan Street, was said to have sold more beer in its inter-war heydays than any other pub in Leeds; some 90 barrels or 25,000 pints in a week. It was the classic city centre beerhouse which catered for men only. It was only as late as the 1970s that ladies were admitted and toilets were installed for them to comply with the law. In 1995 the Joshua Tetley Pub Company that owned *The Whip* decided to change its name and came up with the ludicrous *Fiddler's Elbow*. It caused an uproar in the city and the company was forced into changing it back to its original name at a cost of more than £8,000.

Notes and References

1. *Ducatus Leodiensis*, 1715, p 17.
2. Defoe D, *A Tour Through the Whole Island of Great Britain* Penguin Edition.
3. Fiennes Celia, (ed C Morris) *The Journeys of Celia Fiennes*, p 220.
4. Young A, *A Six Month Tour of the North of England*, p 136.
5. Oral history.
6. Sprittles Joseph, *Links with Bygone Leeds* Thoresby Society, 1969, p 86.
7. Fiennes Celia, *ibid.*
8. Brontë Charlotte, *Jane Eyre*, World Classics, Oxford University Press, 1988, p 94.
9. Godward Brian, *Walkabout*, Leeds Civic Trust, 1981
10. Waterhouse Keith, *City Lights*, 1994 p196.

2. AT THE FLICKS IN LEEDS

by Robert E Preedy

SATURDAY NIGHT AT THE CROWN CINEMA in Wortley, first in the queue meant the best seats. But not necessarily for the best view. Those double seats in the back row were the prize. Sadly this pleasure disappeared when the Crown went to bingo in 1968. Also gone, the ABC Minors Club, the Sunday double bill of 'X' films, and the flit spray.

Up to the early fifties everyone went to the flicks. Then there were forty million admissions a week. Now, even though numbers are increasing, weekly cinema going amounts to only about two million visits. The pattern of entertainment has changed from the habit of yesteryear when the cinemas and theatres of Leeds provided an escape from daily problems. The tram lines gave life more of a certainty. At the end of the 1d. ride lay the glamour of showbusiness. And not only

Figure 1. Alhambra Orchestra Film maker Herbert Pemberton opened his Alhambra Picture Palace in Low Road, Hunslet in 1913. The first film to be shown was described as the greatest coloured film of the age, *Life of Christ*. The orchestra was an added attraction and gave two performances a day. Other suburban cinemas with small orchestras included the Cottage Road and the Lounge. *Author's Collection*

in the city centre. Virtually every suburb saw the Hollywood stars inside their local picture palace. But curiously while hundreds of flea pits have disappeared, and the cable and satellite channel explosion beckons, the cinema business appears healthier now than for three decades (Figure 1).

The multiplex may dominate but local cinemas still survive. And surprisingly behind the scenes the business is still run as it was fifty years ago. The distribution of films from Hollywood to the local cinema is a highly regulated enterprise. A new film demands mass publicity and it has to travel from screen to screen in a way that maximises revenue. The local offices of all the major distribution companies were grouped around Wellington Street, very near to the

Figure 2. A big first run picture could always draw the crowds at the Tower. Here queuing for *The Thing* in October 1952. *R H Whincup*

railway stations. Here the bustling daily business of film supply to hundreds of northern screens, took place.

For over half a century from the twenties to the mid 1970s nearby City Square was the centre for late night swapping of film tins. Every Saturday around midnight, cinema owners would pick up next week's entertainment . . . a newsreel, a support film, and the main feature. Behind this highly social occasion, where much cinema gossip was traded, lay a far from frivolous business which entertained the bulk of the population. In the early days of cinema a film would be sold for a fixed sum. The purchaser could then exploit the celluloid until it literally disintegrated. By the 1920s bigger budget blockbusters needed a more effective system to produce increased revenue. A middleman - the distributor - was born. He negotiated with a film maker and agreed a fixed payment and a percentage of gross revenue. The distributor was responsible for publicity and for the cost of film prints. The cinema owner then booked the film for an agreed duration and percentage of box office take. This practice survives to the present day with a cinema typically paying between 30 per cent and 50 per cent for the screening.

The mechanics of organising the print distribution had a frenetic air. A cinema needs the film still fresh in the public's mind - whilst the distributor only wants to strike a minimum number of prints. Once a new film is released the older releases become worthless, ultimately being melted down for the silver content. Between these opposing demands is the highly regulated supply system (Figure 2).

Until a few years ago the *Odeon* and *ABC* in Leeds would enjoy a four week exclusive run on a film. After that a second wave would release the picture to suburban cinemas like the *ABC Shaftesbury* and *Gaiety*. A third circuit of smaller chains such as 'West Leeds Amusements', with the *Clock, Rex, Lyric and Kingsway,* then picked up the film for a shorter run and a smaller percentage. These days the speed of release has increased dramatically. The shelf life of a film in cinemas now is about six weeks. During the forties a film could still be seen somewhere in the city up to a year after release.

Sunday opening in Leeds was allowed from 1946. For some cinemas this was their salvation. A good double bill could be picked up for a flat fee, and as Sunday proved popular with teenagers, a full house often covered the expenses for the whole week.

Wellington Street became the centre for the trade during the early 1920s with the arrival of equipment companies. By the 1930s new cinemas in Leeds were opening almost monthly. In 1939 Leeds had sixty-eight. Serving all these cinemas were the distributors. In the

Figure 3. The children of Stanningley enjoyed their matinees at the *Pavilion... where the trams stopped.* The picture house survived for fifty years and two months, from February 1920, with Mary Pickford's *Daddy Longlegs,* to closure in April 1970 with *Invitation to a Gunfighter.* The *Pavilion* then went to bingo, but after a fire was converted to offices, retaining the original exterior. *R H Whincup*

short space between City Square and King Street were offices of Columbia, Walt Disney, Paramount, Eros, MGM, British Lion, Exclusive, Republic, Rank, RKO Radio, and United Artists. In nearby Albion Street were Fox and Butchers. Warners, New Realm and Grand National were in Basinghall Street- with Renown and Cinerama in East Parade.

A film salesman would deal with over a hundred cinemas. The bigger the cinema chain the greater their bargaining power. Films were often booked six months in advance. Autumn and winter were the most popular for cinemagoing. Summer was the worst. Holidays tended to be weather dependent, with many cinemas reducing the gamble by booking a 'flat rate' feature. Matinees on Christmas and Boxing Day were hugely popular with youngsters and their busy mums (Figure 3).

For years the ticket price remained very stable. A suburban night at the pictures cost 4d, 6d, or 9d. For this the screen entertainment included a newsreel, a short, trailers, adverts and the feature. Ice cream and sweet sales came during the trailers. On sale a halfpenny bar of Fry's Chocolate, a penny *Pola Maid* and the film-going favourites, choc bars and tubs. Apparently it really was true that the heaters were turned up prior to the arrival of the ice cream girl in her spotlight.

Staff wages in Leeds cinemas during the thirties could total £12 a week. Attendants earnt 10 shillings a week, a doorman 37/6d, and a projectionist £2. Women made up the bulk of the workforce, mostly as part-time usherettes. But if you didn't mind evening and weekend work, it was and remains an ideal way of seeing lots of free movies.

This stable business had developed from the turn of the century and brought the world's stars within reach of millions. But by the 1950s the magic was fading. Television is always blamed but the decline began long before then and related to our changing way of life after the war. Government intervention must also take some blame. The Entertainment Tax, the Quota System, the dollar crisis and the shortage of film stock all took their toll.

The Quota system began in 1927 to provide a stimulus to British production and to counteract the dominance of the cinema screens by Hollywood. The 1927 Act regulated the percentage of British films to be shown and started at a fairly low level of $7^{1}/_{2}$ percent, a figure that was to dramatically increase over the next two decades. By 1930 to 15 per cent, to 30 per cent by 1936 and to its maximum of 45 per cent in 1945, after which it was slowly reduced. The era of the 'Quota Quickie' may have created a backlash against British films. The quality

Figure 4. *News Theatre* interior Photographed in 1938 just prior to opening. The *News Theatre* was housed in the Queens Hotel building, City Square. An hour long programme of newsreels, cartoons, travelogues and the Radio Parade magazine kept railway travellers entertained. The theatre was open from 12 noon to 11pm with admission prices 6d. and I shilling. The cinema became the *Classic* in 1966, the *Tatler Film Club* in 1969, and *Classic* again from 1979 until closure in 1983. *Author's Collection*

Figure 5. Interior Assembly Rooms. The 1100 seater *Assembly Rooms* became the city's first full-time cinema, in 1907. New Century Pictures presented a varied programme of short films at 3 and 8pm daily. In 1958 the name change to Plaza also introduced more adult fare. After closure in 1988, the council began a programme of refurbishment, which sadly was halted through lack of funds. *Author's Collection*

of production becomes the least concern when entrepreneurs are forced by regulation to create a product. The simple difficulty for any control of supply is that the audience is rarely consulted. Cinemagoers had for many years enjoyed the allure of Hollywood and found the new local films to be poorly scripted and frequently lacking in entertainment value.

In spite of the audiences' reluctance to embrace British films, a decade later another *Cinematograph Act* became law. The 1938 document battled in vain to counteract almost total stateside domination. This time 'long' and 'short' films were clearly defined to close a loophole which allowed cinemas to fulfill their quota by showing longer but more tedious British products. To prevent 'quota quickies' from flooding the market, each film would be given a quality test before being registered. An inducement was even offered to the studios to

1951 – 1365 million visits; 1956 – 1100m; 1961 – 575m; 1970 –
193m. The low point was reached in 1984 – 54 million admissions.
Here is a sad roll call of vanished cinemas in Leeds:

Closures in 1953 – Newtown
             1957 – Queen's
                  Electra
                  Scala
             1958 – Gaiety
                  Kingsway
             1959 – Forum
                  Victory
             1960 – Haddon Hall
                  Abbey
             1961 – Lido
                  Gaumont
                  Star
                  Strand
                  Tivoli
                  Clifton
             1963 – Hillcrest
             1964 – Tatler
             1965 – Princess
                  Carlton
                  Savoy
             1966 – Gainsborough
             1967 – Dominion
             1968 – Capitol
                  Lyceum
                  Crown
                  Crescent
             1969 – Majestic
             1971 – Malvern
                  Regent
             1975 – Shaftesbury
             1976 – Clock
                  Rex
             1977 – Odeon Merrion Centre
             1985 – Plaza
             1986 – Yeadon
             1988 – Lyric
             1997 – ABC Vicar Lane faces an uncertain future

Other forms of community activity also suffered. Church

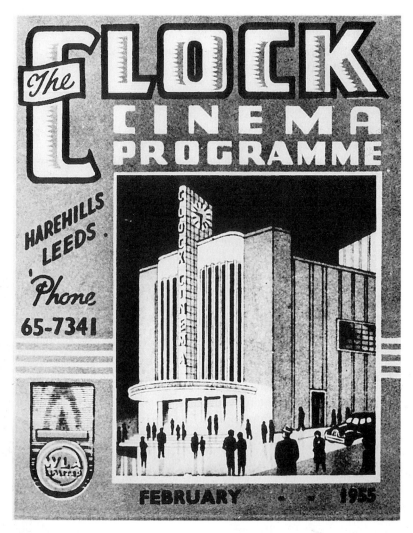

Figure 7. The imposing *Clock Cinema* building at the Harehills and Roundhay Road junction is now in use as an electrical retail shop. Prior to closure in 1986, the owners had bravely struggled for a decade with a full cinema programme. *Author's Collection*

attendances plummeted (Figures 7 & 8). Tram usage declined in spite of a fare reduction from 2d to 1d. The *Evening Post* started a column in 1957 called *Let's switch off the TV and Talk*. Hollywood studios laid off a quarter of their workforce in 1955. The comedy actor Derek Nimmo even remarked that TV viewers should be given no more choice, 'they'll watch trivia given half a chance'.

The Leeds theatres were also badly affected. The *Theatre Royal* was the venue for the first local TV show, *Northern Music Hall*. Featuring Wilfred Pickles and produced by Barney Colehan, this star studded show went out live at 8.00pm on 13 October, 1951. Sadly even this accolade failed to promote a long term future – the *Theatre Royal* closed in 1957. The equally impressive 1750 seater *Empire Theatre* was demolished in 1962.

Recently superior films (or better marketed) and multiplex cinemas

Figure 8. Another fine 1930s suburban cinema, the *Dominion*, Chapel Allerton closed in 1967. Bingo took over until 1996, and a restrictive clause in the sale document procluded any future use as cinema or bingo.

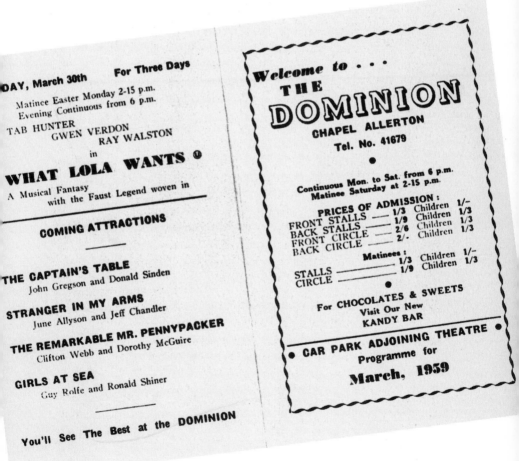

OAY, March 30th   For Three Days

Matinee Easter Monday 2-15 p.m.
Evening Continuous from 6 p.m.

TAB HUNTER
        GWEN VERDON
                RAY WALSTON
in

WHAT LOLA WANTS Ⓤ

A Musical Fantasy
        with the Faust Legend woven in

___

COMING ATTRACTIONS

___

THE CAPTAIN'S TABLE
        John Gregson and Donald Sinden

STRANGER IN MY ARMS
        June Allyson and Jeff Chandler

THE REMARKABLE MR. PENNYPACKER
        Clifton Webb and Dorothy McGuire

GIRLS AT SEA
        Guy Rolfe and Ronald Shiner

___

You'll See The Best at the DOMINION

Welcome to . . .

THE

DOMINION

CHAPEL ALLERTON

Tel. No. 41679

•

Continuous Mon. to Sat. from 6 p.m.
Matinee Saturday at 2-15 p.m.

PRICES OF ADMISSION :
FRONT STALLS ——— 1/3   Children 1/-
BACK STALLS ——— 1/9   Children 1/3
FRONT CIRCLE ——— 2/6   Children 1/3
BACK CIRCLE ——— 2/-   Children 1/3

Matinee :
STALLS ——— 1/3   Children 1/-
CIRCLE ——— 1/9   Children 1/3

•

For CHOCOLATES & SWEETS
Visit Our New
KANDY BAR

___

• CAR PARK ADJOINING THEATRE •
Programme for

March, 1959

have produced a steady increase in attendances. But compare 1996 – 120 million with 1946 – 1640 million. So what future does the cinema have in Leeds? The Warner Brothers, Kirkstall Road Multiplex (opening in 1998) is a confident message that cinema is around for a long time. How the Headingley and city centre cinemas fare remains to be seen.

Small town cinemas like those in Elland, Keighley, Skipton and Wetherby, far away from a multiplex appear best placed to survive. Once a multiscreen complex opens a time bomb ticks under traditional picture houses. But as screenwriter William Goldman once observed 'in the film business, nobody knows anything'. The people of Leeds and their pocketful of money will, as always, decide.

3. A Visit to the Palace

by June Walton Pearce

'THE PICTURES' were a part of life. The programmes were changed twice a week, and as most of them could be reached by walking or by bus, and if expense allowed, it was possible to visit two or three in the space of six days.

The large cinemas in town had organs that rose up through the floor. The organist played medleys of tunes between the films. Often the organs were bright with lights which changed colour. After the war when Sunday viewing wasn't allowed concert parties sometimes put on shows. I remember by grandmother taking me to see some.

The buildings were indeed palatial, and I fear that some wonderful stained glass windows, along with decor and architectural features were lost when a lot of them closed down. To a lot of people the luxury of fitted carpets, plush seating, chandeliers and velvet curtains, was something that could not be enjoyed at home when lino and blackout curtains were the order of the day.

As children, having our pocket money stopped for some mis-demeanour meant no weekly Saturday afternoon at the local cinema, and would result in frantic visits to all the aunts and uncles to see if they had any jam jars they wanted taking back to the shops, as each was worth a penny or halfpenny according to the size. Having no funds often meant that we resorted to illegal means of entry; crawling on all fours under the paybox window, or much pushing or pulling by friends through small toilet windows. The attendents were aware of our scams and if caught we would be ejected. The kids left outside booing and calling at them.

My grandmother would take me and her dog every week to the pictures. Most of the attendents knew her and would let all three of us in. We always sat in the same seats down the left hand side, three rows from the front and near the radiator. *Monty* would lie there very quietly and would share an ice-cream through the interval.

When my uncles came on leave they would send me to book double seats in the dress circle for Saturday nights out with their girl friends, and I used to think it was very romantic. Then, when I got older, part of my courting was spent on the back row too, alternating between the theatre and dancing. Marriage brought children and they were introduced to the big screen, but unfortunately most of the local cinemas had gone by then, and a trip into town was involved. Like most industries the film industry has had its ups and downs, but for a long period now has provided us with some good entertainment, and is enjoying a revival as a pastime. I hope my grandchildren will enjoy it too. By the way, I also have a dog.

A Visit to the Palace

I used to go to the Palace, Savoy and Pavilion too,
Not because I was upper class, it was just the thing to do.
We were always greeted by the commissionaire.
Come rain or shine, he was always there.
It's hard to say which I favoured the most, they were all palatial in style,
With velvet drapes and chandeliers and carpets with one inch pile.

The kids my age on Saturdays, stood in a very long queue.
There was much pushing, and to-ing and fro-ing. You know the way kids do.
Three pence a ticket we paid to get in, to see adventures galore.
And with a mighty heave, and a forward push, we squeezed through the open
    door.
To watch Roy Rodgers and Trigger; Our Gang and Stooges three.
The noise in there was horrendous, as we shouted and stamped with glee.

Of course we did our courting there.
It was usual to book the back row; for the seats were a double chair.
We had to watch for the usherette patrolling up the aisle.
With a flashing torch she'd spotlight you; and stand watching for a while.
Clark Gable, Greta Garbo, Bette Davis, Ginger Rodgers and Fred Astaire.
Gone With The Wind, Blue Angel. We sat and watched them there.
At Bambi, *I cried when I was young; for Mario Lanza, I fell when he sung.*

Twice a week the program was changed
So we were very well entertained.
Then they closed them down. These hallowed walls
Suddenly became Bingo Halls!
There was nowhere for the young to go,
But this is progress, don't you know?
For years we grieved the passing of our local palace.
But now they build great huge ones; like something out of Dallas.

We don't go now, but on tele we view,
All the films. Some old, some new.
We still hold hands sitting on the couch
As we did in days long gone.
When we sat in the back row of the cimema,
In a double seat made into one.

4. A LETTER TO THE EDITOR: READERS' LETTERS TO THE LEEDS PRESS 1795–1850

by David Thornton

ON SATURDAY 19 DECEMBER 1801 a letter from Long Preston in Lancashire appeared in the *Leeds Mercury*. Its author, adopting the somewhat pretentious pseudonym *A Love of Old Fashioned Religion*, deplored the modern way of celebrating Christmas.

> *It is now cards of invitation are sent abroad, great Entertainments are made, the Tea-table, that* Altar of Scandal *is now displayed in the greatest elegance and upon it are sacrificed the characters of thousands.*

It is the kind of statement often made when older people look back nostalgically to an idyllic past that in all probability never existed. That *Mercury* correspondent may well have been indulging in such nostalgia but his letter in some ways symbolised, for many, the age in which he wrote. In 1801 Britain stood at one of the greatest watersheds in its history. Threatened without by the armies of Revolutionary France and within by the awakening leviathan of a people beginning to demand political change, the nation was also slowly undergoing a transformation from what had been predominantly a rural based population dependent upon an agricultural economy, into an urban based society dependent upon manufacturing industries. That *Mercury* letter writer deplored the new celebrations of Christmas; there were others who equally deplored the new society in which they found themselves – but there were also those who saw in that emerging society a vision of a better and more economically satisfactory way of life. No town better reflects those opposing factions than Leeds.

Here was a town that saw its population soar in fifty years from 53,276 in 1801 to 172,270 in 1851.[1] The way it faced up to the social, political and economic problems of rapid industrialisation and population explosion is a microcosm of the way the nation as a whole faced the challenge that the long process, usually described as the Industrial Revolution, placed upon the people of nineteenth century Britain.

Many historians have turned their attention to Leeds at that time. They have graphically analysed the strategies devised to overcome the problems industrialisation generated; they have demonstrated

Figure1. Richard Oastler's letters in the Leeds press on factory reform are among the most important written in the nineteenth century. *Leeds City Libraries*

the political infighting produced as the town itself came to terms with its civic responsibilities. We need not simply rely on secondary sources to understand that period. We can read what the politicians of the day said and what the journalists and the literary critics of the time wrote. But what did the ordinary men and women of Leeds and the West Riding think during that time? What were the issues that dominated their thoughts, the fears they felt and the aspirations they dreamed of?

At a time when many people were illiterate, it has to be acknowledged that the observations on life of much of that population are now as forgotten as the names of the men and women who held them. But others were literate, and some felt passionately enough about certain issues to write to the local press. Thus it is in the columns of our local newspapers that we can uncover the issues that dominated and motivated the people of that period. The correspondence written to the editors of the day is a key that can unlock the past not only of the great and the famous but also of the everyday people of one northern town caught up in the throes of the industrialisation of nineteenth century Britain.[2]

Several relatively eminent people wrote to the Leeds press during this time. Without doubt among some of the most famous and influential letters to the British press ever written during the whole of the nineteenth century were those by Richard Oastler to the *Leeds Mercury* and *Leeds Intelligencer* on 'Yorkshire Slavery.'[3] (Figure 1). His passionate campaign against the employment of children played a significant part in the long struggle for factory reform . There were others. Francis Place, radical reformer and drafter of the People's Charter, wrote to the *Leeds Times* asking 'Is machinery a good or an evil to the working class?'[4] On 4 May 1826, some fifteen years earlier, the younger Edward Baines, already embarked on a Grand Tour of Europe, wrote a strong defence of machinery as he travelled between Rouen and Havre.[5] His address 'To the Unemployed of Yorkshire and Lancashire' and carrying his name, 'because a real name gives an authenticity to the facts communicated,' appeared in the *Leeds Mercury* nine days later.[6] Joseph Pitman, of shorthand fame, was outraged over an 'unwarrantable attack' by the *Leeds Times* and strongly defended his 'new and important Science of Phonography' claiming to have written 200 words a minute with it.[7] The radical politician, Joseph Hume, used its columns expressing the hope that

all the Chartists in Leeds will cordially join the Middle Classes in demanding . . . the just rights of the working classes.[8]

Patrick Brontë wrote several letters to the *Leeds Intelligencer* whilst

Figure 2. Edward Baines. As editor of the *Leeds Mercury*, Edward Baines actively encouraged his readers to write letters to the press. *Leeds City Libraries*

George Turner of Leeds, a disciple of the religious fanatic Joanna Southcott, wrote to the *Mercury* urging its editor to publish a letter from the famous prophetess 'by the command of the Lord.'[9,10]Its editor accommodated the request and this despite the *Mercury*'s policy that 'any correction in the public performance of divine worship is not the business of a Political Journal.'[11]

Politics was the mainstay of that Leeds press. Those politically minded could easily find a newspaper that would offer them a platform from which they could proclaim their own particular point of view, for the town was well served over those years with newspapers that reflected a broad spectrum of political convictions.[12] There was the radical *Leeds Times* edited for a time by the social reformer, Samuel Smiles. There were the *Leeds Patriot*, the *Leeds Independent and York County Advertiser*, the *Leeds Gazette*, the *Leeds Temperance Herald* and the *Leeds Magazine* whose policy was to counteract 'the mischievous tendency of the press . . . and . . . other demoralising influences.'[13, 14, 15] The Tory viewpoint in the town was well represented by the short-lived *Leeds Wednesday Journal* whose first edition rolled off the presses on 6 January 1841. It had been specifically produced because

> *All the Leeds Papers are on Saturday. In many remote places these Papers cannot possibly arrive until Sunday; and that is not a day for political discussion or the amusement of light reading.*[16]

It ran for just eight weeks. Undeterred, Robert Perring, its editor, then announced he would launch the *Leeds Conservative Journal* on 30 April 1842.[17] But without question the leading Tory organ of the day was the *Leeds Intelligencer* which had espoused the right wing cause uninterrupted since its inception by Griffith Wright in 1754. The Whig/Liberal case was presented vigorously by Edward Baines in the *Leeds Mercury* (Figure 2). Baines himself recognised the value of opening up his columns to his West Riding readership. In the very first edition he edited he commented:

> *A letterbox for the reception of any communications with which the public may please to favour us will be placed in the outdoor of the printing office.*[18]

There were, however, certain guidelines laid down by the editors. Both the *Leeds Times* and the *Leeds Mercury* insisted that letters should not be anonymous.[19, 20] Thus many carried the actual name of the writer;[21] others preferred a pseudonym to appear in the paper. Some chose their profession like a clergyman writing on the use of hair powder;[22] some used the theme of their letter as happened in the *Leeds Patriot* when *Theatrical Observer* wrote on the closure of the theatre.[23] And some strictly had tongue in cheek like *Porco Inimicus* writing about the mess pigs were creating on the Lower Headrow.[24] The *Leeds*

Times actually specified the way writers should go about their task:

> *When you describe facts, give your real name to the editor. Write legibly in ink . . . and not on both sides of the leaf . . . Be brief . . . Abstain altogether from questions which any intelligent neighbour can answer . . . consult a dictionary . . . instead of troubling an editor . . . If you wish a letter to appear . . . in any particular paper, don't send it to any other.* [25]

The *Leeds Intelligencer* sniffily refused to print *Calm Observer's* contribution until he learnt to spell whilst the *Leeds Mercury* flatly refused to publish letters that were 'too caustic'. [26, 27]

Although Leeds was considered simply a provincial town, its inhabitants were very much aware of the major national and international political issues of the day. Many took advantage of the opportunity the varied newspapers of the town offered to keep abreast of the changing world in which they found themselves and to follow avidly the innovations in art, literature and fashion, but in particular, it was the machinations of the political world that dominated their interest. It was an interest that is reflected in the subjects they raised in their correspondence through the years. A random selection of examples from the Leeds journals across those years clearly shows the extent of subjects covered: war with France, Napoleon, Luddism, Peterloo, Parliamentary Reform, the Corn Laws, and inevitably income tax, written, on one occasion and with some passion, by *Oud Squair Toas:*

> *Maister Printer – I'll be deng'd if I like th' Property, or t'Income tax, as folk call it.* [28-34]

Some correspondents used the columns of one newspaper to attack another. One writer to the *Leeds Patriot* addressed the editor of the *Mercury* on account of an 'extremely disatisfactory' report in it. [35] In the *Leeds Times* another writer took the editor of the *Intelligencer* to task for publishing a 'slander'(sic). [36] At times a vitriolic war of words burst out between the various papers and in particular between the editors of the *Leeds Mercury* and the *Leeds Intelligencer*. Even the *Intelligencer* letter writers joined in. *A Briton* addressing himself to Baines, the *Mercury* editor, reflected

> *Speak well of you! . . . I would as soon think of giving Belzebub* [sic] *my good word.'* [37]

The *Leeds Patriot* exercised greater decorum confining its critical remarks simply to 'Mr Baines.' [38]

Figure 3. Female workers in Marshall's mill. Many young prostitutes came from the factories of the town.

But there were issues other than the major political ones of the day that needed a public airing, needed complaining about or campaigning for. It was a time of a growing moral awareness throughout society. People were disgusted when a woman was taken to Leeds market one Saturday night with a halter round her neck and sold for five guineas to a man 'well acquainted with her merits.'[39] On another occasion an apology appeared in the *Leeds Mercury* from a man accused of using 'reproachful language' to Rebecca Walshaw and promising 'never to offend again in the like manner.'[40] It was a time when at least one 'elderly gentleman' was carrying out a personal crusade in Leeds against any woman wearing a dress with a low 'back or bosom.' A *Mercury* writer, calling himself *Observator*, warned that the man concerned carried in his hand a 'little instrument' with which he used to stamp on the bare shoulders of any female so dressed the words 'Naked but not ashamed.'[41]

Such trivial concerns for morality should not distract from one of the greatest moral issues the people of Leeds faced during the first fifty years of the nineteenth century; prostitution. In June 1813 the

Leeds Intelligencer carried a letter from *H* complaining bitterly of the 'crowds of young women who infest our streets of an evening' and urged the town to 'restore (Leeds) to its former moral beauty.'[42] Six months later *Agnus Castus*, this time in the *Leeds Mercury*, again raised the issue of the 'swarm of Cyprians which every evening infests our streets.'[43] His solution was to build a Magdalene Hospital or Penitentiary House in the town.

The laws themselves were not adequate, according to another *Leeds Mercury* correspondent, to end this 'torrent of open profligacy and profaness.'[44] There were those who sympathised with these women when they returned to their hovels that were 'devoured with filth . . . and noisome with disease . . . divested from the paths of virtue.'[45] Time and again the need to establish some institution in Leeds to solve the problem was raised. Such a penitentiary would 'restore to society' these women and save their 'souls from death'[46] so wrote *A Friend for the Suppression of Vice* in 1813. Eight years later *Philaretes* returned to the same theme of this

> *unfortunate class of females . . . beguiled in their youth . . . entangled in the snares of a seducer . . . I would inquire in Leeds which supports an Infirmary and House of Recovery . . . would (it) not readily institute a Dispensary for the cure of the distemper of the soul?*[47]

Figure 4. Boar Lane from Briggate in 1867; in the early parts of the century assistants sometimes worked until midnight in shops like these in Lower Briggate. *Leeds City Libraries.*

Figure 5. In 1818 at Leeds Courthouse, later the Post Office, a meeting was held demanding changes to the laws regarding climbing boys. *Leeds City Libraries*

It did; but not until 1842 when the Leeds Lock Hospital was eventually opened at 159 York Street.[48] It was a voluntary project and desperately short of funds as *One of the Management Committee* pointed out in his letter to the *Leeds Times*. It had been set up 'for the unfortunate class of females for whom no . . . provision . . . existed in Leeds' and catered for women from 'neighbouring and surrounding parishes.' The writer pointed out, however, that 'a large proportion of the younger females came from factories of this town' (Figure 3). Its inception had been a success. Some 435 females and children, and 352 males had been restored to health. Of those females 254 were between 15 and 20 years of age.[49] A month later the same writer was back quoting a graphic example of a young maid servant ruined, robbed and then deserted by the 'scoundrel' who brought her to Leeds; harboured by a 'female wretch' who subjected her to drudgery and abuse and finally turned her out onto the streets. It was essential, he argued, that such a hospital needed to be administered by the town.[50]

There were other social evils, not least long hours of work. In 1840 *A Tradesman* reflected in the *Leeds Times* on 'the excellent system of closing shops (Saturday excepted) at 8 o'clock.' Pointing out that most Leeds shops remained open until midnight on Saturdays, he proposed to 'close our shops at eleven o'clock on Saturday nights. (Figure 4)'[51] A London correspondent drew attention to the appalling working conditions in 'the Woollen Manufactory' and the 'dirt and stench to which men, women and children are habituated.'[52] The milliners of Leeds were another group subjected to unreasonable working conditions when women customers expected orders to be completed irrespective of the time of day. As *A Young Milliner and Dressmaker* wrote to the *Leeds Mercury*

> *My Dear Mr Editor – I beseech you to lay aside musty politics for one week . . . which no creature (in our workroom) cares one straw about, pray read a good round lecture to the ladies of Leeds . . . upon their unreasonableness with respect to dress.*[53]

Climbing boys, spending their lives crawling through the twisting chimneys of the homes of the wealthy in order to sweep them, were another group that generated much public sympathy although little positive action was taken to improve their lot. Delaying tactics in the House of Lords and the ineffective legislation of 1834 and 1842 saw little real progress made until the acts of 1864 and 1875 made the employment of climbing boys illegal.[54] Through those earlier years public meetings demanding changes to the law were called. One such was held in the Leeds Courthouse in February 1818 and letters to the press appeared supporting the plea year after year. Some offered alternatives to the inhuman use of children so graphically illustrated in the case of Thomas Lee, the ten year old illegitimate son of an African woman street hawker from Leeds. After her suicide, he was apprenticed to Joseph Haddock, a master sweep, who worked him to the extent that after sweeping seven chimneys in one day, the boy collapsed.[55]

Seven years before the *Mercury* carried that report, a letter had appeared in its columns offering a solution to the problem. A new invention, a 'machine for sweeping chimneys' was described. It consisted of 'a brush, (and) some rods or hollow tubes that fasten into each other.'[56] *Fulgineus* in the *Leeds Intelligencer* quoted Scotland where 'chimney sweepers' boys' had almost been done away with by using a system that 'can be practically adopted in Leeds.' The idea was to pull a broom tied to a rope up the chimney.[57] However, there were arguments that outlawing climbing boys would bring with it its own

Figure 6. Poverty and disease often went hand in hand. Here in the slums of Riley's Court cholera struck in 1832. *Leeds City Libraries*

Figure 7. This new slaughterhouse was opened in 1826 in an attempt to improve the quality of meat. *Leeds City Libraries*

Figure 8. This Henry Burn drawing from Holbeck c1864 shows smoke pollution, which was a serious problem in Leeds from the early years of the nineteenth century. *Leeds City Libraries*

difficulties. Haddock, speaking at the Leeds Courthouse meeting claimed abolition would take away the sustenance of his five apprentices, four of whom were orphans;[58] (Figure 5) whilst a *Master Sweep* bemoaned the effects of the 1842 Act, though the letter does have all the hallmarks of a spoof correspondence:

> *Zir – I ham a numbl individul in the chimbly line wot the nu hact as verry mutch indgured.*[59]

Probably the single most soul destroying evil the town had to face during this time was poverty and letter writers raised the issue through the decades. Indeed the poverty in Leeds, according to *An Old Soldier* was second to none in Europe. He claimed to have travelled to most of the manufacturing towns in France and Belgium including Paris and Lyons, yet

*No destitution meets your eyes such as stares you in the streets of Leeds
... In travelling through Prussia and Holland ... I do not think there
exists as much ignorance and destitution as is now found in Leeds*
(Figure 6).[60]

Compounding that economic paucity were unscrupulous shop-
keepers who were happy to sell contaminated food to an unsuspecting
public; 'a sly way of robbing the public of their money' as one correspondent put it.[61] Other letters appeared giving advice. *E O* in the
Leeds Mercury explained how to test for 'unsound flour;'[62] whereas
Hermes concerned himself with tainted meat 'too long kept' or
'improperly cured.'The solution he offered was to bury it under fresh
earth, leave for a few days and when retrieved it would be 'perfectly
recovered.'[63]The single greatest cause of rotten meat in the town was
the fact that up to 1807 animals were slaughtered on Sundays and
Mondays for the Tuesday and Saturday markets.[64] The problem
lingered on so that one *Leeds Mercury* correspondent wrote urging
more regular slaughtering which would make an improved diet of
fresh meat more readily available (Figure 7).[65]

The worst of all the man-inflicted assaults on the people of Leeds
was the daily pollution pouring from the chimneys of the numerous
factories, mills and domestic dwellings in the town. *Septimus* in the
Leeds Times launched an attack not only on the issue itself but on
the local population.

*Sir – I have been perfectly dismayed at the apathy with which the good
people of this town regard one of the most alarming and frightful
nuisances in existence – that sure and steady destroyer of human life
... the dark and murky cloud ... has I fear choked the lungs of the
Leeds people ... Let the atmosphere be cleared.*[66]

That was not strictly fair. Letters had appeared condemning what *H*
in his letter to the press described as this 'great and increasing evil
which prevails over this and most other manufacturing
towns.'[67](Figure 8). Some writers tried to introduce an air of objec-
tivity. Dircks & Co writing from Manchester pointed out that
economic factors had also to be considered[68] but that some firms like
Messrs Fenton, Murray and Jackson of Leeds had taken positive steps
to reduce emissions.[69] In fact, over twenty years before, Marshall's mill
at Holbeck and the new public baths had taken steps to improve the
situation.[70] Hirst and Bramley had installed a special apparatus to the
same end.[71] When William Pritchard produced an invention to cut
pollution, Benjamin Gott had it installed four weeks later.[72, 73] But

there were others who held a minority even 'childish' point of view on
the subject, if we are to believe the *Mercury* editor's comment.[74] *A
Philanthropist* from Chapeltown was flatly opposed to any public inter-
ference over smoke pollution![75]

Diseases also took their toll. None were more virulent than smallpox
and cholera. In 1796 Jenner's remarkable breakthrough using cowpox
inoculation to combat the ravages of smallpox was greeted with delight
by the informed but with suspicion by many. A Pontefract doctor, John
Haxby MD, despaired in his letter to the *Intelligencer* that so many in
the West Riding failed to take advantage of this great boon to mankind.

> *I am sorry to find the Introduction of it into this Part of the County
> meets with opposition rather than encouragement.*[76]

Eighteen years later suspicion of inoculation, this time against
measles, led *Humanus* to explain these fears away in a letter to the
Mercury.[77] Cholera, that other scourge of nineteenth century Britain
generated its own share of correspondence. The people of Leeds
were all too well acquainted with it, so much so that *H L* made an
interesting observation in the *Leeds Mercury* in September 1825.

> *It is a very remarkable fact that the Disease called Cholera Morbus has
> been more prevalent, and fatal in Leeds, than in any other place.*[78]

The following week *An Old Practitioner* raced into print with his reply.
The reason was obvious why this should be, he explained.

> *The cause is the people in this town* live too well *and take too much
> of Sir John Barleycorn's* 'nappy' *along with fruit and nuts which
> causes ... fermentation in the stomach.*[79]

Other letters urged the need for an antidote for scarlet and typhus
fevers[80] whilst *Dew Ben* raised the dreaded subject of hydrophobia.[81]

One sure way to produce a healthier society was to support the
already hard pressed Leeds General Infirmary in fund raising. One
Mercury writer brought this to the public's attention in 1802. But the
only way success could be truly achieved was to establish a society that
was educated enough to come to terms with the difficulties it faced.

Education was the way to improve the nation generally. It would
disseminate the ignorance and prejudice that pervaded so much of the
lower classes or so many believed. Even so, schemes to rectify the situation did not go unchallenged. 'Let the poor be educated as they have
hitherto been,' wrote *No Changeling* in the *Leeds Intelligencer* in 1810.
He wanted no truck with Joseph Lancaster and his 'deep-laid
schemes.'[82] The following week he was back on the attack. Before

Lancaster embarked on his schemes of public education he should 'study *Spelling* – in which . . . he appears most miserably deficient.'[83] More enlightened policies prevailed, however, and in 1811 a Lancasterian school opened for boys in the old Assembly Rooms in Kirkgate.[84] A girls' school opened the following year.[85] Nor were children with disabilities overlooked. Handicapped children were admitted to the schools[86] but deaf children were not always so lucky. One writer signing himself *A Deaf Boy* urged his readers to 'consider the miseries of the deaf.'[87]

Adults, too, were not overlooked. In 1816, and with some jubilation, *J T* from Bradford was delighted to announce that a school for adults was to be opened in Bradford on Sunday nights 'for people of mature age.'[88] But adult education could itself present problems as *J S* from Huddersfield pointed out;

> *Adults are not easily persuaded to expose their ignorance . . . let the poor be met in their own habitations.*[89]

Education was not only needed for the working classes. The middle classes, too, were eager for intellectual improvement. It was a series of letters to the *Leeds Mercury* that brought about the establishment of the Leeds Philosophical and Literary Society. A grateful *Leodiensis* wrote thanking the *Mercury* in March 1819 for helping to get the society off the ground.[90] A week later, Di Vernon wrote of her delight that such a society had been formed but urged that women should also be admitted.[91]

A sound infrastructure was essential if this burgeoning industrial town of Leeds was to become a success and paramount in its need was the provision of an adequate and pure water supply. A *Water Drinker* aptly summed up the need in the *Leeds Mercury*.

> *Everyone must acknowledge it is of great importance that the Town of Leeds should be well supplied with water . . . The Inhabitants of Leeds should be well supplied with* pure water *and at a reasonable price.*[92]

Townsman writing in the *Leeds Patriot* expressed the same feelings five years later saying it was

> *a matter of regret that the inhabitants of Leeds were not supplied with water of a wholesome quality.*[93]

But *Aquarius* in the *Mercury* identified why that water might not be wholesome. If his language is somewhat archaic, his theme has a very modern ring about it. The use of lead pipes for carrying water, he claimed, had 'disadvantages very serious.'[94]

Figure 9. Salamanca and Middleton miner. Murray's engine Salamanca c1814. That same year letters proposed building a similar steam operated railway from Leeds to Selby. From *Walker's Costumes of Yorkshire. Leeds City Libraries*

Improved facilities meant better transport and in particular better maintained highways. Streets and roads were regular themes which letter writers addressed. One writer calling himself simply *Y* claimed that the 'footpaths are intolerably bad . . . New Road End . . . is scarcely passable.'[95] *NW* in the *Leeds Patriot* was puzzled why the south side of Wellington Bridge had 'a good flagged causeway' and yet the north side was nothing but 'mire and clay.'[96] Not only should thoroughfares be passable, it would be an advantage if streets carried names in 'legible characters' was one suggestion.[97] Street lights too were a cause for concern. They may have been a 'beautiful and economic mode of lighting' according to *R J Engineer*[98] but what use was that if 'the lamps are so shamefully neglected at this end of town.' *Constant Reader* was referring to Park Lane.[99] Still irate, he was back in the columns of the *Mercury* three years later penning his thoughts on the 'twinkling dimness of our street lamps!'[100] There were a few less than enthusiastic about street lighting. John Kaye wrote expressing his concern about the effects of gas lights on general health.[101]

Writers were more fervent in their support for that newly emerging form of transport, railways. *Mercator*'s oft quoted letter to the *Leeds Mercury* in 1802 considered the 'superior advantage of railways' and suggested building a horse drawn one from Leeds to Selby.[102] In 1812 both the *Leeds Mercury*[103] and the *Leeds Intelligencer*[104] brought to public notice the trial run of a steam engine on the 'Middleton Iron-railway,'(Figure 9). A couple of years later there were several suggestions in the press to build a steam railway between Leeds and Selby using a 'Patent Steam Carriage, as now in use at Middleton Colliery.'[105] The estimated cost to build it ranged from £300 per mile to £2500. However, *XYZ* in putting the latter putative price, did stress that the engine would be capable of carrying 100 tons at 3–4 miles per hour.

Here was a new society emerging from an old one, perhaps at times, even carrying an indication of a more civilized and humane one to be. In 1813 the *Leeds Intelligencer* published an account of the execution of three Luddites for the murder of millowner William Horsfall in 1812. An *Attentive Hearer* described the melancholy scene in York when at

> nine yesterday morning Mellor, Thorp and Smith ascended the scaffold . . . 'I hope the world will forgive me.' These were his [Mellor's] last words. Never was there a sight more awful.[106]

Throughout the 1840s the radical *Leeds Times* carried editorial after editorial condemning the 'awful sight' of capital punishment. But it was Patrick Brontë writing from his bleak and windswept Haworth Parsonage ten years previously, who so pithily and succinctly expressed the feelings of the abolitionists in a letter to the *Leeds Intelligencer*. He saw

> the urgent necessity of the revision and amendment of our criminal code . . . bloody executions . . . pollute our land . . . they distress the thinking and humane.[107]

Thinking people continued airing their views and identifying injustices. Such a one was *Laone*. She penned her thoughts in March 1841 to the *Leeds Times,* concerned at the inequality of the laws with regard to women. The paper stressed it was a letter 'by a woman.'

*Laws have been passed most injurious to the interests of women, both
as females and citizens . . . It cannot be asserted that women are indifferent to political existence . . . there are many women in England who
think.*[108]

Thus through those formative years, as Leeds moved towards
becoming a major industrial centre, did the men and occasionally
women of the town, present their views in the columns of the local
press on a plethora of subjects with passion, perception and humour.
The editors of the respective journals in which their letters appeared
fulfilled a vital role in offering an opportunity of free speech as the
nation groped slowly and hesitatingly towards the Parliamentary
democracy that would emerge in the twentieth century. Of course,
there were occasions when editors had neither the space nor the inclination to publish some of the letters received. Few, however, were
rejected for the reason Baines gave in the *Leeds Mercury* of February
1812.

*When a man and wife quarrel it is said the best recipe for producing a
reconciliation is to kiss and be friends . . . cannot indignant Laura and
repentant Simon . . . [settle their affairs] . . . without obtruding them
on the public?*[109]

Notes and References

1. Birt, Kevin & Grady, Steven, *The Illustrated History of Leeds* (Derby: Breedon Books) 1994 p 258.
2. The conductor of a newspaper was frequently referred to as a 'printer' but by 1803 the word
'editor' was being used according to the *Oxford English Dictionary*. In fact the *Leeds Mercury* used
the expression earlier – see 11.4.1801; and the *Leeds Intelligencer* 26.10.1795; the *Preston Review* as
early as 16.11.1793.
3. Oastler's letters commenced in the *Leeds Mercury* 16.10.1830.Then 'having been treated cavilierly
by the Junior Editor of the *Leeds Mercury*' he switched his correspondence to the *Leeds
Intelligencer*, commencing publication 24.3.1831.
4. *Leeds Times*, 11.12.1841.5.WestYorkshire Archives, Baines MSS 1–41.
5. WestYorkshire Archives, Baines MSS 1-41.
6. *Leeds Mercury*, 13.5.1826.
7. *Leeds Mercury*, 2.12.1843.
8. *Leeds Mercury*, 22.4.1848.
9.*Leeds Intelligencer*, 16.9.1826, 20.5.1829, 5.2.1829, 6.5.1830.
10. *Leeds Mercury*, 9.6.1804.
11. *Leeds Mercury*, 27.10.1804.
12. The Chartist paper, the *Northern Star*, although published in Leeds was in reality a national
rather than a local paper.
13. See *Leeds Mercury*, 1.12.1827.
14. Published by H W Walker from 7.1.1837 it became *The Temperance Advocate*, a monthly magazine, in January 1838.
15. See the *Leeds Times* 6.6.1840.
16. The only extant copy of the *Journal*, the first, is in Bradford Reference Library.
17. An advertisement appeared in the *Leeds Times*, 30.4.1842.
18. *Leeds Mercury*, 7.3.1801.

19. *Leeds Times*, 16.1.1841.
20. *Leeds Mercury*, 20.2.1808.
21. One example of an author giving his name is W J Stears writing on machinery in the *Leeds Independent* 11.10.1825.
22. *Leeds Intelligencer*, 16.3.1795.
23. *Leeds Patriot*, 28.11.1829.
24. *Leeds Mercury*, 10.10.1818.
25. *Leeds Times*, 22.3.1841.
26. *Leeds Intelligencer*, 27.4.1807.
27. *Leeds Mercury*, 5.5.1810.
28. *Leeds Intelligencer*, 9.3.1795.
29. *Leeds Intelligencer*, 14.1.1815.
30. *Leeds Mercury*, 9.5.1812.
31. *Leeds Mercury*, 11.9.1819.
32. *Leeds Mercury*, 30.1.1830.
33. *Leeds Times*, 21.12.1839.
34. *Leeds Intelligencer*, 12.2.1816.
35. *Leeds Patriot*, 26.9.1829.
36. *Leeds Times*, 21.12.1839.
37. *Leeds Intelligencer*, 15.2.1808.
38. *Leeds Patriot*, 26.9.1829.
39. *Leeds Mercury*, 26.5.1804.
40. *Leeds Mercury*, 25.1.1800.
41. *Leeds Mercury*, 13.7.1816.
42. *Leeds Intelligencer*, 7.6.1813.
43. *Leeds Mercury*, 2.10.1813.
44. *Leeds Mercury*, 10.2.1810.
45. *Leeds Mercury*, 12.6.1813.
46. *Leeds Mercury*, 15.5.1813.
47. *Leeds Mercury*, 6.1.1821.
48. Charlton, R J *Charlton's Directory of the Borough of Leeds 1847* (Leeds: C A Wilson & Co for R J Charlton), 1847 p 465.
49. *Leeds Times*, 8.8.1846.
50. *Leeds Times*, 19.9.1846.
51. *Leeds Times*, 30.5.1840.
52. *Leeds Mercury*, 18.1.1812.
53. *Leeds Mercury*, 17.9.1825.
54. Hill C P, *British Economic and Social History* (London: Edward Arnold) 1985 pp 186–187.
55. *Leeds Mercury*, 3.5.1823.
56. *Leeds Mercury*, 20.4.1816.
57. *Leeds Intelligencer*, 8.04.1816.
58. *Leeds Mercury*, 14.2.1818.
59. *Leeds Times*, 2.7.1842.
60. *Leeds Times*, 25.1.1840.
61. *Leeds Mercury*, 19.11.1825.
62. *Leeds Mercury*, 14.2.1816.
63. *Leeds Mercury*, 23.5.1812.
64. Mayhall, John *The Annals and History of Leeds, and Other Places in the County of York* (Leeds: Joseph Johnson), 1860.p.215.
65. *Leeds Mercury*, 16.6.1821.
66. *Leeds Times*, 5.4.1845.
67. *Leeds Mercury*, 29.1.1820.
68. *Leeds Times*, 15.1.1842.
69. *Leeds Times*, 16.4.1842.
70. *Leeds Mercury*, 13.5.1820.
71. *Leeds Mercury*, 28.10.1820
72. *Leeds Mercury*, 21.1.1821.
73. *Leeds Mercury*, 17.2.1821.
74. *Leeds Mercury*, 6.3.1824. Baines commented that he would publish this 'childish and oppressive' letter shortly. It was his stated policy to publish letters he did not necessarily agree with if they remained within the bounds of decency.
75. *Leeds Mercury*, 13.3.1824.
76. *Leeds Intelligencer*, 1.12.1800.

77. *Leeds Mercury*, 17.1.1818.
78. *Leeds Mercury*, 17.9.1825.
79. *Leeds Mercury*, 24.9.1825. A 'nappy' was an archaic word for a foamy alcoholic drink.
80. *Leeds Mercury*, 31.1.1818.
81. *Leeds Mercury*, 13.11.1819.
82. *Leeds Intelligencer*, 15.10.1810.
83. *Leeds Intelligencer*, 22.10.1810.
84. *Leeds Mercury*, 12.10.1811.
85. Anon, *Education in Leeds* (Leeds: Leeds Education Committee), 1926 p 8.
86. *Leeds Mercury*, 12.10.1811.
87. *Leeds Intelligencer*, 9.12.1811.
88. *Leeds Mercury*, 23.11.1816.
89. *Leeds Mercury*, 16.11.1816.
90. *Leeds Mercury*, 13.3.1819.
91. *Leeds Mercury*, 20.3.1819.
92. *Leeds Mercury*, 21.1.1826.
93. *Leeds Patriot*, 19.9.1829.
94. *Leeds Mercury*, 27.1.1810.
95. *Leeds Mercury*, 6.2.1819.
96. *Leeds Patriot*, 20.11.1824.
97. *Leeds Mercury*, 29.10.1825.
98. *Leeds Mercury*, 28.3.1818.
99. *Leeds Mercury*, 14.1.1815.
100. *Leeds Mercury*, 3.10.1818.
101. *Leeds Mercury*, 7.2.1818.
102. *Leeds Mercury*, 16.1.1802.
103. *Leeds Mercury*, 27.6.1812.
104. *Leeds Intelligencer*, 29.6.1812.
105. *Leeds Mercury*, 30.7.1814, 13.8.1814.
106. *Leeds Intelligencer*, 11.1.1813.
107. *Leeds Intelligencer*, 6.5.1830.
108. *Leeds Times*, 20.3.1841.
109. *Leeds Mercury*, 15.2.1812.

5. THE HEATONS OF CLAREMONT

by Dorothy Payne

THE DIARIES OF JOHN DEAKIN HEATON, MD (London) FRCP JP are first mentioned in the *Memoir of Dr John Deakin Heaton* written by Sir Thomas Wemyss Reid, who was editor of the *Leeds Mercury* from 1870 to 1887. He was asked to write this Memoir, by the Heaton family, after Dr Heaton's death in 1880. The Memoir was published in 1883, three years after the death of Dr Heaton (Figure 1). The following extract from Wemyss Reid gives a tantalising look into the annals of the Heaton family . . .

A hundred years hence, the laborious and comprehensive story told by Dr Heaton in the seven or eight closely written quarto volumes, each of many hundred pages, which formed the work of so many years, will be exceedingly valuable as a picture of domestic life in an English provincial town in the reign of Queen Victoria . . .

A further extract from the Memoir leads us into the Society which is the subject of my article.

Figure 1. Dr Heaton's bookplate showing his coat of arms. *Author's Collection*

It was shortly after their return from Paris, in the beginning of 1856, that Dr. and Mrs. Heaton took the first steps in a matter which led to a not inconsiderable change in the course of their daily life in Leeds. Up to this time they had continued to reside in the house in East Parade which had been provided for him by his father when he began practice in the town. Now, however, circumstances led them to contemplate the purchase of a larger detached house, situated on the north side of Woodhouse Square, which was at the time still almost in the suburbs of Leeds, and in the most fashionable quarter of the town. A man's house, it is justly said, is always an indication of his character, and the house which Dr. Heaton was about to purchase, and which under the name of Claremont subsequently became so well known to the inhabitants of Leeds and to many persons of distinction in all parts of the country, affords no exception to this rule . . .

Figure 2. *Claremont,* sometime after it became the headquarters of the Yorkshire Archaeological Society in 1968. *Author's Collection*

Figure 3. Dr J D Heaton –from the Memoir by Wemyss Reid. *Author's Collection*

The move to *Claremont* (Figure 2) was to change the Heaton's life style, according to Wemyss Reid, as the occupier of a large and commodious house, occupying a most convenient situation, he was brought into contact with a wider circle than he previously knew. We are told that

The visitors' book at Claremont contained the names of many who are known to the world at large . . .

John Deakin Heaton (Figure 3) was an eminent citizen of Leeds in the nineteenth century; he was President of the Leeds Philosophical and Literary Society and Chairman of the Council of the Yorkshire College (now the University of Leeds). At various times he was physician to the Public Dispensary, the House of Recovery and the Leeds General Infirmary;

Figure 4. A handbill advertising the circulating library run by John Heaton from his bookselling, printing and stationery business in 1845. *Author's Collection*

he was also a lecturer and treasurer at the Medical School. Dr Heaton and his sister Ellen were the children of John Heaton, bookseller, of Leeds, they were born at 7 Briggate in a house attached to their father's shop and warehouse (Figure 4). According to Dr Heaton, this was the last house to be lived in at street level in Briggate. Ellen was the elder by one year, her birthday was 18 November 1816 and her brother was born on 23 November 1817.

Dr Heaton's wife Fanny, was the daughter of another John Heaton, (Figure 5) Stuff Merchant, who was a partner in the firm of Pease and Heaton of Park Lane, Leeds. The two families were not related. The couple were married at St George's Church, Leeds on 3 April 1850, Ellen Heaton and the bride's sister Marian were the bridesmaids. The Groomsmen were Fanny's brother Aldam Heaton and Andrew Fairbairn, son of Sir Peter Fairbairn. Fanny and Marian were the elder sisters of John Aldam Heaton, he was always called Aldam by the family, and this was the name he used throughout his career.

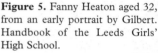

Figure 5. Fanny Heaton aged 32, from an early portrait by Gilbert. Handbook of the Leeds Girls' High School.

Aldam Heaton (Figure 6) moved to Bradford in 1855, after the closing down of the stuff business that Aldam and his father had been carrying on together. It was in June of that year that he married Miss Ellen Morley who had been the governess to Sir Peter Fairbairn's children. They had met as close neighbours of the Fairbairns in Little Woodhouse, As a result of this courtship Aldam was estranged from his family which resulted in his move to Bradford. During his time in Bradford Aldam became involved with John Ruskin and the controversy over the new Wool Exchange Building. In 1861 he moved to Bingley with his wife and two daughters, renting a lovely old house with extensive grounds. The house was called *Woodbank* and it was here that Dante Gabriel Rossetti came to stay when he painted Mrs. Heaton as *The Lady of Woodbank*. Rossetti's first stained glass windows were made

for this house. These were three small panels. In 1875 he moved to London where he was to work with the eminent Victorian architect Norman Shaw. Adam Heaton had premises in Bloomsbury where he employed about seventy workers.

Figure 6. John Aldam Heaton *Author's Collection*

Figure 8. Ellen Heaton's House, 6 Woodhouse Square, now the Swarthmore Adult Education Centre. *Author's Collection*

He designed wallpapers, fabrics, furniture and stained glass. He did the interiors for many of Norman Shaw's houses and he also designed church furnishings. He died in Hampstead in 1897.

We must now return to our Miss Heaton, (Figure 7) sister and aunt to the Heaton menage. The brother and sister appear to have had a reasonably happy relationship, but in

Figure 7. *Miss Ellen Heaton,* pair by Thomas Richmond, 1849. *Reproa courtesy of Thoresby Society.*

later life she became a great trial to him, because of her oddities, which he very annoyingly never really tells us about. At the age of six they attended the same day school. Ellen was a clever child, she was later educated at a school kept by the Misses Plint in Hanover Street. Finally she was sent to a boarding school in Mirfield 'to be finished', by the Misses Waltham. In 1827 her father retired from business and he moved to 31 Park Square, where he died in 1864.

Ellen was now a lady of independent means and Dr Heaton acting as her trustee purchased four houses in Woodhouse Square on her behalf and she went to live at No 6 (Figure 8). No doubt he came to regret this, as it was so near *Claremont,* and she only had to walk up through the garden, whenever she felt like it. Being rich and without family commitments she was able to travel, she spent months at a time living in Rome and London. In 1867 she visited Poland and Russia, where she stayed in St Petersburg and Warsaw. She had aspirations to becoming a poet; her brother was very scathing about her artistic abilities and her love of pre-eminence. She moved in artistic circles, and numbered John Ruskin, D G Rossetti and Elizabeth Barrett Browning among her friends. Dr Heaton gives us the impression that Ellen inflicted herself on celebrities, on one occasion, attaching herself to the Royal party of Queen Victoria and Princes Beatrice, at the International Exhibition at South Kensington in 1871.

At times she was a great trouble to her brother, yet he admits that

Figure 9. Plan of Little Woodhouse showing the houses of the friends and family. Redrawn and computer originated by D Wycherley, from the Ordnance Survey of Leeds 1906 scale 1:25000.

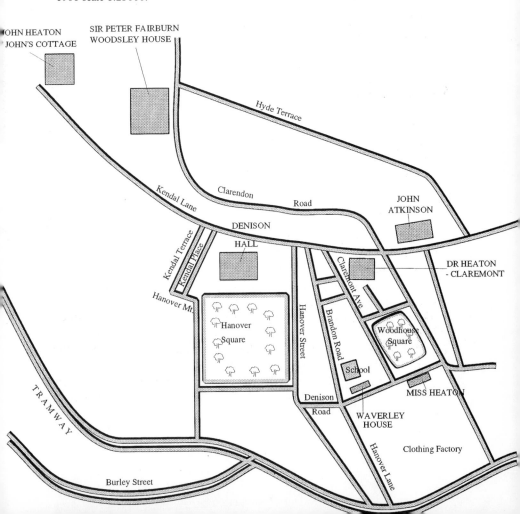

she was a kind aunt; she was generous and would often pay for her nephews and nieces to travel abroad with the family, so that they would not be left behind. She was a patron of the arts, and purchased paintings by Rossetti, Turner and Arthur Hughes, on the advice of John Ruskin. These paintings are now in the Tate Gallery. In 1871. She commissioned a portrait of Elizabeth Barrett Browning, by Field Talford which she presented to the National Portrait Gallery. Her door was always open to local artists, who would bring their portfolios for her to see. Miss Heaton was on the executive committee of the Yorkshire Ladies Council of Education, where she was secretary of the health committee. In 1875 she was involved with University Extension Lectures, and annoyed her brother by offering to pay 3p admission to as many working men who would attend lectures. It was all too much for her brother, in writing to Fanny on 20 February he says . . .

> She has now determined to give a public tea to all working men to come and be addressed by Foxwell. She says she doesn't care what it costs her. She is also determined to pay no attention to anything I may say and she is not going to be made uncomfortable by me. She says she is busy all day and has not time to stop here and talk to Helen. I fear she is rather mad. I fear I am as busy as Ellen; I hope with rather more advantage and a good deal less craze . . .

After his sister Ellen and brother-in law Aldam, Fanny's, sister Marian must have seemed quite tame, she was married to John William Atkinson, who was a solicitor. His father and grandfather both called John were also solicitors. They lived in a large house near the bottom of Clarendon Road, now called *Little Woodhouse Hall*. It had been known as the *Old Judges Lodging* (Figure 10). The Judges being

Figure 10. The Atkinson House. It was the Judge's Lodging from 1864 until 1913, and is now called Little Woodhouse Hall. *Author's Collection*

housed there from 1864 until 1913. Dr Heaton was very proud to have them for his neighbours. The Atkinsons produced several plans for the development of Woodhouse Square and were responsible for the construction of Clarendon Road in the late 1830s. It was because of this connection with the Atkinsons that the Heatons purchased *Claremont*.

Marian and John William, were married on 1 October 1851; he was made a partner with his father and Mr Dibb, (later Dibb Lupton). They also, moved into Woodhouse Square, living on the South West corner in the house now known as *Waverley House* (Figure 11).

So here in 1856 we have Dr and Mrs Heaton moving to 23 Clarendon Road, an eighteenth century merchant's house, which he named *Claremont* (Figure 12). Over the years he made several alterations, adding bay windows to some of the downstairs rooms, Minton tiles in the hall, and an elegant skylight with his

Figure 11. *Waverley House* in the south west corner of Woodhouse Square. The family home of John William Heaton and his wife Marian, sister of Fanny Heaton. *Author's Collection*

coat of arms over the front door. He was later to buy the kitchen garden with glasshouses from the then owner of *Denison Hall*, Mr

Figure 12. *Claremont* c1878, showing the extent of the land before the sale of 1894. *Author's Collection (Courtesy of Nicholas Swire)*

Figure 13. St John's Cottage. Family home of John Heaton, stuff merchant. Now demolished it was on the site of St Michael's College. *Author's Collection*

Sykes Ward. This enabled him to convert his own kitchen garden into a croquet lawn, extending his land on the west side. In front of the house lawns stretched as far as the square, adding to the character of the house. At that time Woodhouse Square consisted of elegant Georgian houses on the south side. In Clarendon Road and the surrounding area new villas and large terrace houses were being built.

The Heatons were living in this fashionable area, surrounded by relatives and friends, although Aldam had left Leeds, his father and his aunt Miss Rimington lived further up the hill at *St John's Cottage*, which was a large house with farmlands (Figure 13). This house now demolished stood on the site of *St Michael's College*. At this time the most elegant house in the area was *Woodsley House* (Figure 14), where Queen Victoria was to stay when she came to open the Town Hall on 6 September 1858. It was the home of Peter Fairbairn, Mayor of Leeds who was knighted by the Queen on that occasion.

At the time of the move to *Claremont*, the Heatons had three children, Helen Frances (Helen) aged six, Marian (May) aged four and John Arthur Dakeyne (Arthur) a baby of five months. They had previously been living at 2 East Parade, in the house purchased for Dr

Heaton by his father as a suitable residence for a newly qualified doctor.

It must have been a lively household, Fanny had been away to school in Malvern, she was used to travelling and entertaining. They sang and played the piano, many programmes of musical evenings are displayed in the diaries. They travelled widely in Britain and on the continent. Dr Heaton and Fanny went on several Cook's Tours, sometimes with Thomas Cook himself. They were constant churchgoers, attending various denominations when away from home. Dr Heaton had low church leanings, and he frowned upon Fanny and Helen, for being carried away with Catholic services when on holiday (he thought she got these tendencies from her brother).

Dr Heaton was a caring father and a loving husband, he wrote to Fanny daily when away from home, or as was often the case when she was away recuperating after some illness or other. He encouraged his children to lead useful interesting lives, the girls were educated as well as the boys, it was a great disappointment to him that they studied harder than their brothers and seemed to be more successful. He supported his wife, when she held a large party for governesses at *Claremont*, to meet Mr Fitch of the Royal Commission for School Enquiry. This was to enable them to discuss the subject of University Middle Class Examinations for girls, in Leeds (Figure 15). They were successful in their endeavours and in December 1869, May sat the Cambridge Local Examination, which she passed obtaining her certificate, being specially approved in French.

Aunt Ellen and the older children often accompanied Dr Heaton to conferences and meetings of Societies such as the British Archaeological Institute, and the British Association, among others. At the British Medical Association's Annual

Figure 14. *Woodsley House.* The home of Sir Peter Fairburn, now *Fairburn House.* *Author's collection*

UNIVERSITY EXAMINATIONS FOR GIRLS.
LADIES' MEETING IN LEEDS.

The improvement of middle-class education has for some time occupied a large share of public attention. The great efforts made by our educational societies, assisted in many cases by State aid, to promote education among the manual labour class, have resulted in the production of schools in which the education given contrasts most favourably with that imparted in schools of far higher pretensions, and attended by scholars moving in a totally different social position. It cannot now be said that education is beyond the reach of the poor, but it is a just ground of complaint that their children are receiving as a class an education superior to the children of their employers. So general has this complaint become, that a Royal Commission is occupied in making inquiry into the condition of middle-class schools, while teachers themselves are actively engaged in endeavouring to obtain a Registration Act, to protect themselves from the intrusion of charlatans. The Universities of Cambridge and Oxford are rendering great assistance to the movement, and by their scheme of annual local examinations offer to teachers and parents a standard by which school-work may be impartially tested. During the first few years these examinations were held a popular feeling existed that teachers would neglect the greater part of their school in order to prepare clever boys for prizes and certificates. The contrary has been the case. An exceptional success may attend a teacher who so acts, but continued success cannot be secured by such means. The effect of the examinations is to introduce throughout schools a graduated programme of work not conceived by individual predilections, but devised by highly qualified members of our chief Universities. The benefit of the examinations is thus extended to those who are not candidates. In consequence of the great success of the scheme as regards boys' schools, the Universities of Cambridge and Edinburgh have opened their examinations to girls. Last year local examinations of the pupils of ladies' schools were held at Brighton, Bristol, Cambridge, Manchester, London, and Sheffield testimony of the examiners respecting their _____ satisfactory. The West Riding has never b____ in taking advantage of any educational m___ Saturday last, through the kindness of D___ meeting of ladies resident in the chief towns ___ and interested in the education of girls wa___ house, Claremont, Leeds, for the purpose of ___ above subject, with Mr. J. G. Fitch, M.A., As___ missioner of the Schools Inquiry Royal Com___ Henry H. Sales, Hon. Sec. to the West Riding ___ Board; and Miss E. Davies, the authoress of ___ on the social and intellectual advancement ___ After luncheon, the subject for consideration ___ duced by Dr. HEATON, who remarked that, al___ meeting was held in his house, neither Mrs. ___ himself should be regarded as its originator. It w___ that ladies would more readily enter into a disc___ private room, and he was ever ready to assist an___ of public welfare, hence the invitations which ___ issued. As regarded the University examination___ they must all feel that a test of the efficiency o___ struction given in their schools was alike va___ teachers and parents. On his part he not only s___ willing for his children's knowledge to be tested, bu___ value any honours they might gain. Mr. Fitch h___ been good enough to turn aside from his very heavy duties, not only as one of Her Majesty's Inspectors of Schools, but as Assistant-Commissioner of the Schools Inquiry Royal Commission, to attend their meeting, and he no doubt would enter very fully into the matter before them. Dr. Heaton then called upon *Mr. Fitch.*

THE great success which has attended middle-class examinations for boys has induced Universities of Cambridge and Edinburgh to ex___ the scheme also to girls' schools. On Saturd___ meeting of ladies resident in the chief towns o___ West Riding was held at the house of DR. HEATO___ Leeds, to discuss this question, and MR. J. E. F___ M.A., Assistant-Commissioner of the Schools Inc___ Commission, MR. SALES, Hon. Sec. of the West Ri___ Educational Board, and MISS DAVIES, authore___ works on the social and intellectual advancemen___ women, attended. Mr. Fitch spoke at some len___ explaining the character of the examinations and ___ advantages resulting from them, and, after a di___ sion, it was decided to form a committee to supe___ tend the examinations which will be held in this t___ in December.

Figure 15. Left: Newspaper cutting reporting the meeting. Comments about the success of the project were added to the left hand page at a later date.

Figure 16. Next page: Diary of Dr Heaton. An excellent example of his work. On the right hand page is his current account.

Below: The invitation to the meeting.

Cambridge Univ. Middle-class Examination for Girls.

J. G. Fitch, Esq., M.A. (of the School Inquiry Royal Commission), and other gentlemen, have kindly consented to meet several ladies interested in the Education of Girls, at the House of Dr. Heaton, Claremont, Leeds, on Saturday, Sept. 8th, 1866, at One o'clock p.m., for the purpose of advocating and discussing the above subject.

LUNCHEON WILL BE PROVIDED.

The favour of the attendance of
is particularly requested.

An early answer is desired, addressed to Mrs. Heaton.

184

Sept.ʳ 1866.   Result of the war in Germany.   Meeting of Governesses at Claremont, on the Middle Class Exam.ⁿˢ for Girls.   Mʳˢ Priestly at Harrogate.

Italian allies have by no means so successful against Austria in the South. The result is that Austria will be nearly driven out of Germany, which will be absorbed by Prussia, & Italy will have Venetia handed over to be added to her kingdom.

The third effort to lay an electric cable between Ireland & America has proved successful; And the Great Eastern ship has just succeeded in picking up the end of the second cable, which was lost in mid-ocean, and splicing it to another to be carried to the American shore.

On Saturday, Sept.ʳ 8., Fanny had a large party of Governesses of Young Ladies Schools, assembled at Claremont, to meet Mʳ Fitch of the Royal Commission for School Enquiry, & Miss Davies, (sister of Rev.ᵈ Llewellyn Davies) to advocate & discuss the subject of University Middle-Class Exam.ⁿˢ for Girls. — This was arranged by the wish of Miss Davies, who wrote to Fanny about it, & herself came to us the day before, for the sake of being present. We had about 30 ladies present, for whom Fanny provided a handsome lunch in the first place, after which they all adjourned to the Drawing Room, where I made a short speech in the first place, opening the subject, & introducing Mʳ Fitch and Miss Davies, after which Mʳ Fitch spoke at some length, — and after that Miss Davies; & various ladies then made remarks and inquiries; after which the company broke up, all "much gratified" but variously impressed as to the subject advocated.   In the evg. Fanny had some visitors to meet Miss Davies.

During the latter part of the month, (September) and during October, I had frequently to go to Harrogate, to see Mrs Priestley, of Wales, (George Shaw's sister,) who, with her husband and two daughters, was staying there, at Cumberland House, and was consulting me professionally, on account of her health. She is a confirmed invalid, but she returned to Wales, in November, certainly much better in health than she had been for long, previously.

On the 24th September, Dʳ Hare's two little boys, aged about 2 & 3 years old, came here with their nurse, to stay with us for a month, during Mrs Hare's confinement; and Florence Sunderland, from Barnsley, — a girl of 15 years of age, — came to stay with us for the same time, to help Fanny to take charge of them.

About this time, there were some meetings of the gentry of Leeds, to decide upon holding an Art & Industrial Exhibition in the New Infirmary Buildings before its appropriation to the permanent use of an Hospital. — It had been understood that the building would be ready for use as an Hospital in 1867,

Meeting in Leeds, in July 1869 he took the chair at the public dinner.
They all made annual visits to London to the Royal Academy visiting
exhibitions and museums. There were many family outings to the East
Coast, Bridlington, Whitby, Redcar and Scarborough. Dr Heaton was
a shareholder in the *Grand Hotel* in Scarborough and as chairman of
the board had many problems with the finances and the construction
of that building.

The Diaries consist of seven volumes which are half-bound in black
leather with marbled covers. Each volume has two red labels on the
spine, the upper one having the initials J.D.H. embossed in gold, and
in some instances the appropriate years are given on the lower panel.
They are neatly and closely written on thick blue paper in black ink.
Strictly speaking they are not diaries, they are his autobiography,
which makes them both interesting and confusing. He started the
diaries in 1859, three years after his move to *Claremont* saying

> *In this month of May 1859 I commenced writing this Autobiography;*
> *which I have now* [Nov. 1863] *brought down to the date of the time*
> *I commenced it . . .*

The first volume covers forty years from 1817 to 1863, and relates the
early history of his family and his own early life in Briggate. He tell us
of the birth of his sister in 1816 and his own birth a year later. He
writes about their school life, his own progress through university, and
his early training to become a doctor.

At the time of his death he was a year behind with his writing, as
this very sad entry by his wife shows.

> *Devonshire House, Harrogate, Sunday July 11th. 1880. I continue*
> *the abstract of my beloved husband's diary with much hesitation and*
> *misgiving – my hand writing is unsuitable – I do not know how much*
> *he would himself have written here of it – but I believe he would wish*
> *me to complete it, and I have the material for doing so. I resume the*
> *narrative of Wednesday July 16th. 1879 and as I shall copy from his*
> *daily notes it will be understood that he is writing in the first*
> *person . . .*

The last entry was on the 24 March 1880 and it concerns his eldest
son

> *Arthur came home this morning arriving somewhere about 6, &*
> *retired to sleep in the drawing room where he was not to be disturbed.*
> *When he awoke he had his breakfast & went out to hunt forthwith,*

so that I did not see him up to the time of writing this . . .

Then in Fanny's own words:

The end Alas!

After Dr. Heaton's death in 1880 Fanny lived there until her death 1893, having survived him by thirteen years (Figure 17). His will stated that after her death or re-marriage the house was to remain unsold so long as any of his children wished to live there. By this time the surviving children had all left Leeds, and Alan Baldwin Heaton the only unmarried Heaton no longer wished to live there. This was in April 1894, and it marks the end of *Claremont* as a desirable residence with a large garden. The property was sold to the architect James Charles, he paid £4,200 for the house together with 9455 square yards of land. This led to the gradual developing of the present

Figure 17. In Memoriam card for Fanny Heaton 17 September, 1893. *Author's Collection*

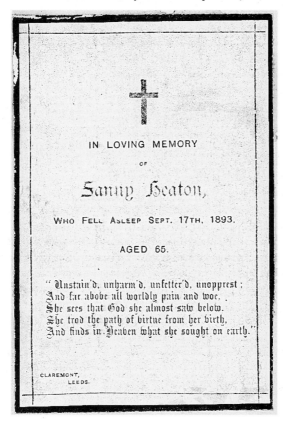

IN LOVING MEMORY

OF

Fanny Heaton,

WHO FELL ASLEEP SEPT. 17TH, 1893.

AGED 65.

" Unstain'd, unharm'd, unfetter'd, unopprest :
And far above all worldly pain and woe, .
She sees that God she almost saw below.
She trod the path of virtue from her birth,
And finds in Heaven what she sought on earth."

CLAREMONT,
LEEDS.

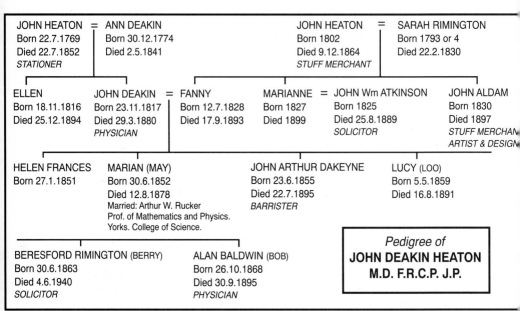

Figure 18. Copy of the Heaton pedigree showing the Heaton connection with John Heaton, the stuff merchant's family. *Drawn by B Payne.*

street plan within the Victorian boundary of *Claremont*. John William Charles, the son of James Charles lived at *Claremont* until 1907. It was sometime after this that it became the *Claremont Nursing Home*, still remembered today by many people. The Nursing Home continued to exist until just before it was purchased by the Yorkshire Archaeological Society in 1968. When all the internal partitions and plumbing were removed, the house was virtually as Dr Heaton had left it.

Miss Heaton must have felt these changes very much, but we might think that she still carried on organising people and bustling about Leeds, but at a much slower rate. She was seventy eight when she died on Christmas day 1894, having outlived her brother and his wife and two of their six children. The following year her eldest and her youngest nephews died and it was her nephew Beresford Rimington Heaton, who inherited her paintings which were bequeathed to the nation after his death in 1940. They are now in the Tate Gallery. She is buried in the family grave which is the only surviving grave in St George's Church yard.

Appendix 1
Selected exerpts from the diaries of Dr John Heaton c1860–1878.
Cook's tours

As we have seen, the Heaton's went on several Cook's Tours, travelling on the Continent and in England and Scotland, sometimes under guidance of Thomas Cook himself. Dr Heaton appears to have been quite satisfied with the excursions, giving us very detailed descriptions of the places visited. He had all the problems of booking ahead for accommodation, which didn't always come up to expectations, being the only gentleman usually with female relatives along as well as Fanny, he was the one who had to make do with the poorest rooms. Poor Fanny was never very well, she was always a worry to him, so he took the greatest care of her. He packed a daily travelling bag for her, which would contain oranges, biscuits and brandy. She always bore up well, and with great determination. Nevertheless he was always pleased to be home. He usually concluded by finding that they had found the cost economical, gave the daily mileage travelled, and was grateful that everything was well at Claremont during his absence.

1860.

. . . *On Friday Sept. 7th. Fanny & I & Marian left Leeds to accompany a public Excursion, escorted by Cook, to Cornwall & Devonshire. We reached Bristol that night, & secured the two last bedrooms at the Railway Hotel. The following day we travelled all day on the broad – gage, passing Bridgwater, Taunton, Dawlish, Teignmouth, & Plymouth, which we reached after three o'clock. There we changed for the narrow gauge, & crawled slowly along, crossing the famous Saltash viaduct, & reached Penzance after 9 o'clock, where we secured accommodation at Balls' Hotel in consequence of my having written beforehand . . .*

. . . *Whilst at Torquay, we called on Mr & Mrs Wolfe; the former having been a curate at St George's under Mr Sinclair, & latter a daughter of Mr Pease, were both well known to us. Mr. Wolfe has a large handsome church here, which I believe he was partly instrumental in building with some of his wife's money. We heard him preach in it on Sunday. I have nothing very remarkable to record of*

Torquay . . .

. . .We had been struck previously by the scarcity and dearness of fruit but in Exeter we found a profusion of most beautiful fruit very cheap. We brought away with us 6 dozen of the finest apricots I ever saw, for preserving. In the afternoon of Tuesday, we went by train to Bristol, being now decidedly on our way home. We staid at the Station Inn, which was hot & crowded & rendered more noisy by a body of Rifle Volunteers from a review at Gloucester, who drank beer & smoked, & the band actually played under the windows until midnight . . .

. . .Wednesday was devoted to a visit to Bath, familiar to Fanny and Marian from their having been at school there, & they particularly wished to revisit some of their old haunts & recall old associations there . . .

. . .Afterwards we had our dinner; & returned to Bristol . . .

We had to rise early the next morning at half past 5, to be ready to start at 6.30. Owing however, to some confusion at starting consequent on the number of passengers, we were not fairly off till 7.0 'Clock. Other delays occurred in picking up passengers at succeeding stations, and from the accommodation in the train being insufficient. And consequently upon the loss of time the whole train was placed in circumstances of the greatest possible hazard, from which we escaped without any accident only by a hair's breadth. At one station where we stayed we heard a call that we must get on as the Express was after us! At the next station there was again delay; & at the station next to this we were to be shunted on to a siding to allow the Express to pass us. In shunting we had to back across the main line, to a siding on the other side; & during the whole of this operation with a very long and heavy train, it is evident we were liable to be run into by a train on either the up or down rails. Many heads were looking anxiously out of the windows while this operation was being slowly effected. At length I exclaimed, now we are safely off the main line. And immediately, a coal train ran past at a moderate speed, on the rails we had last cleared, in the direction opposite to that we were travelling; & then the Express rushed along at a tremendous speed on the same rails which we had hitherto pursued our journey and which we had just left. Thus were we & many others mercifully preserved from frightfull destruction

Fanny had been a good deal agitated by the anxiety which was general till our safety was proclaimed, & by the narrowness of our escape; and she was made faint & poorly from which she did not fully recover that day. However we reached home safely in the evening, where we found the children well, & all apparently right. We had travelled about 800 miles in the course of a fortnight; and although we had been liberal, without extravagance, in our living ect., our actual travelling expenses, independently of any purchases, were only 11 guineas each . . .

Family life.

1863.

. . . On Monday, June 29, I took Helen to London in order that Mr. Lintott might extract some of her teeth which were decayed and gave her much pain. Fanny was pretty well, at this time, and not immediately expecting her confinement. On our way to Town a shocking occurrence took place. The train was unexpectedly stopped at Newark (that not being a station at which it should have stopped in ordinary course, being an express train) and a man was taken out of a 2nd. class carriage and laid upon the platform apparently dead. Thinking that he might be in a fit, I got out & went to him, when I found that he had just before shot himself through the head, and was quite dead. The blood was trickling from his head, and a thin cloud of steam rose from it into the air. Two other passengers were with him in the same compartment, to whom he was quite unknown; of course they had been much startled by the explosion & shocked by the occurrence; it was very well that there were two others, to prevent any suspicion against one. He was evidently a foreigner, & had a ticket in his pocket taken at Edinburgh for London but there was no evidence to show who he was. His two companions staid at Newark to give evidence at the inquest. It afterwards was shown that he was a Frenchman; apparently respectably connected, but in pecuniary difficulties, from which he had relieved himself of in this remarkable way, leaving a wife and children. He did not seem to be above 40 years of age. We reached Suffolk Place without further adventure in the forenoon, having departed by a very early train, and I at once went with Helen to Mr Lintott, who extracted two teeth. Then we called on the Hares, in Langham Place, and I then took Helen to the Polytechnic Exhibition where we saw The Ghost *performed in better style than at the Leeds Music Hall, and some curious conjuring tricks, and a foreigner, Herr Susman, gave some curious imitations of the songs of various birds, and the voices of other animals. After dinner we went to the Old Water Colour exhibition; and after tea we called on Dr. &*

Mrs. Hare in Brook St., and Helen wrote a letter to her Mama, &
my sister called on us at our lodgings. So we had a very busy day. The
next morning I had a letter from Fanny to the effect that she thought
her confinement was coming on, & she wished me to return home. As
I had to take Helen to the dentist again, I went with her after
breakfast to take a hasty glance of the Royal Academy Exhibition, on
our return from which I found a telegram from Marian that Fanny
had given birth to a fine boy at 9.40 that morning (June 30th) and
was doing well. After that I took her to Mr Lintott's, where, after
calling twice and waiting a long time, we got our business transacted.
We left London at 5, and reached Leeds at 10.15; the carriage was
waiting to take us to Claremont. We found Fanny doing well, &
cheerful, and the baby well and lively. On the whole Fanny went on
well & recovered nicely . . .

Figure 19. The Claremont Ball. A dance programme for one of these balls. Balls were
a regular entertainment in Leeds during the Victorian period. The cards were carried
by the men. Spencer's band appears to have been the superior band in Leeds at that
time. *Author's Collection*

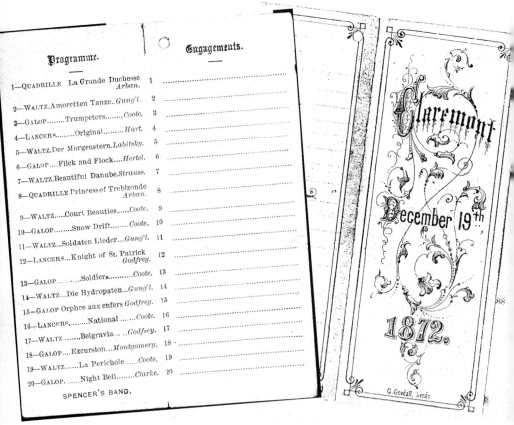

Evening entertainment.

1872.

... *On December the 19th. There was ball at Claremont for the benefit of the rising generation* (Figure 19). *We had upwards of 80 acceptances, and the whole house was disarranged to meet the requirements of the occasion. The Dining-room was converted into the ball-room, by taking up the carpet, and covering the floor with Holland; and the Green-room was emptied of furniture & converted into a supper room. The Library was the Tea-room. Arthur returned home from school, this very day. Janie Roberts & her brother from Sheffield, Miss Holt from Harrogate, & Miss Landon from Kippax staid at Claremont till the following day, so that our house was well filled that night. The company broke up at about 2 o'clock. Fanny went about all day, though so great an invalid and did not seem to be worse for her exertions* ... (Figure 20)

Figure 20. Dr and Mrs Heaton at *Claremont* c1864.
Courtesy of Nicholas Swire

August 5th. Friday.

1864.

On the following day Saturday, the Judges arrived to open the Assizes on Monday. This being the first occasion of Assizes being held in Leeds, it occasioned considerable excitement, & some special formality was observed ; A procession was formed from the Ry Station to the Town Hall consisting of the High Sheriff's [Mr Gascoigne of Parlington] *state carriage, javelin men, trumpeters and footmen, and several private carriages, & a great mob of the people. At the Town Hall the Judges opened the commission and thence proceeded to the Judges Lodgings, which are Mr Atkinsons old house at Little Woodhouse, which together with Mr Dibbs house, which is attached, the Town Council have purchased. So that we are very near neighbours of the Judges, and hear their silver trumpets every morning during the assizes . . .*

Sources

Andrew Saint, *Richard Norman Shaw.*
Virginia Surtees, *Sublime and Instructive.*
Brian and Dorothy Payne, (Extracts from the Journals of John Deakin Heaton, MD).
Thoresby Society Miscellany Vol. 15 part 2.
Brian and Dorothy Payne, *Claremont Guide,* Yorkshire Archaeological Society.
T Wemyss Reid, *Memoir of John Deakin Heaton.*
Malcolm Hardman, *Ruskin and Bradford.*
K E Procter, *Leeds Girls High School Part 1, 1876–1906.*
Letters and Journals of John Deakin Heaton, private collection.

6. ST CHAD'S, A HOME FOR WAIFS AND STRAYS: A HISTORY OF HOLLIN HALL, 1894–1996

by Samantha J Fisher.

I STOOD ON THE TARMAC OF the car park, facing the front door of the old red brick building I have always known as Hollin Hall. As I looked up at its broken windows and the roof which was open to the sky, I wondered at the story that lay behind this big, silent, empty building that had stood here for a hundred years and more. It was this idle thought that led me on a quest into the past which I found both fascinating and rewarding.

My search took me further back into the past than the building of Hollin Hall. It all began with the founding of an organisation then known as The Church of England Society for the Providing of Homes for Waifs and Strays in 1881.

One day in 1881, a young Sunday school teacher by the name of Edward de Montjoie Rudolf came across two of his pupils begging on the streets of London, instead of attending Sunday school. Mr Rudolf made various enquiries and uncovered the sad facts that their father was dead and the family was struggling to survive without his vital income. Rudolf realised that there were many children in the same position. Poor and needy and desperate for help, many of these children had no relatives to turn to, no one who would or perhaps could care for them financially. So they would often take to the streets

Figure 1. Glebe House. St Chad's Home in August 1890. *Children's Society Archive*

and beg from passers-by. The only other option was the workhouse which had a terrible reputation. It was cramped and filthy and full of disease. Families made destitute that entered through its doors were all too often separated and likely to remain so until they died in squalid penury.

Rudolf did not want children to experience this terrible fate. So he formed the idea for child care in a warm comfortable homelike environment. He approached the then, Archbishop of Canterbury, Archibald Campbell Tait (1868–1883), who gave the idea his backing. In 1882 The Church of England Central Homes for Waifs and Strays was registered. They opened their first two homes shortly afterwards with just thirty-four orphaned children and a yearly income of £740.

However, it was soon painfully obvious that the need for these homes was great. The number of homes rose quickly from two in 1882 to thirty-four by 1890. One thousand five hundred and fifty seven children were living in the care of The Society, and it had already found 2, 658 children places to live with families of their own. Sadly there were still many more children needing care and waiting for help. So it was that in January 1889 another home was opened. This was The Society's twenty-ninth home and it was known as the St Chad's Home for Waifs and Strays in Far Headingley, Leeds. However the home was not the place we know today as Hollin Hall. It was first located in a building known as Glebe House which stood at the top of Hollin Lane, a short distance from Hollin Hall (Figure 1).

The home was opened officially by Lady Balfour and dedicated by the Reverend Dr Smyth of St Chad's Parish church. There was a small ceremony with a number of well known people of the community in attendance. Among those present were; Mrs Lucy Beckett(wife of Ernest William Beckett MP),a member of the very well known Becketts family in Leeds, Reverend H D Barrett, Miss Stansfield, the Lady Superintendent of the home and several of the local clergy. This home was specifically for girls. There already were two other homes open in the area; the Becketts home and the Bede home for boys. All these were well supported by many in the community, who saw this as a Christian duty of Victorians. But I think people genuinely wished to help these unfortunate children. These homes were similarly run to all the other homes under the Society's care. They were well managed and for the most part self supporting, but donations were always welcome.

This particular home was to be a little different in that the girls who would reside here would probably never find it easy to gain useful employment in the big wide world due to their delicate constitutions

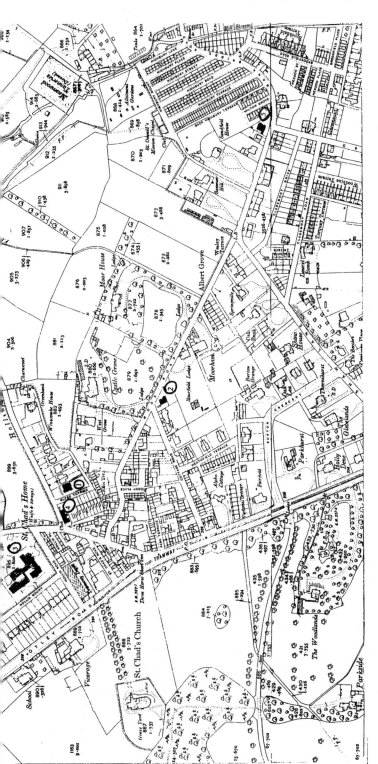

Figure 2. Map showing the position of all the sites. *The Author*

KEY

1. **Glebe House.** The site of St Chad's home for waifs and strays.
2. **Moorside.** The site of the original laundry.
3. **St Chad's Home for Waifs and Strays** – later Hollin Hall.
4. **St Chad's school** c1892.
5. **Monkbridge House.** Where the girls slept prior to the building of St Chad's.

or disabilities. They were however given training in various housecrafts to help bring in an income to the home, and if any were reasonably fit and able they might possibly find a place at a knitting factory or in domestic service. They were also given a good general education with time to spare for informal activities and recreation. About thirty girls resided there under the chaplaincy of Dr Smyth, vicar of St Chad's Parish church (Figure 2).

All the girls were employed in the useful occupation of stocking knitting and laundrywork. These were cottage industries and helped to earn money for the home. Glebe house was where the stocking knitting industry was set up. The whole of the ground floor was fitted out for the purpose of making stockings of all kinds. There was the machine room where nine machines were installed. Each machine could make seven pairs of stockings a day. Then there was the finishing room where all the newly knitted stockings were sent to be finished. This was known as 'toeing' and had to be done by hand. The girls were very skilled at this. In fact some of the girls were so adept they won a bronze medal and diploma at the Worlds Fair in Chicago in 1893. After the stockings had been finished off they were pressed with a hot iron over a specially shaped block called a last and then passed on to the storeroom where they were sorted into pairs, carded and sent for inspection by the forewoman. When she was happy with them they were wrapped in bundles and put in the storeroom ready for sale. The industry was organised and managed from the office along with the general day-to-day running of the home. The stockings were all made from the best quality yarns of Paton and son of Alloa, and sold to all manner of people. Even Royalty were known to have bought some of their hosiery. The girls made a wide range of socks and stockings from their diversity of yarns. Ladies' and babyies' silken hosiery, cashmere stockings, gentlemen's shooting socks and even coarse socks which

Figure 3. Advertisement in Our Waif's and Strays newsletter, February 1899, showing the range and prices of the knitwear produced by the girls. *Children's Society Archive*

Ladies' black cashmere stockings, 2s. 9d.; Scotch fingering, 1s. 6d.; Children's woollen stockings from 1s. 9d.; Ladies' black silk stockings, best quality, 9s. 6d.; Ladies' silk and wool stockings, 4s. 6d.; Gentlemen's Scotch fingering shooting stockings, 3s. 6d.; Gentlemen's Scotch fingering bicycle stockings, 2s. 6d.; Gentlemen's woollen socks, from 2s.; Boys' heather fingering, 1s. 6d.; Babies' silk socks, 1s. 6d.

Figure 4. Glebe House. The original home. *The Author*

were for the inmates of Reformatories and Industrial schools. Winter was usually their busiest time of year. In 1890, they sold £1075 worth of hosiery. In the following year they sold over a £1,000 worth of goods. The most they made in a year were 11, 100 stockings! (Figure 3)

So life continued quite successfully for the girls of the St Chad's home in Far Headingley. By 1891 it was becoming obvious that the present home was just too small. The girls worked at Glebe house at their stocking knitting but went to Moorside on Moor Road, just around the corner, to carry out the laundrywork. Further down the street, Moor Road joined Monkbridge Road. Halfway along which was situated Monkbridge House where the girls slept. It was apparent that not only was the home too small, but that it was also time consuming and inconvenient trekking from one place to another for their daily routine (Figures 4 and 5).

Figure 5. The original site of St. Chad's School in Hollin Lane. *The Author*

So it was agreed that a new home must be built. A site was chosen and proposals made and passed to this end. But money had to be raised to pay for the new building. So patrons of St Chad's, in whose parish the home stood, organised the raising of funds. The Waifs and Strays Society also had supportive organisations that helped to raise funds for the home. These included a Needlework Association, an Association of Friends and the Children's Union all dedicated to helping those in need. They held sales at the home of all the crafts and produce they made including the stockings made at the home. They had musical evenings, coffee mornings, buffets and dinners One such fund raising event which proved very popular was called Pound Day. This was where anyone who wanted to could take part. All they had to do was bring in a pound in weight of anything they could think of that would raise money, or bring in a pound in money. Larger donations were made by the wealthier and more eminent people. One such gift was from Mr Ernest William Beckett MP.

Figure 6. Mr E W Beckett, MP JP.

Mr Beckett was a member of the prosperous and eminent Becketts family in Leeds. He was born at Roundhay on 25 November 1856. He had a formal education at Eton and Trinity College Cambridge after which he joined the family banking firm of Beckett and Co. in Leeds. He loved the arts and travelled widely. His other great interest was politics. He became Member of Parliament for Whitby in 1885 (Figure 6).

In 1883 he married Miss Lucy Tracy Lee from New York, daughter of Mr William P Lee. Together Mr and Mrs Beckett made Kirkstall Grange their home (today Kirkstall Grange is better known as the Grange at the Becketts Park site, now a training college for students). Both Mr and Mrs Beckett were patrons of St Chad's church and showed great interest and concern for others less fortunate than themselves. Lucy Beckett in particular paid close attention to the well-being of people in the community. She was quite often present at functions and visited people who were sick and disabled. She was a conscientious supporter of the scheme set up for employing a parish nurse and contributed financially towards her upkeep.

Lucy bore Mr Beckett three children; Lucille, Muriel and Ralph. Each birth was a notable event in the community. After Ralph's birth the bells of St Chad's rang out in celebration on Sunday 3 May 1891. It was mentioned in the parish magazine and in church that

In Memoriam.

LUCY TRACY BECKETT,

Born, 1864;

Died May 9th, 1891.

is with the deepest regret and sadness that we have to place on record the death of 's. Ernest Beckett, an event which has cast a gloom over the whole parish and brought true d deep sorrow into the hearts of all.

The circumstances of her death are already well known. On Sunday, May 3rd, she gave birth her first son, Mr. Beckett's heir, and at first seemed to be going on well; but on Wednesday change for the worse took place, and she gradually sank, and passed away peacefully on turday afternoon.

She was laid to rest in the quiet country churchyard at Adel on the following Friday afternoon, idst every sign of grief and sympathy on the part of the large assembly present. The funeral ocession was met at the gate by the Rector of Adel (Rev. C. H. Owen), and the Vicar (Rev. F. Hoyle), together with the S. Chad's Choir. Inside the Church—which was beautifully corated with some of the many crosses and wreaths of flowers that had been sent—the Choir ng the 90th Psalm, and after the Lesson, which was read by Mr. Owen, the hymn, " Nearer, y God, to Thee," was feelingly sung. Then in a solemn pause, the " Dead March " was played; d immediately after the procession passed out of the Church, singing the familiar hymn, Jesu, Lover of my Soul," on the way to the grave, amidst a heavy down-pour of rain, which fortunately lasted throughout the remainder of the service.

Preaching on Sunday, the 10th, the Vicar said—" Less than a week ago the joy-bells ere rung in honour of the birth of her first son; and to-day the muffled peal that lls us to Church announces that she has passed away, and that two sorrows—the aviest that can befall a man—have fallen upon her husband within half a year. It as a life that seemed to have so much before it—of happiness, position, and sefulness. For it was her earnest desire to use what God had given her for the welfare of hers. Her Christmas contribution for the Sick and Poor was a constant gift. She was warmly terested in the scheme for providing a Parish Nurse for the Poor, and just before leaving home e gave the first subscription that was received for the purpose. Nor were these mere matters : form or duty, for it was her earnest desire to take a personal interest in the lives of the village eople; and at her own request I had given her the names of some of the aged and sick whom e wished to visit on her return home—that return which was never to take place."

The most deep and real sympathy is, we feel sure, felt for Mr. Beckett in his sad bereavement; d we trust that " the God of all comfort " may give the consolation which He only can bestow.

Figure 7. *In Memoriam* tribute to Lucy Beckett in *St Chad's Parish Magazine*, St Chad's Church.

Sunday. But by Wednesday Lucy was desperately ill. She never recovered and died the following Saturday, 19 May at twenty-seven years of age. She was deeply mourned by all who knew her and for the loss of all her good work and efforts to improving life for others.

She was buried in a quiet country churchyard in Adel. It was as a memorial to his wife that Mr Beckett MP made the tremendous donation of £3,000 towards the building of the new home. In the parish magazine of June 1891 he makes mention of his intention to gift the building works this money. The estimated total cost of building the new home was £6,000. By the time the home was opened most of this money had been raised (Figure 7).

The home was to be dedicated to Lucy Beckett's memory and on 6 November 1893 the formal opening ceremony of the start of the building works took place at the site. After a short service in St Chad's Church, on the opposite side of Otley Road from the home, a small procession of people made its way down to the site. Mr Beckett was present with his three children, Lucille, Muriel and Ralph, together with the architect Mr Hobson, Mrs Lee of Kirkstall Grange, Miss Stansfield, who was the Lady Superintendent of the home, the matrons and all the resident girls from the home. Prayers of dedication were said over the site of the home, by the Vicar of St Chad's, after which the architect presented the three Beckett children with small hammers. Each child in turn approached the foundations and formally laid a stone carved with their initials saying, *In the Name of the Father, the Son and the Holy Ghost, I lay this stone to the glory of God and in the memory of my dear Mother.* Ralph was all of two-and-a-half years old by this time! Today you can still see the memorial stones inlaid in the walls below the windows and to either side of the front door. Over the front door can be seen the crest of the Becketts family; three boars' heads surrounded by an ermine tails trim (Figure 8).

As from November the building of the new home got under way. The new home did not include the laundry immediately, this was to be added at a later date, at a further cost of £1, 500. The laundry work was still carried out at Moorside on Moor Road. Nor did the amount

Figure 8. Beckett family crest over the door. *The Author*

of money raised for building works cover the cost of actually furnishing the home. This was to be achieved by yet more fund raising events and donations and sales of hosiery made by the girls.

The building progressed satisfactorily and by late 1894 was finally complete. On 1 December 1894, the new St Chad's Home for Waifs and Strays was opened. The official opening ceremony was amazingly well attended by people from all walks of life; from the local community to wealthy and prominent notables in general society. The event had newspaper coverage from the *Leeds Mercury* and the forerunner to the *Yorkshire Post*. The Bishops of Richmond and Wakefield were there to bless the home as were the Vicar of Leeds; Dr Talbot, the vicar and the curate of St Chad's, the Rev J F Hoyle and the Rev F N Hardwick; the matrons and children from the Bede Home, the Beckett's Home and St Chad's Home. A large procession was formed after a service at the church, which walked down to the home, marching along behind the banners depicting their homes. Girls and boys from the Childrens Union marched with them to the music of the Adel Reformatory band. Even the fire brigade made an appearance. Everyone crowded round the front of the new building to watch the opening and dedication of the new home by the Bishop of Richmond. He led the ceremony to the front door. There Lucille Beckett, eldest daughter of Mr Beckett MP stepped forward with a brand new key and opened the front door. Now formally open, everyone was allowed to go in and inspect the whole building. Curiosity satisfied they were offered tea in the hall and invited to attend a sale of the homes' socks and stockings along with Christmas cards, produce and crafts.

The new home was to house sixty girls and their home industries; stocking knitting, catering and later laundry. To either side of the hall, upon entering the home, were two offices where the Lady Superintendent managed the day to day running of the home. At the far end of the hall a room opened out into a spacious area. On one side were three arches, in the centre arch was placed a replica statue of *Christus Consolator* by Bartel Thorwaldsen. At the west end of this part of the hall was a magnificent fireplace. A chimney piece beautifully carved from oak was given by Mr Beckett, from Kirkstall Grange. He also gave a portrait of his wife and two eldest daughters to the home, but they are sadly no longer in the building. Furniture and fittings were given by the Honourable Henry Butler. Beds could be bought for £10 and presented to the home by anyone who so wished. Sometimes people had small brass plates fixed to the bedsteads with the benefactors name etched upon it. The Children's Union bought

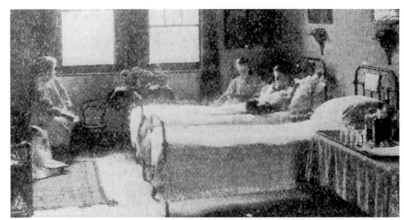

Figure 9. One of the sick wards, February 1899. *Children's Society Archive*

Figure 10. Girls' Hall. Recreation hour February 1899. *Children's Society Archive*

Figure 11. In the playground, February 1899. *Children's Society Archive*

some of the beds with the money they raised from selling their craft-works. Friends donated pictures and bedspreads and anything imaginable that helped to make the home a warm and welcoming place for the children to live.

Because a lot of the girls were frail or disabled in some way, two hospital wards were created, one upstairs on the first floor and another at the top of the building. The first floor ward had four beds and a prayer desk where the sister read to her charges morning and evening prayers, and the chaplain, Dr Smyth gave a short service once a week. Next to the ward was the bathroom and further on the dispensary. Many of the children needed daily medication. The second ward on the second floor had an isolation ward next to that, for serious and suspicious illnesses. However, the home did have an arrangement with the main Leeds hospitals to take and treat their seriously ill children (Figure 9).

Friends and associates of St Chad's home took it upon themselves to decorate the home creating an amiable and pleasant atmosphere. The big hall downstairs was decorated by a 'friend' of the home. This room was where the girls took their meals and spent their leisure time (Figure 10). They had open cupboards with pigeon holes for their personal belongings. These were covered by red curtains. The hall looked south-west over the playground which had slides and swings and a pond for recreation (Figure 11). Next to the girls' hall was the kitchen which had a huge cauldron in it, on the boil all the time for instant teas and breakfast. Having the kitchen here also helped those girls who were in training for domestic service by learning to cook and clean and manage household duties. These girls went on to find

Figure 12. Workroom interior at St. Chad's at Glebe House c1890. *Children's Society Archive*

Figure 13. Workroom interior at St Chad's Glebe House c1890. *Children's Society Archive*

service in the big houses in the area or in the catering service elsewhere. Near the kitchen was the wardrobe room. This was where the
girls learned to sew and mend and alter clothing donated to them.
They also made the clothes that the children wore at the home. If the
donations couldn't be used they were sold on to raise an income for
the home (Figures 12, 13, and 14).

On 13 July 1896, the new laundry was opened at the back of the
home. The girls would go there after breakfast and begin the daily task
of laundering the clothes. The laundry was brought to the home on
Mondays, sorted, laundered, re-packed and returned on Fridays. This

Figure 14. The new knitting room at St. Chad's, Hollin Hall February 1899. *Children's
Society Archive*

must have been a highly organised part of the home's industries, as they took care of laundry belonging to at least eighty of the large families in the surrounding area. Near the laundry where the clothes were washed were other rooms for drying and ironing and re-packing in big baskets.

The building of the home had finally brought all the children and their work together under one roof. This made it much more convenient economical and efficient than before. The home continued to be run successfully by a Lady Superintendent and her matrons through the First World War right up to the eve of the Second World War. They contributed to the war effort whenever they could.

In 1915 England was into its second year of The Great War. On the home front large buildings were used as hospitals to take all the casualties of the war. One such building used as a military hospital was Becketts Park Training College. The St Chad's home, close by, was doing its share to support the boys at the front. In four months they made 6,000 pairs of socks for the troops to wear, besides their normal output of 8, 527 socks and stockings. In 1914 they made a total of 13,611 pairs of socks and re-footed 390 pairs, presumably for those returning to the front! They helped in other ways too, taking on more children through the Church of England Society, orphaned by the war. Many of the boys from the Bede Home were called to war. Sadly some of those never came home.

During the war years one of the matrons of the home retired. Miss Barter had been with St Chad's Home for twenty years helping to make it the success it was. After the war, in the early twenties, life was hard but the home still managed to prosper through its own efforts and the help of friends in the community. They held many events, some were purely social, others money raising. They held musical soirées and reading evenings, bazaars and sales. A Girl Guide troupe met regularly in one of their rooms once a week. During the days they went regularly to school and church at St Chad's.

When the home was situated at Glebe house at the top of Hollin Lane, it was literally just across the road to school. The original school was the very first building on Hollin Lane. Now it is a stained-glass craft shop, a barbers and a hairdressers. The school moved to Otley Road and then to West Park.

Every day the girls could be seen walking to school in two straight lines, smartly dressed in their reefer coats and red berets. One gentleman, Mr A Johnson, remembers them playing in the playground at St Chad's school where he went as a boy. He also remembers the old horsedrawn laundry wagon that meandered through the streets of Headingley collecting the washing in huge wicker baskets, from the doors of the big families. The wagon owner was a Mr Howard. He and his covered wagon would leave the stables in Authorpe Road, Monkbridge to collect his bundles and deliver them to the laundry at St Chad's home. The laundry was at the rear of the home so he took his wagon round by Hollin Mount and in through the gates to the back door.

The home carried on its self-supporting work until the outbreak of the Second World War. Then it was closed and commandeered as an ARP (Air Raid Precautions) station and supplementary ambulance station by Leeds City Council. It was run by a Superintendent ARP officer and office staff, with the help of part-time ARP officers and ambulance workers, during the day. No one as yet knows where all the children from the home went. As an ambulance station, men and women from all walks of life offered up their cars and vans to be used as ambulances, parking them on the nearby roads. They served the main hospitals and also First Aid Outposts such as the one at St Chad's Primary school on Otley Road. During the day the building, which had become known as Hollin Hall, was used by the auxiliary forces. By night the ambulance crews took over. In the hall tables were laid out for the volunteers to pass the time waiting for 'the call'. There was food in the kitchens and the muted strains of radio music drifted by in the background. Upstairs the rooms were laid out as sleeping dormitories for those just coming off shift or doing a quick turn around. Every day the Deputy ARP officer for Leeds, Mr H Young, also UXB (Unexploded Bombs) Disposal Services expert, visited the hall to give instruction on the use of gas masks and what to do in the event of various types of gas attack. He also taught the basics of what to do in the event of a bombing raid. As it turned out Leeds was actually bombed very little during the war years. The odd bomb was off-loaded as the returning German bombers passed by overhead. There was only one serious bombing raid on Leeds when ninety tonnes of bombs were dropped, during 14–15 March 1941.

After the war Hollin Hall remained empty for several years until it was bought and used by the Yorkshire College of Housecraft. It was then that a teaching block was built onto the back of the hall near the laundry, so that students could put the theory of their work into practice. The college became known as the 'Pud School', presumably because of the famous Yorkshire Puddings, although many housecraft colleges around the country were christened with the same or similar titles. The name stuck for a long time. The college merged with the Leeds Polytechnic which more recently became Leeds Metropolitan

Figure 15. Weetwood Primary School

University. Students remained there until 1992 when they were moved to other halls of residence and the building was sold back to the Education Authority. Now Hollin Hall has been refurbished as Weetwood Primary school for children, aged four to eleven, with a nursery school recently included (Figure 15).

Today the playground is alive with the laughter and shouts of the children, an echo of the past? The bell rings at 8.55 am for the beginning of school. All the children line up in their classes and walk quietly into school. The door closes behind them, opening a new chapter in the history of the building once known as St Chad's Home for Waifs and Strays, a hundred years ago.

Chronology of Events

1881/2	Church of England Society for the Providing of Homes for Waifs and Strays was formed.(two homes opened with thirty-four children)
1883	Marriage of Mr Ernest William Beckett to Lucy Tracy Lee.
1891	3rd May: Ralph Beckett was born, youngest of three children. Two older sisters Lucille and Muriel.
1891	9th May: Lucy Beckett dies of childbirth fever at twenty seven years of age.
1891	June. Extract from *St Chad's Parish Magazine* showing the dedication of the new home to Lucy Beckett's memory.
	Account of the Church of England Society's work.
1893	St Chad's original school building closed and sold at auction.
1893	6th November: Opening ceremony of the building works on the Hollin Hall site. The three Beckett children laid stones with their initials on.
1894	1st December: St Chad's Home for Waifs and Strays was formally opened.
1917	10th May: Ernest William Beckett MP (Lord Grimthorpe) died.
1933	29th May: Edward de Montjoie Rudolph (Founder of the C of E Waifs and Strays Society) died aged 82 years.
1938/1939	St Chad's Home is closed and commandeered by the military for use as an ambulance station.
1941	14th/15th March Leeds suffered its worst bombing of the war.
1945	Home left empty for several years.
1950	Education Authority purchased Hollin Hall with a view to adapting and providing accommodation for sixty students and facilities for housewifery and laundry work. Was used as hall of residence for students until sold.
1995/1996	Refurbished as Weetwood Primary School and opened in January 1997

Notes and References

Main Sources
St Chad's Parish Magazines vols: 1890–1891
1893–1894
1895–1896
1933–1934
Kelly's Directory of Leeds for ; 1891, 1894, 1897(pp 31, 824),1921, 1938, 1940–47.
Phillip Elston *Old Far Headingley* printed by A. Wigley and son Ltd.
Leo Connell. *A Century of Teacher Training in Leeds 1875–1975* Leeds Metropolitan University.
Leo Connell *A History of Modern Leeds by Derek Fraser.* Manchester University Press.
Making Lives Worth Living Magazine Our Waifs and Strays, The Children's Society
Yorkshire Evening Post, 1894
The Leeds Mercury, 1894
Yorkshire Evening Post, 1941
W H Scott *Leeds in the Great War,* by Library Arts Committee
O/S maps of 1893, 1894. Far Headingley area of Leeds.

Acknowledgements

Many thanks to Mr Alfie Johnson for his amazing knowledge, his personal memories and all his help in providing information and references; to St Chad's church for the loan of their Parish magazines; to Mr H. Young for allowing me to interview him about his memories of Hollin Hall during the Second World War; to the Archivist of The Children's Society, Mr Ian Wakeling and his assistant archivist Dawn Burnett for the wealth of information which they sent. Photographs by kind permission of The Children's Society Archives. Thank you to the staff of Leeds Central Lending Library, specifically the Local History Library for their help and advice on literature and old maps. Thank you to Judith Marsden of Leeds Metropolitan University

7. NOTHING BETTER: A SHORT HISTORY OF THE CITY SCHOOL OF COMMERCE

by Lynne M Stevenson Tate

THE FIRST HALF OF THE TWENTIETH century has seen some fascinating shifts in the types of employment available to the majority of the population of Britain. In particular there has been the one from jobs in the industrial and manufacturing sector, to those in the clerical and business sectors. Prior to 1914 most clerical and business posts were held by men, but the huge casualties engendered by the First World War, meant that increasingly, the junior office posts were filled by women and girls. The remaining male office workers were accommodated in the more senior supervisory and management grades. This period also saw the emergence of schools and colleges whose curriculum was solely designed to cater for the clerical, accounting and book-keeping needs of the business community. One such school was the City School of Commerce which was established in 1923 and closed in 1964. The City School of Commerce was only one of the many that were established in Leeds between 1900 and 1939 (Figure 1).

Figure 1. Frontage of the City School of Commerce c1940 after rebuilding. *Author's Collection*

In the 1901 Trade Directory for Leeds there are three establishments listed that offered specific commercial education; the Leeds
Civil Service Institute and the Northern Institute, and the
Commercial Evening School.[1] By the outbreak of the First World War
in 1914, a number of other private commercial schools had been
established in the city, raising the total to seven.[2] By 1929 this figure
had risen to eleven; with at least one of the private High Schools
offering some business courses (The Grammar School advertised that
there were specialist tutors in shorthand and book-keeping on their
staff from 1921). The real 'boom' times for commercial schools
and colleges, offering full-time or part-time tuition were the 1920s and
1930s. The various Trade Directories show that between 1920
and 1939 twenty-two separate establishments were set up in this
period. Some only lasted a year or so before they closed or were amalgamated with other schools. Up until the outbreak of war in 1939,
between eight and eleven schools and colleges are listed at any given
time (see Appendix 1 for a complete list). Pitmans' opened a school
in 1920, and by 1927 there was not only a designated School of
Accountancy (1921), but also a School of Banking and a School
of Insurance (all three were run from the same address). The
American rival to the Pitman method of shorthand writing, Gregg,
opened a school in 1929.

Most towns and cities have areas which, historically, are associated
with one particular aspect of industry or commerce. Chartres and
Honeyman state that in Leeds by the late 1890s

Insurance, banking and legal services became concentrated in the area
between Park Row and Briggate; while warehouses and merchanting
was [sic] *located predominantly in*
Wellington Street and Park
Square.[3]

It is no coincidence then that many
of the commercial schools and
colleges that appeared in the first
half of this century were sited near
or around these areas.

The origins of the City School of
Commerce in Leeds, can be found
in Huddersfield (Figure 2). The

Figure 2. Central (Kaye's College) 70 New
North Road, Huddersfield which opened on
27 January 1938. *Author's Collection*

Central, or Kaye's College, sited at Byram Building, Station Street and Westgate prior to its relocation to New North Road Hudderfield in 1937, had been founded by the Kaye family in 1907, and by the early 1920s was well-known as offering a high standard of commercial education. The founder, Norman Kaye, emigrated to Australia in 1911, leaving his brother Leonard to run the school.[4] During the early 1920s Leonard Kaye was joined in partnership by two other fully qualified accountants, Joe Lee and Frank Wood. They had all previously met when Lee and Wood attended the Huddersfield Technical College before the First World War, where Leonard Kaye had been a lecturer. After the war Frank Wood attended a teacher training course at Leeds University and obtained a teaching diploma (Figure 3).

Figure 3. The College principals and civic dignitaries at the opening ceremony of the Central (Kaye's) College in 1938.
Back row, *left to right:* Mr Frank Wood (Principal), Canon A L Leeper, Councillor A L Bennie Grey JP, Mr Leonard Kaye (Principal), Mr Joe Lee (Principal). **Front row:** Mayoress of Huddersfield Miss Willis, Mayor of Huddersfield Alderman Alfred Willis and Mrs J Lee. *Author's Collection*

As has been previously noted, the 1920s were an especially favourable time for expansion in the area of commercial education, and the partners decided to expand into other towns and cities. Leeds was chosen as the first site, and the City School of Commerce opened in the summer of 1923 in Portland Chambers at 91 Woodhouse Lane. A year later the school moved to 105–107 Portland Crescent, where it remained until 1931. It offered to boys and girls tuition in all commercial subjects and one language, French. The introduction of a language into the curriculum was Frank Wood's innovation. He had had to learn some French as a naval clerical rating when posted to Calais between 1914 and 1918.[5] He had then kept up the language after the war by attending evening classes. Leonard Kaye moved to take charge of the Leeds school, Joe Lee ran the Huddersfield branch and Frank Wood spent some time between both before moving to the Leeds school permanently in 1931. An early pupil remembers teachers at the school being Dennis Lord, who taught Pitman shorthand and English language; and Miss Margaret 'Peg' Hazel who taught all the typewriting. Miss Hazel could also maintain and effect repairs to the machines on which she taught. Leonard Kaye taught book-keeping and commerce.[6]

In the early 1930s the partners opened a school in Bradford. This commercial school, also called the City School of Commerce, was initially situated in Morley Street, and then latterly in Little Horton Lane. The partners also bought an established girls' secretarial school situated on North Parade, the Bradford Girls' Secretarial College. This was eventually amalgamated with the City School of Commerce. The head in Bradford was Irene Oldham, who was the sister-in-law of Joe Lee; she was ably seconded by Jessie Freeborough, who continued to work in Bradford until the school closed in the 1970s.[7]

Expansion was not considered just in terms of opening up new schools in different towns. In Leeds, as elsewhere, the partners were on the look out for the possibility of acquiring and incorporating other existing commercial schools. In the early part of 1931, the partners bought the business and premises of Clarke's College Ltd. First opened in 1912, at Hillary Place, it was then sited on Blenheim Terrace from 1922. An early entry in the Trade Directories gives its full title as being 'Clarke's College Ltd. – the Civil Service and Business University of London'. When the City School of Commerce bought out Clarke's, they retained the use of the name and, until the war it was known as the 'City School of Commerce, incorporating Clarke's College'.

Later on that same year, 1931, a second school was acquired. This was De Grey College. For a number of years De Grey's was nominally run as a separate business, even when relocated from Eldon Terrace to 17 Blenheim Terrace. Both De Grey's and the City School of Commerce shared the same teachers, and the name of De Grey as a separate establishment, only disappears when the new extension at the rear of 21 Blenheim Terrace was opened in 1940. The original owner of De Grey, a Mr H E Richardson, was retained as a member of the teaching staff at the City School of Commerce, but his main duties appear to have consisted of visiting the homes and parents of prospective pupils. He appears to have left the school around 1939 or 1940, as his name no longer appears among the teaching staff in the school magazines of 1940.[8]

In acquiring this latter school the partners not only took over a commercial school, but also a small private High School department for children over ten years old. According to an early advertisement in the *Leeds Trade Directory* for 1930, in addition to the usual commercial subjects of shorthand, typewriting, book-keeping, accountancy, business methods, commercial law and auditing, De Grey staff also taught more academic subjects such as handwriting, arithmetic, english, geography, geometry, algebra and foreign languages for 'matriculation and professional preliminary exams.[9] Previous to this acquisition, the City School of Commerce had not developed a separate high school department of its own, unlike its sister college in Huddersfield. The assimilation of De Grey brought the two schools more in line. Only in Bradford did one of the two schools there remain solely a commercial college for girls.

From the mid 1930s onwards the City School of Commerce could now offer two types of education for parents to choose from, and a child was entered either for the Commercial department or the High School department. In 1939 the High School consisted of six forms for the eleven to sixteen year olds, with a separate junior form for those under eleven. The Commercial and Secretarial department also had six forms, one of which catered for pupils who were over sixteen and had passed their School Certificate. These pupils were given a rapid, one year intensive commercial training course. This training consisted of shorthand, typewriting, book-keeping and business methods.[10]

By 1939 the City School of Commerce entered its pupils for the examinations of the R.S.A. the London Chamber of Commerce, and the Faculty of Teachers in Commerce.

After 1907 there had been a gradual increase in the proportion of children continuing with education beyond the ages of twelve and fourteen, from 7.5 per cent in 1914 to 20.6 per cent in 1938.[11] With so many other schools competing for potential pupils ways had to be found of publicising the school and recruiting pupils. The City School of Commerce, in common with others, advertised itself through the local papers. Two past pupils of the school from the 1930s remember that their first contact came thus. What in particular appealed to both families was the fact that two-year scholarships were being offered to candidates who successfully sat, and passed a competitive examination. There does appear to have been a sliding scale of scholarships and bursaries. Jack Halstead, a pupil from 1930 to 1932, was one successful candidate who obtained a full scholarship. At the end of his two years at the school he was unable, through family circumstances, to afford to be articled to a practising accountant. He therefore accepted Leonard Kaye's offer of training to be a teacher of commerce. In return for free tuition Jack Halstead agreed to stay and join the school staff. After qualifying in 1936 he was sent to teach at the Bradford school. He returned to teach in Leeds in 1938.[12]

Educating a child beyond elementary school was an expensive matter for many working-class families before 1944. The 1918

Education Act had abolished fees to elementary school and had raised the school leaving age from twelve to fourteen. School fees to the City School of Commerce in the 1930s were about £30 a year (about £10 a term); by the 1960s this had risen to between £100 to £135 per year (about 33 to 45 per term). For working-class families who wished their children to 'get on', this would constitute a large proportion of the family income. The scholarships and bursaries offerred by the schools to 'able' children were one of the ways that helped parents to achieve some degree of enhancement for their children. Mary C, a past pupil, sat an entrance examination in 1934

> *I went and sat an exam. An entrance exam, and a sort of scholarship and got the fees reduced . . . But we'd to . . . buy all* [the] *own, . . . books, of course. All* [our] *text books that you needed. And all the paper that* [you] *used. Your shorthand notebooks; typing paper . . . You'd to pay the first day, and I got a bill for two pounds, fifteen shillings and something. Me mother nearly died!* [13]

The school stocked and sold a variety of Waterman fountain pens. Those pupils who were taking shorthand were all expected to buy one as pencils were not allowed.

> *And they expected you to buy a Waterman pen. And they were a guinea!* [14]

However, pupils could pay a shilling a week to enable them to purchase one. One student remembers when, after leaving school, she went to sit to take her first dictation in her new job, clutching her Waterman pen, she was sent back to her desk to get a supply of lead pencils because her boss was fed up with his dictation being interrupted when the fountain pen ran out of ink. After that, she hardly ever used her fountain pen again, and certainly not for dictation. [15]

There was also the cost of the school uniform. In the 1930s for the City School of Commerce this consisted for both boys and girls of a dark green blazer with vertical gold and white stripes, and a striped school tie. For the boys the rest of the uniform consisted of grey trousers, white shirt and a green cap. The younger girls wore white or cream blouses with a green gymslip while the older girls wore green skirts. All the girls were expected to wear green felt hats and gloves outside. The summer uniform for the girls was a regulation pattern green print cotton dress with either a straw hat or a panama, with a hat band in the school colours. The colours for the schools in Huddersfield and Bradford were blue, gold and white.

The crest of the school appeared on both the cap and hat badges as well as on the blazer pocket (Figure 4). There was a gold lamp of learning with a red flame, standing on top of two red books on a black background in the top third of the badge. The bottom two-thirds consisted of a black, gold edged chevron, over a field of green (again blue for Huddersfield and Bradford). There were three white Yorkshire roses on the chevron. The whole badge was edged with gold. The motto for the school given in a scroll underneath was *Ne Plus Supra*, which was generally translated as *Nothing Better*.[16]

Figure 4. The school badge and motto. *Author's Collection*

An important service offered to the students who studied at the commercial schools was the placement service. At the end of a student's period of training, the school offered to find a place for each student. Various firms registered with the school and students were advised about what jobs were on offer and about the level of remuneration that they themselves ought to expect for their personal level of attainment.

> . . . *the firms in those days used to apply to the commercial colleges. And you were sent to various interviews, from there . . . And, [I] got instructions that I hadn't to . . . take less than fifteen shillings a week. 'Cos sometimes you only got ten and six or twelve and six. In fact I went to Marlbeck Tailors, and I could have had that job, but they [the school] said I hadn't to take less. So I ended up working for a firm up Hudson Road.*[17]

This service, particularly through the years of the depression, and up to the Second World War must have been very welcome to many families. Having at least one child in relatively secure, non-manufacturing employment would have lightened the family burden considerably.

Evening classes in commercial subjects had long been offered by many educational establishments in Leeds. The commercial schools had, perforce, to offer the same. Many of the pupils who had attended the City School of Commerce returned there in the evenings for a time after leaving the school to study for higher qualifications or to learn new skills required by their employers. The evening classes run at the City School of Commerce were in commercial subjects only (Extra tuition for the High School department took place on Saturday mornings). The evening classes were held on Mondays, Wednesdays and Fridays; generally between six and eight pm. Latterly the staff who ran these evening classes were eligible for compensatory time in lieu. Up until the late 1950s the teaching of these evening classes had been part of teachers' contract.[18]

The commercial school also had shorter summer breaks than did the High School; only four weeks off in August. During those four weeks some of the commercial teachers had to be available to man the school office for one week at a time on a rota basis. They were also there to take calls from prospective employers and the parents of pupils. Teaching staff were also expected to be flexible in where they worked. They could be asked to cover staff shortages in the other colleges. This led to some movement of staff in the early days between all three colleges. Jack Halstead taught at Bradford and Leeds; Lawrence Leake came to Leeds from the Huddersfield school; Jessie Freeborough went from Huddersfield to Bradford; Leonard Kaye from Huddersfield to Leeds and Frank Wood from Leeds to Huddersfield and back to Leeds again.

With the amalgamation of Clarke's and De Grey's with the City School of Commerce, the number of pupils rose to about one hundred and fifty. The numbers continued to rise steadily through the rest of the 1930s and 1940s. At its peak there were approximately 350 pupils on the rolls, with about 14 teaching staff. This made for an average class size of between 20 and 25. This pupil teacher ratio was about the national average for private secondary schools between 1911 and 1938. Secondary schools in the state sector generally had larger classes; between 30 and 40 was the norm there.[19]

The teaching staff at the City School of Commerce were fairly typical for the time, being a mixture of qualified and unqualified teachers. The number of unqualified teachers in the state sector was diminishing constantly through the 1930s and 1940s. Private schools were gradually becoming the only establishments that were willing to employ uncertificated teachers. At the City School of Commerce, most, if not all those who taught the commercial subjects were members of the Faculty of Teachers in Commerce. On the High School side the situation is not so clear. What is certain was that qualified teachers were paid according to the Burnham Scale (This was the official pay review body for the teaching profession at this time). In 1947, a newly qualified teacher at the school remembers her salary as being around £272 per annum.[20] For those who failed to qualify for Burnham Scale rates, their pay was a matter for negotiation.

In 1940 the extension to the premises at Blenheim Terrace was completed. Originally there had been only six classrooms here. Three on the ground floor and three on the first floor, with a caretaker's flat

Figure 5. Interior of one of the new classrooms c1940. *Author's Collection*

in the basement. After building the extension five new classrooms were added. These classrooms were created by dividing up the new space by means of folding glass and wood partitions, which unfortunately did not prove to be sound proof. When these partitions were folded back a large assembly hall could be created. Cloakroom and toilet facilities were accommodated on the lower floor of this extension. The junior and high school divisions of the school were generally housed in the extension (Figure 5).

The commercial school continued to be housed in the front of the building. After the alterations had been completed there still remained two classrooms on the left hand side of the hall corridor on the ground floor and the first floor levels. A long classroom, the typewriting room, was on the first floor on the right of the corridor, above the principals' office, and the secretarial office that occupied the right-hand side of the ground floor. Two further classrooms had been created at the front of the basement out of the former caretaker's flat.[21]

Another facility offered at the City School of Commerce after the extension was built was the 'model office'. This also seems to have been called by the title of Secretarial Services, and appears to have been staffed on a half-day rota basis by the Senior Commercial class prior to the being 'placed' with various firms. These were under the supervision of Miss A Bentley (a former pupil) and Miss

Figure 6. Three typewriter artists identified as being Joyce Rushforth, Dorothy Metcalf and Ann Bentley, pictured with their creations at an open day at the school c1939. *Photograph used courtesy of Yorkshire Post Newspapers Ltd.*

E MacConachie, the principal's secretary. In this office the pupils, all girls, undertook the day-to-day routines of genuine office life. Here they manned the telephones, typed the principals' correspondence, filed, cut stencils and duplicated forms and various documents, and dealt with incoming and outgoing post. It was here that they put into practice all they had learnt in the previous two or three years in their commercial classes (Figure 6).

From the summer of 1938 until midsummer 1940, the four schools published magazines. These were *Commercity* for the City Schools of Commerce in Leeds and Bradford; *Centrakaylian* for Central Kaye's College in Huddersfield and *The B.S.C Student Magazine* for the Bradford Secretarial College for Girls. A past teacher believes that the production of the magazines was the work of the Senior Commercial class in each of the schools. All the schools contributed to the central portion of the magazine. The outer four pages front and back were given over to the individual concerns of each particular school. The production of the magazines was abandoned in 1940 because of wartime paper shortages, and was never taken up again after the war was over (Figure 7).

All the principals were freemasons and prominent members of the local business communities in the various towns where their schools were active. Leonard Kaye was a noted amateur horticulturalist whose speciality was roses; Joe Lee was a keen golfer. Frank Wood in particular was very active in many Leeds concerns. He was a member of the Leeds Rotary Club and was involved with the Leeds Rugby League Football Club up at Headingly. Two former players of Leeds R.L, Arthur Clues and H E 'Bert' Cook taught and coached the boys for a time in cricket, rugby swimming and gym. After the war a full time mistress, a Miss Capewell, was employed to teach the girls hockey, tennis, swimming and gym. As a former teacher at the schools says

> It certainly made the school after the war a very thriving enterprise. And there were pupils coming there who did not get into a state, Grammar school; but who later blossomed, you know, as they do; late developers. And got school certificates which they otherwise would never have got, if they [had] stayed in their Secondary Modern schools. So it did a good job; and I was very glad to have been a part of it. [22]

"COMMERCITY"

STUDENTS' MAGAZINE

OF
THE CITY SCHOOL OF COMMERCE,
21, BLENHEIM TERRACE, LEEDS, 2.
Midsummer. 1938.

THE
CENTRA KAYLIAN
STUDENTS' MAGAZINE
of
CENTRAL (KAYES') COLLEGE, 70, NEW NORTH ROAD, HUDDERSFIEL
No. 1.
Mid...

"COMMERCITY"
STUDENTS' MAGAZINE
OF
THE CITY SCHOOL OF COMMERCE
and Smart's Institute,
35, Morley Street, Bradford.

STUDENTS' MAGAZINE

BRADFORD SECRETARIAL COLLEGE FOR GIRLS,
20, NORTH PARADE, BRADFORD.
Vol. II No. 1
Summer 1939

Figure 7. School magazines titles from the associate colleges between 1938 and 1940.
Author's Collection

On Saturday 6 July 1941, Leonard Kaye died aged sixty-three. His death was announced in the *Huddersfield Examiner* and the *Yorkshire Post* the following week. Two years earlier in March 1939, Norman Kaye, the founder of Kaye's College had died in Australia, whence he had emigrated. The partnership continued with Frank Wood and Joe Lee until after the war when Northern Tutorial Services, a private limited company was set up. The other partners in

Figure 8. Mr Frank Wood, taken in the office of City High School May 1948.
Photograph used courtesy of Mrs M Clues

this venture were Malcolm Lee, Joe Lee's son, and Irene Oldham. The partnership continued running the schools until at some point in the 1950s when Frank Wood bought the City School of Commerce and City High School outright from the partnership (Figure 8).

In the immediate post-war period Frank Wood began to change the emphasis of the school from being predominantly a commercial school, to one offering a broader, more general high school curriculum. The number of commercial pupils declined steadily from 1939 onwards until the ratio of pupils in each division became two-thirds high school to one-third commercial. In 1947 the entry in the *Leeds Trade Directory* shows for the first time this change of emphasis. From now on the school was listed as the City High School and School of Commerce.[23]

Through the 1950s and early 1960s Frank Wood, and then after his death around 1958, his daughter Muriel Clues, aimed at offering a Grammar School type of education(Figure 9).Unfortunately Her Majesty's Inspectors of Schools could not grant Grammar school status to the school as they could not overlook the lack of facilities for the teaching of science, nor the lack of on-site or near-site sports or gymnasium facilities.[24]

During the late 1950s and ealy 1960s many local authorities began, in response to growing demands from both parents and the industrial and commercial sectors, to offer more full and part-time courses in the Colleges of Further Education. Jack Halstead was one of the growing band of commercial teachers to change from the private sector to the state sector. In 1954, after eighteen years teaching in the Bradford and Leeds branches of the City Schools of Commerce (broken only by service in the Royal Air Force during the Second World War) he left the City High School to take up a position as Assistant Lecturer in Commerce at the then Harrogate Technical Institute. Part of his brief was to set up a secretarial training course for post O-level students of sixteen and over. He took with him the

Figure 9. Mrs Muriel Clues nee Wood. She regularly wore her gown while teaching in school, and the hood when officiating at speech days.
Courtesy of Mrs M Clues

idea of the 'model office' as it was set up at the City High School; in fact he believes that it was his advocacy of the use of the 'model office' as an integral part of the course syllabus that predisposed the inter-viewers in his favour. The course in Harrogate later came to be regarded as the premier post A-level secretarial course in the area of the West Riding Local Education Authority prior to the local government reorganisation in 1974 when Harrogate was relocated within the boundaries of North Yorkshire.[25]

Private schools which offered the type of High School education up to School Certificate and later GCE standard as the City High school did, found themselves under pressure from the burgeoning state sector, as the new Comprehensives came on stream. Most of these new schools began to match the syllabus of the City High School subject for subject up to GCE O-level standard. This, combined with the fact that the new schools were all state funded and therefore free, effectively sounded the death knell for many of the fee-paying schools.

The early 1960s saw a steady decline in the student roll until it reached the point where it was no longer an economically viable concern. The City High School and School of Commerce closed its doors at the end of the summer term in 1964. By February 1965 Mrs

Figure 10. Frontage of Austick's University Bookshop c1975. *Courtesy of Mr P Austick*

Clues had sold the site to the Austick brothers, owners of the University Bookshop at 172 Woodhouse Lane. After a few alterations the new Austicks University Bookshop opened for business on its new site in October 1965 (Figure 10).

Appendix

The commmercial schools and colleges are listed here by the year of their appearance in the Trade Directories for the city of Leeds. These directories are held in the Local History Library at the Central Library in Leeds. Dates of amalgamation with other schools are given in brackets after the name of the school. The original site of the school and any subsequent removal from their original sites are given in the end column.

1901	Commercial Evening School	Cookridge Street
1901	Leeds Civil Service Institute (see Skerry's 1906)	7 Commercial Buildings Park Row
1901	Northern Institute	10 Park Row, then 9 St George St (1909)
1902	Leeds Schools of Shorthand	3 Park Lane, then 5 Park Lane (1923)
1906	Skerry's Civil Service College	48 Albion St, then 28 Guilford St (1908) then 92a Ablion St (1909)
1909	Henderson's	18 Park Lane, then 9 Park Lane (1923)
1911	North Leeds Commercial College	7 Louis St
1912	Clarke's College Ltd – The Civil Service & Business University of London (see City School of Commerce after 1931)	1 Hillary Place, Woodhouse Lane, then 21 Blenheim Terr
1913	Bankers Correspondence Institute	City Chambers, Infirmary St
1915	County Commercial School	20 Park Row
1916	De Bear	Atheneum Building 9 Park Row
1917	Tempest, Toothill & Tempest (see Leeds School of Shorthand)	
1920	Central School of Commerce	91 Woodhouse Lane
1920	Newton Arnold	303 Roundhay Road
1920	Meadows College of Business Science	25–26 Greek St
1920	Pitman School	1 Cookridge St
1921	School of Accountancy	Standard Building, City Square
1921	Yorkshire Secretarial Training	5 De Grey Terrace, then 18 Blenheim Terrace (1929)
1923	City School of Commerce	Portland Chambers, 91 Woodhouse Lane, then 105–7 Portland Cres (1924) then 21 Blenheim Terrace (1931)
1925	School of Banking	Standard Building City Square
1925	School of Insurance	Standard Building City Square
1929	De Grey College (see also City School of Commerce after 1931)	13 Eldon Terrace, then 17 Blenheim Terrace
1929	Gregg School	77–9 New Briggate
1929	Leeds Education Committee School of Commerce	77 Woodhouse Lane
1932	South Leeds Commercial and Modern College	40 Malvern Road

1938	Business Training School	28 Blenheim Terr, Woodhouse Lane
1938	Fenton Secretarial Training	69 Otley Road
1940	North of England Secretarial College	12 Lands Lane
1947	Northcote School	145 Town St, Leeds 12

Notes and References

1. The trade directories referred to in the text are the *Barrett*, *Kelly* or *Robinson* trade directories of Leeds, which are to be found in the Local History Library of the Central Library in Leeds.
2. The term 'private' is used in this article to mean that the schools and colleges were not under the direct supervision of the local education boards. They were run as a business which provided the main source of income for its owners. They were of necessity all fee paying schools even after the 1944 *Education Act*.
3. Chartres J & Honeyman K *Leeds City Business*, Leeds University Press 1993 p 15.
4. *Centrakaylian* magazine, 1939.
5. Interview with Muriel Clues, 19.4.96.
6. Interview with Jack Halstead, 12.6.96.
7. *Commercity* magazines 1939 & Interview with Jack Halstead, 12.6.96.
8. Interview with Jack Halstead, 12.6.96.
9. *Kelly's Trade Directory*, 1930.
10. *Commercity*, 1940.
11. Halsey A H, *British Social Trends since 1900*, Macmillan Press, London, 1988, p 240.
12. Interview with Jack Halstead, 12.6.96.
13. Interview with Mary C May, 1995.
14. *Ibid.*
15. *Ibid.*
16. Interview with Muriel Clues, 19.4.96.
17. Interview with Mary C May, 1995.
18. Interview with Muriel Clues, 19.4.96.
19. Halsey A H, *British Social Trends since 1900*, Macmillan Press, London, 1988, p 252.
20. Interview with Evelyn Balmforth.
21. *Commercity*, 1940.
22. Interview with Peter D, June 1996.
23. *Kelly's Trade Directory*, 1947.
24. Interview with Muriel Clues.
25. Interviews with Jack Halstead, 12.6.96.

Acknowledgements

Mr Paul F Austick, Mrs Evelyn Balmforth, Miss Mary C, Mr Peter D, Mrs Muriel Clues and Mr Jack Halstead.

I am extremely grateful to all those who allowed themselves to be interviewed for the article. Little is actually left on printed record of the City School of Commerce, and it is due to those brave people who allowed me to tape record our interviews that most of my research has been drawn. My deepest thanks are reserved for those. I would also like to thank the librarians in the Local History Library in Leeds for their patience. A special word of thanks to Mr Jack Halstead, whose previous experience as Senior Lecturer in Secretarial Studies at the Harrogate College of Further Education stood him in good stead as he read my draft and kindly, but firmly corrected my spelling and my grammar.

8. WOODHOUSE MOOR

by Edna Bews

STRANGERS TO LEEDS are quite often puzzled as to why "t'Moor", as it it affectionately known locally, is not called Woodhouse Park, but in fact time is the culprit; and in days gone by the area was much rougher and wilder. It has only been tamed over the last century-and-a-half with the growth of the population of Leeds.

Little is known about its early history but it is possible there there may be traces of Iron and Bronze age settlements, and it is said that there were ramparts at some later date; no doubt commemorated in the name of the road which runs between Woodhouse Lane and Woodhouse Street, separating the two rough areas on the right when leaving the city. The larger of these areas bordering Hyde Park, Woodhouse Lane and Woodhouse Street is known as the 'cinder moor' while the grassy part near Cathcart Street is the 'Low Moor'. In my younger days cattle were grazed there. The part bordering Raglan Road and Woodhouse Lane was often referred to as the 'swing moor', for at the beginning of this century there were swings of a sort, making it I suppose, one of the earliest children's playgrounds. It is hard to imagine now that the busy A660 was once a mere track across open land leading from the town centre to Otley. The larger part of the moor on the left of Woodhouse Lane has seen more development than the right hand side, which remains much as it has been over the last century.

In the early seventeenth century the moor was surveyed by the London Corporation which surprisingly owned Leeds at that time. Coal was found and subsequently mined by the bell-pit method which involved sinking a small shaft down to the seam and then spreading out once the coal was reached.

In 1643 the country was in the grip of the Civil War and in January of that year Bradford and Leeds witnessed a clash between the two antagonists, the Royalists being led by Sir William Saville and the Parliamentarians by Sir Thomas Fairfax. After various manoeuvres the Parliamentarian army came down from a northerly direction and assembled on the moor, near where the University is now, which in those days would be a good vantage point overlooking the town. Thankfully there were very few casualties when the two factions eventually met. I lived for a time overlooking this site and sometimes,

WOODHOUSE MOOR

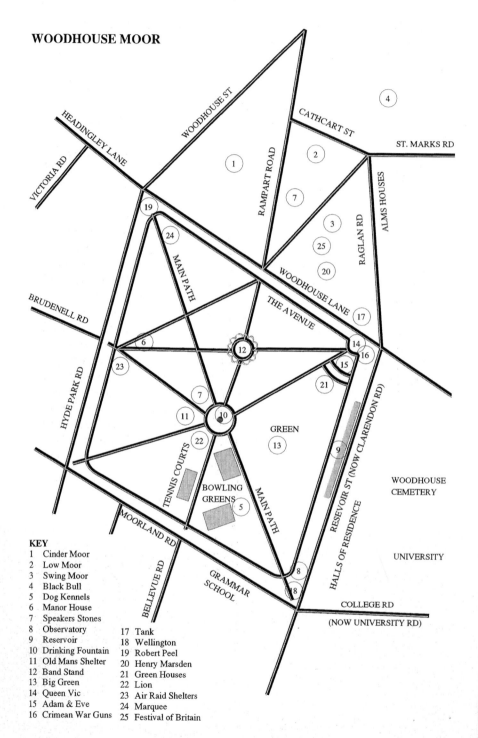

KEY
1 Cinder Moor
2 Low Moor
3 Swing Moor
4 Black Bull
5 Dog Kennels
6 Manor House
7 Speakers Stones
8 Observatory
9 Reservoir
10 Drinking Fountain
11 Old Mans Shelter
12 Band Stand
13 Big Green
14 Queen Vic
15 Adam & Eve
16 Crimean War Guns

17 Tank
18 Wellington
19 Robert Peel
20 Henry Marsden
21 Green Houses
22 Lion
23 Air Raid Shelters
24 Marquee
25 Festival of Britain

Figure 1. Map showing the position of Woodhouse Moor and the various points of interest in the article. *Based on the Ordnance Survey of Leeds 1906 scale 1:25000. Re-drawn and computer originated by D Wycherley*

on a bitterly cold 23 January, it was easy to imagine this skirmish.

In 1645 the plague arrived in Leeds and the various markets moved up onto the moor when it was realised that congestion in the town centre was causing the disease to spread. Pest houses, which were the forerunners of isolation hospitals, were built on the 'swing moor' near the almshouses on Raglan Road. A fifth of the then population of Leeds (which was recorded as being 6,500 in 1645) died in this outbreak.

The moor has always been a rallying point and at the turn of the eighteenth century when invasion by the French seemed a very real threat, the Leeds Volunteers mustered there. By all accounts it was a rather chaotic business with horses, carriages and men milling about, but thankfully their services were not required.

On a lighter note Woodhouse Feast has been held on the low 'moor' and the smaller 'moor' for centuries (Figure 1). The Feast was, and still is a fair, though for the locals in times past it was the event of the year. It took place on the week nearest to the 21 September, and people came to visit their friends and relatives in the area from afar. Roast beef and red cabbage was always served for Sunday Dinner that weekend, along with other delicacies of the age. The pubs around, notably the *Black Bull* situated on Raglan Road (but now demolished) held various competitions and activities; one such was climbing a greasy pole to win a joint of meat. There were many side shows, boxing booths, small circuses and fortune tellers, and on Saturday evenings it was difficult to move in the vast crowds that milled around. The air was full of exciting pungent smells; not least of which was smoke and oil from the steam engines and the various food stalls around. One or two attempts have been made this century to move the event

Figure 2. View of Woodhouse Moor early 1900s, showing the main path from College Road to Hyde Park Corner. *Editor's Collection*

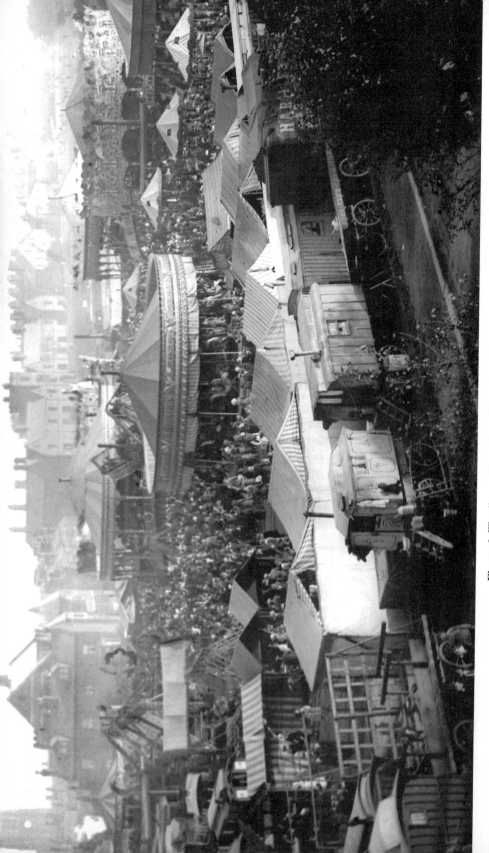

Figure 3. Woodhouse Moor Feast, September 1915. *Author's Collection*

Figure 4. Fountain and 'Parliament'. Woodhouse Moor early 1900s. *Author's Collection*

elsewhere, due to complaints about noise and rowdiness, but it has soon gravitated back to its natural home. At Whitsuntide there used to be a smaller fair but this was moved to Easter and was held on the 'swing moor'. Although the main fair is still held, it is a shadow of its former self (Figure 2).

Horse racing was held on the moor in the mid-nineteenth century though after a jockey had been killed one year the practice seemed to die out. There also existed a Leeds Hunt and the dogs were kept in kennels in a row of cottages near the Belle Vue Road entrance to the main moor. I believe it was called Sportsman's Row. From the 1840s it was possible to buy home-made wines and nettle beer there, and I'm sure it would have been a popular rendezvous on Sunday afternoons for the locals to stroll along the first rough path.

Near the Brudenell Road entrance stood the Manor House, which eventually became the home of an optician who re-named it *Myrtle Grove*. He had a revolving light fixed in a prominent position and on dark nights he employed a boy to work the contraption so that if he was returning home at a late hour he had something to guide him over the moor. In the end *Myrtle Grove* became a public house.

In the absence of radio and television, and with only the news-sheets of the day to keep people informed of current affairs, political meetings took place on open spaces. To accommodate this, large blocks of stone were placed in suitable positions so that speakers could be seen and heard. At one time there were eight such stones on Woodhouse Moor in various situations, and one or two still remain. At election time wooden stands were erected called hustings (a word still used in respect of canvassing). In May 1857 a stand collapsed killing two people. This must have happened around the time that the Town Council bought the moor from the then lords of the manor for £3,000, and the whole area became a public park. Then began the task of taming the wilderness.

Early in the 1900s, as part of the parks development, an observatory was built at the University end of the moor by the Leeds Astronomical Society and the University. This was in use until the last war. A feeder reservoir for the city was sited on Reservoir Street, now Clarendon Road, but, due to one or two tragedies, this was eventually grassed over. A long path led from College Road, as it was then, to Hyde Park, and it used to have ornamental wrought iron arches with lamps suspended from the middle of them. These features commemorated the coronation of King Edward VII (Figure 4). Midway along the path was a Victorian fountain surrounded by a ring of trees and seats. This was also a meeting place for the local men, as well as a round shelter on the slope towards Hyde Park Road (Figure 4). More paths appeared, as did iron railings. And as every park of any size had a band-stand, Woodhouse Moor was no exception. It stood not far from the fountain with a broad path joining the two, and was sited on a large circle of concrete. What pleasures it brought to the local community! On Monday evenings the band, most likely the Leeds Model Prize Band, played all the latest dance tunes and couples danced round the surrounding circle of concrete. Enclosing this were seats for the more sedate and then on the outer edge was an ever circling promenade of young people – a good meeting place for the

Figure 5. Adam and Eve Gardens, Woodhouse Lane early 1900s. *Author's Collection*

Figure 6. First World War tank at the corner of Raglan Road and Woodhouse Lane post 1919. *Author's Collection*

boys and girls of Woodhouse. On Sunday afternoons and evenings it was the older generations who had their entertainment with more classical music being played; but still the parade of youngsters around them at the back. Occasionally in the summer there would be a military band and a small charge was made for a seat. These concerts took place mainly on a Wednesday. At the entrances to the park men stood with square canvas containers in which you dropped a penny, or two pence for a programme.

On the big expanse of grass near the bowling greens various functions took place. There was a particularly big one attached to the police forces centenary in 1936. At the entrance to the moor, where the statue of Queen Victoria now stands, were the Adam and Eve gardens; so called after the two statues of a boy and girl (Figure 5). They were taken away in 1936 as they were damaged, but the gardens and the name remained. Just in front of them was an enclosed circle containing Russian guns and cannon-balls from the Crimean War. These were originally in an alcove at the side of the path nearest the

Figure 7. Statue of Sir Henry Marsden. *Author's Collection*

reservoir and were brought there with a certain amount of ceremony. There was even a captured Russian dog in the procession!

After the First World War a tank clanked and rumbled its way up from the city in 1919 and was deposited at the corner of Raglan Road and Woodhouse Lane (Figure 6). Local youth found this and the guns a great playground. But the tank and guns were removed, along with the arches and railings, to be melted down to help the war effort during the Second World War. It was after the Crimean guns went that the statue of Queen Victoria was moved from outside the Town Hall to the moor. At about the same time the statue of the Duke of Wellington, and Sir Robert Peel were also moved to the moor together with the statue of Sir Henry Marsden, which was taken from its situation at the top of Albion Street. Marsden was a respected mayor of Leeds in the 1870s. He at least did have a local connection as his home was at the top of St Mark's Street, and this later became the Motor Club before being demolished. Marsden's monument now stands near Raglan Road on the 'swing moor'(Figure 7).

There used to be some quite pretty greenhouses between the gardens and the big green. The gardeners in those days grew their own plants and there was a creditable display of some of the more exotic examples in one of the glasshouses. These came to a sorry end in

Figure 8. Statue of the Lion with the snake. *Author's Collection*

Figure 9. The Victorian Bandstand, Woodhouse Moor c1900. *Author's Collection*

February 1962 when a hurricane struck and caused widespread damage. Another memory going back to the last century was the statue of the lion with a snake that stood on a mound near the main entrance (Figure 8). It still exists, although now moved to the children's play area. It has been painted many colours to liven it's appearance since then. There also used to be an owl sculpture, but that has since vanished.

The Second World War brought many alterations. All the shrubberies and alcoves with seats near Reservoir Street were opened out. Opposite the top of Brudenell Road air-raid shelters were built underground (one wonders what future archaeologists will make of those). Then, of course, came the allotments on the lower slopes; some of which survive to this day. As the war got under way a searchlight battery appeared on the old 'swing moor', but mysteriously moved just before the big air-raid in March 1941. Bombs fell where the battery had been. On a happier note a big marquee was put up on Hyde Park tennis courts where dancing and concerts carried on. The bandstand seems to have declined in use over the war years and in fact was replaced by a more modern wedge-shaped edifice in the 1950s. This never had the same appeal as its Victorian predecessor and was, in its turn, pulled down (Figure 9).

After the war came the Festival of Britain in 1951, and although the main event was held in Battersea Park in London, a travelling version visited the main cities in the country. The venue in Leeds was the old 'swing moor', which acquired new paths for the event, and these are still to be seen (Figure 10).

The main purpose for the exhibition was to arouse the population's will to get back to a normal life style after the war, and as it was also the centenary of the Great Exhibition which had been held in London in 1851, it was felt to be a convenient time to do this. In the week previous to the visit, a decorated tram toured the city, complete with a revolving globe, and with pictures of the main industries in Leeds. The show itself was opened by the then Princess Royal, on 23 June, 1951. The route up Woodhouse Lane was lined with thousands of people; five or six deep in places. To welcome the Princess Royal there were members of the Household Cavalry and the Guards Regiment. All aspects of living were represented in the exhibition itself. There were in fact five thousand exhibits, one of which was a Corridor of Time, with sixteen pendulums swinging across the ages and winking out in lights our scientific progress. Another exhibit was a Chamber of Invention, Discovery and Design, which was like a 'Frankenstein's' laboratory. Household goods and fashion parades, as well as a children's section were to be seen; not forgetting an outdoor pursuits show. The shops in town had various displays and competitions and there was an atmosphere of excitement and hope for the future. At the time it was suggested that people bought well chosen souvenirs and saved them to be brought to light again in 2051! I wonder how many people have these memento's still!

In subsequent years an 'Ideal Homes' exhibition was held on the moor. One year the exhibition was opened by the film star Diana Dors.

Many memories come flooding back of the happy times spent in our local park and I'm sure that generations to come will enjoy it too. Now of course, it is the haunt of students from the University and as they come from many different countries, these memories will spread throughout the world.

Figure 10. Entrance to the Festival of Britain Exhibition, Woodhouse Moor June 1951. *Author's Collection*

9. THE MOSAIC OF ST AIDAN'S

by Barrie Pepper

WITHIN ST AIDAN'S CHURCH IN HAREHILLS is one of the nation's little known art treasures. This imposing, but certainly not handsome, red brick church houses a 1,000 square foot mosaic which provides the backdrop to the altar and helps pick out this unassuming inner city church from the ruck. The work by Frank Brangwyn, one of the noted Royal Academicians of his day, was first mooted in 1909 and took until 1916 to complete.

The church itself was built between 1891 and 1894 at a cost that was originally estimated at £10,000 but which finished up much nearer £20,000. It was built to serve an area that was being rapidly urbanised. It is a basilica-type church suitable for congregational worship and in the original plans it was intended to have a tower but this was not regarded as essential and has still not been built. The architects were Messrs Johnson and Crawford Hick of Newcastle.

The first vicar was the Reverend Samuel Mumford Taylor who was later to become Archdeacon of Southwark and then Bishop of Kingston upon Thames and a Residentiary Canon of St George's, Windsor. The church opened on 13 October 1894, and was consecrated by the Bishop of Richmond.

St Aidan's centenary was marked by six weeks of celebration culminating in October, 1994 with a High Mass at which an address was given by the Archbishop of York. In that time many people saw the mosaic for the first time and heard or read of its fascinating story.

In 1909 a parishioner, Robert Hawthorne Kitson, offered £100 each year for ten years for his friend the artist Frank Brangwyn to design and decorate the eastern apse of church. He was a nephew of the then vicar's wife and his brother Sir James Kitson was Lord Mayor of Leeds. After a long period of consultation Kitson convinced the Church authorities that Brangwyn had the right appreciation of the unusual architecture of St Aidan's and it was decided to depict in tempera the life of St Aidan on the back wall of the apse. It would be a continuous picture showing periods of his ministry.

In 1910 Brangwyn started painting the central portion of the apse. He continued, haphazardly for two years before he publicly indicated a long-felt worry. The atmosphere of Harehills was smoke-ridden and filthy. He wrote:

> *It was a bright summer day in London, but when we got to Leeds –*
> *although the sun still shone – it was like seeing things through a*
> *moulded glass; no shadows were cast on the ground. I would never had*
> *believed it if I hadn't seen it. I suggested to Kitson that no painting*
> *could exist in such an atmosphere.*

He asked if he could start again using mosaic and marble. William
Mason, the newly appointed Vicar, agreed particularly as Brangwyn
was to pay part of the additional cost himself. In the artist's own
words:

> *I had to add lots more 'oof' out of my own pocket for the rest. Anyway*
> *it was better than wasting the work and money on what in a year or*
> *two would be like brown paper.*

The work moved to London. Brangwyn employed Sylvester Sparrow,
an experienced glass painter as his superintendent. He in turn used
the firm of Henry Rust to execute the mosaic and 40 young women
from the poorer areas of Battersea were trained in the delicate art of
setting the tesserae. Brangwyn's full sized cartoons were reversed and
the cut pieces of vitreous were stuck on face down. When a sheet was
complete it was taken to Leeds where it was cemented to the wall,
the backing paper was soaked off and after cleaning the mosaic was
grouted with cement.

The work took longer than expected but was finished in 1916 and
unveiled on the anniversary of the consecration, 13 October.
Arguments about who actually paid for the work continued for
another four years. Correspondence between Brangwyn and the
Vicar was not acrimonious but certainly not friendly. On one
occasion Brangwyn wrote: '... *pay up and look big!*'

The mosaic is seen at its best on a bright winters day at noon when
the sun shines through the nave windows. Rodney Brangwyn, the
artist's great nephew, explained:

> *When the sun shines and flecks it with warm beams of light its*
> *gorgeous texture is released. It bursts into life; its forms become*
> *discernible, its figures shed their mystery and reveal on their faces*
> *expressions of hope and piety.*

The mosaic displays four periods in St Aidan's life but not in any
particular order. They are from left to right:

> *St Aidan feeding the poor*

Figure 1. The arrival of St Aidan in Northumbria. *Author's Collection*

Figure 2. Detail from the arrival of St Aidan. *Author's Collection*

The arrival of St Aidan in Northumbria (Figures 1 & 2)

St Aidan preaching (Figures 3 & 4)
and the death of St Aidan

Mildred Gibb wrote a fine history of St Aidan's in 1954 to mark the Diamond Jubilee of the Church. In it she quotes Brangwyn as saying:

> *I have tried to put all I could feel into it.*

He may not have been referring to his St Aidan's work but as she pointed out the words were certainly apposite. She gave her own description of the setting:

> *Especially notable is the fine treatment of the gracefully balanced tall trees arranged in ably poised groups over the entire panel surface, giving dignity and unity of purpose to the whole design. The setting has the beauty of the English countryside in springtime; rich green grass, decked with great bluebells, wild purple anemones, a spray of budding apple blossom gleaming white against the dark background, yellow and mauve tulips in the immediate foreground.*
>
> *To the left is a pug dog with studded collar; in the centre are white plumaged geese, and a final happy detail of the familiar scene is*

Figure 3. St Aidan preaching. *Author's Collection*

conceived in the four yellow, new-born goslings, suggesting the eternal fruitfulness of nature.

The chancel walls were also decorated but in more muted colours in keeping with the pious nature of the figures which mark the words of St Matthew: *Come unto me, all ye that labour and are heavily laden and I will give you rest.* A display of stars on the south wall appears to be just that, but closer examination will show that they spell out the letters F B and that the artist has signed his great work (Figure 5).

Among the many famous people who have viewed the mosaic are Her Majesty Queen Elizabeth and Prince Phillip, the Most Reverend George Carey, Archbishop of Canterbury, Lord Healey of Riddlesden, and the late Sir John Betjeman, the Poet Laureate.

The original cartoons were returned to Brangwyn who held on to them for twenty-five years after which he presented them to the monastery of St André near Bruges the city in which he was

Figure 4. Detail from St. Aidan preaching. *Author's Collection*

born. He was a member of the Royal Academy, was knighted in 1956 and died at his home in Sussex in 1956 at the age of eighty-nine.

Sources

Rodney Brangwyn: *Brangwyn*
Mildred Gibb: *History of St Aidan's Church, Leeds, 1954*
Anon: *St Aidan's Church, Leeds and the Brangwyn Mosaics, 1983*
Barrie Pepper, *A Goodly Heritage, 1994*
St Aidan's Parish magazines 1891–1994
West Yorkshire Archives: Correspondence between Brangwyn and Vicars of St Aidan's

Figure 5. The mosaic and the altar. *Author's Collection*

10. BRAMLEY TAKES OFF

by Anthony Silson

SO MANY BRAMLEY BUILDINGS HAVE BEEN erected since 1930 that a stranger might be forgiven for dismissing the place as a mere twentieth century suburb of Leeds. Yet the stranger would be wrong. Impressive public buildings such as the Baptist Sunday School (1894), surely one of the largest in England, and the splendid Swimming Baths (1904) suggest Bramley was already an important settlement by the beginning of the twentieth century. Indeed Bramley was then a small town and its urban character had begun to emerge as early as 1830. The change was associated with three decades of astonishing population growth made all the more noteworthy as it occurred when domestic manufacturing was still dominant in Bramley. So this article seeks some understanding of the great growth in population size, between 1801 and 1831, in Bramley Township.

The township was large and within it lay not only the core settlement of Bramley but parts of Pudsey, Rodley and Stanningley. Adjacent to Bramley Township were the Townships of Horsforth and Headingley in the north, Armley in the east, Farnley in the south and Pudsey and Calverley (with Farsley) in the west (Figure 1).[1]

Population Change.

In Bramley Township population growth accelerated during the eighteenth century leading into a period, between 1801 and 1831, when the rate of increase was greater than at any other period in its history.[2] So rapid was this growth that, between 1801 and 1821, Bramley Township grew faster than any of its adjacent townships and of these, only Headingley grew faster than Bramley between 1821 and 1831 (Figure 2).[3]

Over half of this increase in population size in Bramley Township may be attributed to inward migration (Table 1).

Table 1

Estimates of the percentage of population growth in Bramley Township attributable to:

	Natural Increase	In-migration
1801–11	36	64
1811–21	37	63
1821–31	34	66

Location of Bramley

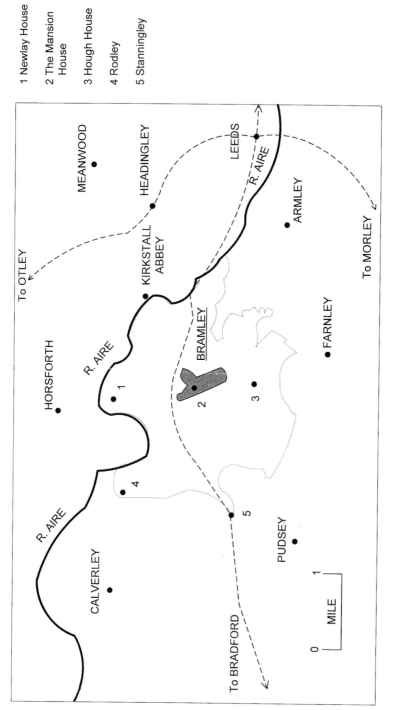

1 Newlay House
2 The Mansion House
3 Hough House
4 Rodley
5 Stanningley

Boundary of Bramley Township

Main built up area of Bramley settlement, 1820

Turnpike Road, 1800

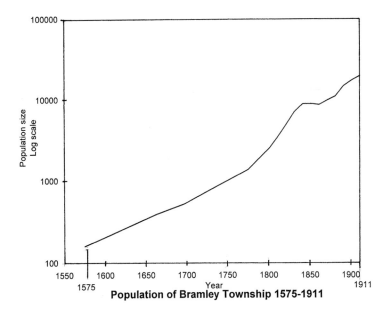

Figure 2. The population of Bramley Township, 1575 - 1911

Most migrants had probably been born near Bramley. The earliest year when details of migration are available is 1851. In that year, of the Bramley residents born outside Bramley, a third had been born in the adjacent townships, and four fifths had been born within 30km. of Bramley centre.[5]

Robert Spurr settled in Bramley in 1831.[6] If he was typical of other early nineteenth century migrants to Bramley then the pattern of movement was complex. Spurr was born in Ossett, only a short distance from Bramley, but he moved many times before settling in Bramley. In 1825 he had walked to Liverpool and back to Ossett in search of work but without any success. Spurr managed to find work in Hunslet and then in Leeds before illness forced him back to Ossett. When he had recovered he spent a few months making boots in Gildersome. Spurr then records that I 'wished again to try my weel of fortune elsewhere'.[7] This wish again led him to Leeds where he found work. When his firm moved to Meanwood, Spurr followed. After eighteen months, with little work and his wages owing, Spurr moved to Rodley where there was 'all kinds of folly from morning till night'.[8] When a bailiff called with a writ for his master, Spurr moved to another part of Rodley where he had a miserable existence. This brought him to work in Bramley settlement where Spurr found happiness in the hymns sung in Mr Pickard's workshop and in having his wages paid on time. Later he was to establish his own boot making business in Bramley. This account also shows that, whilst the search for work had led Spurr to leave Ossett, it was chance rather than foreknowledge that brought him to Bramley. That said, Spurr settled in Bramley because he found work there.

Not everyone in Bramley Township was so fortunate. The number of poor families probably increased so that some of the growth in population lacked an economic basis of support.[9] Nevertheless there was an increase in the number of people in employment between 1801 and 1831, especially in manufacturing and trade.[10] Irrespective of whether chance or intent brought migrants to Bramley, opportunities for work, encouraged them and, for that matter, many native born, to remain in the township.

The Economic Bases Underlying Population Growth

Quarrying, farming and manufacturing were the bases on which the economy rested in Bramley Township in the early nineteenth century.

At that period the most important quarry was Bramley Fall.[11] Quarrying had increased there when the Yorkshire section of the Leeds and Liverpool canal opened in 1777.[12] People worked as 'mineral getters' and in support services. John Rogerson, a stone merchant at Bramley Fall, had a joiner's shop, three blacksmiths' shops and four stables to assist his quarrying business. Nevertheless quarrying provided full-time work for only about sixty people in 1823.[13]

Small though it was, quarrying's contribution to the economy almost equalled that of farming. Agricultural change was to have some bearing on manufacturing. Some 670 acres (27 per cent of the total area) of Bramley Township were Commons and Waste in 1790 but in that year an Act of Parliament was passed to divide and enclose these areas.[14] However it was not until 1799 that the awards were formally made.[15]

Apart from this, agriculture did not influence population growth as the numbers in farming decreased slightly between 1801 and 1831.[16] And with only low numbers in quarrying, the key economic influence was manufacturing. Table 2 suggests that population size increased as the number of mills and other works increased between 1774 and 1830 in Bramley Township. This relationship is statistically significant and is also likely to be causal. For example, in 1727 Lawrence had stated that the building of fulling mills at Calverley Bridge had tempted cloth-makers to come and settle in Calverley.[17]

Table 2

YEARS WHEN MILLS AND OTHER WORKS WERE IN EXISTENCE IN BRAMLEY TOWNSHIP.

	Present by 31st December in the year of:-				
Works name	1774	1800	1810	1820	1830
Ross Mill	Q1	Q2	Q3R	Q4	D2 D3
Company Mill		Q2	Q3R	Q4	B2
Hill Top Tannery		A	M	B1	D2
Newlay Whiting Mill		A	M	B1	D3
Hough Mill		WRRD	Q3R	Q4	D2 D3
Cape Mill		j	R	Q4	D2
St Helen's Mill			Q3F	Q4	D2 D3
New Mills			Q3F	Q4	D2
Globe Foundry			c	D1	D2 D3
Belle Isle Mill			Q3R	Q4	D2 D3
Waterloo Woollen Mill				Q4F	D2
Waterloo Corn Mill					S B2
St John's Mill					S B2
Wellington Mill					D2F
Stanningley Foundry					WRRD$_2$
Allenbrigg Mill					F
Total Number of Mills and other Works	1	6	10	11	16
Population Size	1378	2562	3484	4921	7039
in the year of:	1775	1801	1811	1821	1831

Key for the letters (full details are given in reference[18].)
The letters are the sources for the dates.

Q	Quarter Session Order Books.
A	An Assessment in Bramley, 1794.
WRRD	West Riding Register of Deeds.
j	Jenkins DT The West Riding Wool Textiles Industry, 1975.
R	Rogerson J Diaries.
F	Factories Inquiry Commission, 1834.
c	Carr ET Industry in Bramley, 1938.
M	Taylor J Plan of Township of Bramley, 1811.
B	Bramley Overseers of the Poor Rate Books.
D	Directories.
S	Survey of Bramley, 1823.

Of the types of industry shown in Table 2 there was only one tannery and that was built well before 1800, so its impact on population growth from 1801 to 1831 was negligible. The Globe Foundry opened shortly after 1800 and so made some contribution to population growth. No other foundry opened until the 1820s so the impact of engineering, though greater than tanning, was small.

The inescapable conclusion is that it was an expanding woollen textile industry that formed the economic basis for the rapid growth in population. Yet this is easier to assert than to substantiate as the statistical record is incomplete. A domestic woollen textile industry had long existed in Bramley Township.[19] During the late eighteenth century and the earliest years of the nineteenth century the number of clothiers had markedly increased.[20] By 1818 there were slightly more cloth manufacturers in Bramley Township than in any adjacent township.[21] Thereafter there was a slight decrease.[22] Unfortunately evidence for the key years between 1806 and 1818 is lacking. Much more evidence exists concerning the scribbling and fulling mills which, up to 1830, were almost exclusively a part of the domestic industry.

Table 2 shows changes in the number of mills. To some extent the number of mills could have grown because of increased demand from clothiers. Equally, though, as the number of mills grew so the area became more attractive to clothiers, encouraging those present to remain and others to migrate to Bramley. Robert Myers considered proximity to mills would encourage cloth manufacturers to buy his recently built properties.[23] As the number of mills increased, employment in mills increased, and so population growth was further supported.

Table 3

Location Quotients of Woollen Textile Mills in existence by 31st December in the year of:

Township	1800	1810	1820	1830
Armley	1.03	0.77	1.33	1.51
Bramley	1.56	2.11	2.07	2.16
Calverley (with Farsley)	0.53	0.40	0.52	0.52
Farnley	0.94	1.42	1.21	0.92
Headingley	1.22	0.92	0.99	0.75
Horsforth	1.03	0.77	0.66	0.50
Pudsey	0.78	0.90	0.77	1.37

(A value of more than 1.00 is over-representation: under 1.00 is under-representation. Sources see reference [24].)

Table 3 shows that by the end of each of the years 1800, 1810, 1820 and 1830 mills were over-represented in Bramley Township. Furthermore after 1800 Bramley Township's relative significance increased. Its greater share of mills helps to explain why its population grew faster than any of its adjacent townships between 1801 and 1821.

Possible advantages for the increase in mill numbers.

Some textile mills including *Hough, Belle Isle, Waterloo* and *Wellington* were steam powered from their inception and by 1823 only *Ross* was wholly water driven.[25] Despite the importance of steam power there is no record of any coal mining in the township after 1801 and the coal used in Bramley's mills came from Farnley, Adwalton, Rooley

Figure 3. The location of mills and other works in Bramley in 1800.

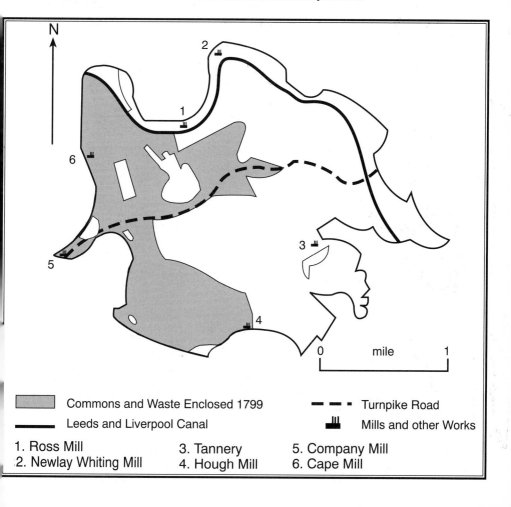

Commons and Waste Enclosed 1799	Turnpike Road
Leeds and Liverpool Canal	Mills and other Works

1. Ross Mill   3. Tannery   5. Company Mill
2. Newlay Whiting Mill   4. Hough Mill   6. Cape Mill

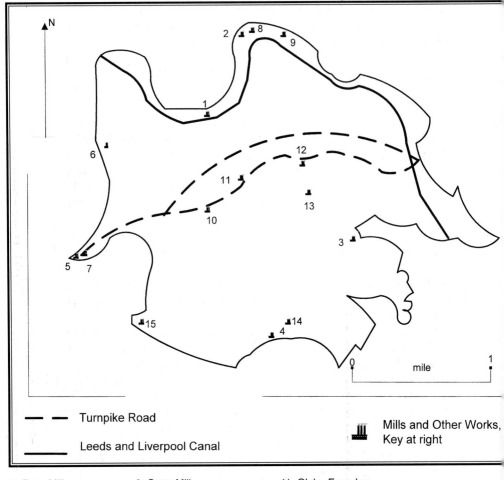

Figure 4. The location of the mills and other works in Bramley in 1830s.

- 1. Ross Mill
- 2. Newlay Whiting Mill
- 3. Tannery
- 4. Hough Mill
- 5. Company Mill
- 6. Cape Mill
- 7. Old Foundry, Stanningley
- 8. St John's Mill
- 9. St Helen's Mill
- 10. Belle Isle Mill
- 11. Globe Foundry
- 12. Wellington Mill
- 13. Waterloo Woollen Mill and Waterloo Corn Mi
- 14. New Mills
- 15. Allenbrigg Mill

and Bierley.[26] Whilst it was an advantage for Bramley Township to be near these coal supplies, of the adjacent townships, Farnley actually mined coal and the others (with the possible exception of Horsforth) were as near to coal as Bramley Township. So Bramley Township had no local relative advantage in terms of proximity to coal.

Compared with Farnley and Pudsey Townships, Bramley had the advantage of the Leeds and Liverpool Canal but it does not seem to have been much used to bring coal to Bramley's mills. Rogerson used horse pulled carts to bring coal to his mill. Some mills such as those at Hough End, were too far from the canal for it to confer any advantage (Figure 3).

Of greater importance was an improved road, the Leeds, Bradford and Halifax turnpike, part of which was located well within Bramley Township (Figure 3).[27] Four mills, *Company, Belle Isle, Wellington* and *Waterloo* were located on, or close to this turnpike (Figure 3) which helped bring wool to Bramley and take cloth to the Leeds Cloth Hall. No doubt the turnpike was used to bring coal from Rooley and Bierley as their coal pits lay near the road.[28]

However the turnpike road is far from sufficient to fully account for the growth of mills in Bramley Township. Road surfaces were not necessarily all that good.[29] Furthermore *Hough End* mills were a considerable distance from the turnpike, whilst Headingley Township, with a turnpike provision better than Bramley's in 1800, gained only one mill after 1800.

Pudsey suffered from a shortage of available land for textile industrial growth in the early years of the nineteenth century.[30] In contrast Bramley Township had the important advantage of a large area of land just enclosed by 1800. Former Commons and Waste provided sites for some mills,(Figures 3 & 4). *Hough Mill,* even though built in 1797, was sited on part of the former Commons and Wastes perhaps by agreement prior to the formal awards of 1799.[31] *Wellington Mill* and *Allenbrigg Mill* were sited on part of the former Commons and Wastes, and *Cape Mills* probably was so sited. [32, 33] The 1799 enclosures also reduced pressure on existing improved land in Bramley Township and so some of its many freeholders released land for clothiers' premises and for mill building.

Good sites for the building of mills were available in the Township. The river Aire was the source of water for *St Helen's mill.* Compared with the Horsforth side of the Aire, at Newlay, the Bramley side had a much larger expanse of gently sloping land which made it easier to build *St Helen's.* Down river, at Kirkstall, much of the riverside gently sloping land was occupied either by the Abbey or by mills built just before 1800 on land leased to James Graham, so sites for later mill building would be difficult to obtain in this part of Headingley Township.[34] *Wellington Mill* was sited where underground water was available.[35] At Hough End two Farnley Beck tributaries provided water and gentle slopes for *Hough Mill* and *New Mills*.

The site advantages must, though, be qualified. *New Mills* and *Cape Mills* each needed a pond to store the trickles of water in their nearby becks.[36] *Belle Isle* and *Waterloo* mills were not sited where natural water supplies occurred and so depended on artificial ponds.[37] And available sites were not unique to Bramley Township.

Nevertheless none of the adjacent townships possessed that combination of available building sites, many freeholders, a large area of recently enclosed land and a turnpike road that were enjoyed by Bramley Township. It was a powerful combination but it needed people who would realise these advantages early in the nineteenth century. And there were, at that period, just such Bramley people who, with different motives and backgrounds, decided to build mills.

The Builders of Mills.

Table 4

WOOLLEN TEXTILE MILLS BUILT BETWEEN 1797 AND 1830 IN BRAMLEY TOWNSHIP.[38]

Date Built	Name of Mill	Built by:
1797	Hough	John Lister, Samuel Barker and John Haley
1799	Cape	John Pollard
1802	St Helen's	John Pollard
1804	New Mills	Thomas Pawson and John Haley
1807	Belle Isle	Thomas Rogerson and Charles Lord
1816	Waterloo	John Haley
c.1823	St John's	John Pollard
1823	Wellington	Thomas Stead, Isaac Haley and John Barker
1830	Allenbrigg	Company

The mills built between 1797 and 1830 (Table 4) are most likely to affect population growth between 1801 and 1831. Even *Allenbrigg* may have been built too late to have had much effect on population growth at this period. Briefly, Allenbrigg was built by a very large number of clothiers who bought shares to provide the capital to build the mill.[39] Of the remaining eight mills, the name of John Pollard is linked with three, and John Haley played a part in another three. On these grounds alone Pollard and Haley merit attention. Moreover they represent different attitudes to mill building; by also including

Thomas Rogerson, all the approaches to mill building during the period are represented.

John Pollard senior(s) and John Pollard junior(j) were descended from a long line of substantial land-owners, one of whom, Richard, had obtained one fifth of the Horsforth part of Kirkstall Abbey estate after the monastery was dissolved by Henry VIII.[40] By the time John(j) was born, in 1763, the Pollards held land in both Horsforth and Bramley and lived in *Newlay House,* Bramley.[41] This considerable estate was further increased when large plots of land, stretching from Half Mile in the south to the canal at Rodley in the north, were granted to Pollard in the 1799 enclosure awards.[42] Pollard(s) was a merchant but Pollard(j) was an esquire or a gentleman, one of five so designated in Bramley Township and the only one to have built mills.[43] As befitted his station, his home included a wine cellar. He took part in the township's business, being a frequent witness to the signing of deeds and trustee for Bramley School.

It is not certain whether it was the father or the son, or both, who built *Cape Mills* (Figure 5). The son probably built *St Helen's Mill* and definitely built *St John's*. Bramley's residents of today know of the family through Pollard Lane which leads to the toll bridge John(j) erected in 1819 at Newlay. The tolls that Pollard would expect from the use of his bridge show Pollard was an investor. Therefore it seems highly likely that the Pollards perceived mill building as an investment opportunity and as a means to improve the value of their estate. This

Figure 5. Cape Mills. The opening between the lower and taller buildings was the location of the wheel which provided the drive for the machines. *Author's Collection*

assessment is strengthened by the fact that Pollard, (s or j) rather than working all the mills themselves, leased several. *Cape Mills* was leased to John Vickers and later to Abimelech Hainsworth who, with his brother, Joseph, probably bought the mill in 1813.[44,45] For several years *St Helen's Mill* was leased to Musgrave and Company.[46] This practice continued when the newly built *St John's* dyehouse and fulling mill was leased. In 1823 William Mason was the tenant of *St John's*.[47]

The choice of mill names, after 1800, provokes thought. *St John's* is a later partner of *St Helen's*. The name might merely indicate affection for a lady called Helen. However for John(j) to designate himself as a 'saint' hints at eccentric arrogance. Such a trait would hardly be surprising in view of Pollard's lonely and isolated existence at Newlay House, after his father died in 1816. If Pollard had some degree of arrogance it might explain why, at the age of sixty, he decided to work *St Helen's* himself when Musgrave and Co. ceased to be tenants in 1823. Pollard(j) was never a cloth-maker and he seems to have had no experience in the woollen industry when *Cape Mills* and *St Helen's* were built. Indeed the choice of water power at *Cape Mills* scarcely seems wise when the mill pond was fed by so small a stream as Bagley Beck. Whatever their technical deficiencies, the Pollard family built more mills than the Rogerson family despite their prior knowledge of woollen textiles.

The diary kept by Joseph Rogerson has earned him a place in posterity that his work alone might never have achieved. *Belle Isle Mill*, the workings of which he supervised and so valuably recorded, was created by his father, Thomas, who was a drysalter and by Charles Lord, a millwright.[48]

Charles Lord was keen on money. He paid very close attention to *Belle Isle's* accounts and once, in Joseph Rogerson's opinion, made an unreasonable charge for some millwright's work.[49] Therefore, some of Charles Lord's motives in joining the venture are clear. By being part-owner of a mill, Lord secured a reliable source of work. In addition, part of the mill's profits would increase his income and so enable him to enjoy a high standard of living. Certainly in 1823 his home and workshop were highly rated.[50]

Belle Isle opened on 1 January 1807, but Thomas Rogerson had made the decision to build the mill much earlier. Even with money saved from his drysalting business, Thomas needed extra capital. Not only had he to find a partner but, when found, he and Charles Lord still needed the extra financial assistance provided by James Oddie, a stone merchant, and possibly a friend, and by Joseph Ackroyd, an Armley clothier.[51] Compared with John Pollard, Thomas Rogerson owned only a small amount of land so a suitable site had to be found and then bought.

The decision to build was probably taken in the winter of 1802/03 when Joseph Rogerson was twenty-one and John, his brother, would soon become of age.[52] Thomas would have hoped that by building a mill his sons' economic prospects would be enhanced and made more secure through the greater diversity that a mill would offer. The Rogersons belief in economic diversity is evident in the brothers' occupations. Joseph was a farmer, a drysalter, manager of *Belle Isle* and, by 1818, a cloth manufacturer.[53] John was a woolstapler, stone merchant, and, by 1830, the owner of a grocer's shop.[54] Thomas was concerned not only for his sons' future but for his own. He hoped that some of the profits from a mill would support him in his retirement. His hope was realised in 1813 when he gave his share of the mill to Joseph and John but received an income of £150 a year in return.[55]

Despite *Belle Isle's* success the Rogersons built no more mills. With his handsome income Thomas lived in comfort in his imposing *Mansion House,* just off Town Street (Figure 6).[56] Perhaps his sons had enough to do without building other mills. And as Thomas seems to have been the driving force behind the building of *Belle Isle,* by the time sufficient capital had accumulated to finance another mill that force was spent. At least it had given Bramley an additional mill at a time when few mills were being built elsewhere in the West Riding.[57]

Something of the self-made empire-builder characterised John Haley. Unlike Pollard, Haley had no large estate when he first became involved in mill building. At that time, Haley, unlike Thomas Rogerson, was a young man so if Haley chose, and he did so choose, he had many years ahead of him to build mills.

First and foremost Haley was a cloth-maker or cloth manufacturer and therein lies the clue to his motivation.[58] By owning a mill Haley

Figure 6. The Mansion House, Bramley Town Street. *Author's Collection*

could control the main processes in his cloth making business. No doubt he found it cheaper to use his own mill than pay others to scribble his wool and full his cloth. The building of one mill can be accounted for in these ways but the reasons why he built several mills are more complex and best emerge through a discussion of his working life.

As a young man he needed partners to help finance his business ventures. Around 1791, Haley in partnership with Mr Whitley, owned a horse mill used to scribble wool.[59] By 1797, and only thirty years old, Haley had entered into a new partnership with Samuel Barker (the elder) and John Lister to build *Hough Mill,* the first wholly steam-powered mill in Bramley.[60] Haley was an ardent Methodist and a sympathy for Methodism probably brought together the partners and their several financial supporters, including Samuel Barker (junior) a woolstapler and Thomas Stead a clothier.[61]

On 1 January 1802, the partnership was dissolved.[62] Evidently Haley had become discontented for, whilst Lister remained at *Hough Mill,* Haley sold his share to William Farrer.[63] One can only speculate as to the source of Haley's discontent. Lister was partly a stone mason, and Barker, though a clothier, may have been something of a sleeping partner, for, after the dissolution, he had no more than a financial interest in the mill.[64] Haley might have felt that, for his efforts, his returns were too low and he had too little time to spend on his cloth-making business.

Whatever the reasons, the dissolution was important as it led to another mill being built in Bramley as Haley had to begin again. This time his partner was Thomas Pawson, another Methodist and a Farnley woolstapler. Aided by a mortgage, Pawson and Haley built *New Mills* which opened in 1804.[65] The mill prospered and shortly after 1815 Haley became the sole owner.

By 1813 Haley had decided to build another mill, named *Waterloo* when it opened in 1816.[66] Haley may have been anticipating the day when he would need extra accommodation for power loom weaving and when he would need to be closer to Bramley's labour supplies. Meanwhile the mill would, he hoped, prove a sound investment; for initially it was not so much for his own use, as for leasing. The Methodist connection continued when *Waterloo Mill* was leased to a fellow Methodist, Mark Smith, formerly of *New Mills.*[67]

As Haley was already part owner of *New Mills,* ambition must have played its part in his decision to build another mill. He was a thrifty employer. Of the mills recorded in the district in 1834 his workers were amongst the lowest paid and had the shortest holidays (a mere four days a year). Even these were unpaid and there was no sick pay provision.[68]

Yet Haley does not seem to have sought money to enjoy a luxurious life. Though he died, at the age of ninety, in *Waterloo House*, in 1823 he was living in *Hough House*.[69] Whilst this was certainly no cottage, it was rated far lower then Pollard's Newlay House and that, in turn, was ranked lower than Thomas Rogerson's Mansion House.[70] Haley's ambition hinged upon his interest in textiles for their own sake and upon the influence he could yield and the good he could do. Consequently John Haley's name headed the list of subscribers for the distressed poor.[71] He donated flour to the value of £10, though admittedly it was probably made in his own, *Waterloo*, corn mill. Above all he was generous to the Methodist cause. In 1811 he gave £150 in land for a dwelling-house for Methodist Preachers and, in 1839, donated £315 to the Wesleyan Centenary Fund.[72]

About 1830 Haley built another mill on the Waterloo site.[73] By 1834 he was scribbling, slubbing, spinning, weaving and fulling in his mills.[74] He was the only mill-owner, with the exceptions of Varley at Stanningley, and Gott at Armley to be using power looms in Bramley and its adjacent townships in 1834.[75] Haley may not have been the most generous of employers but his was no mean achievement, having built, between 1797 and 1830, one corn mill and four textile mills. Between 1831 and 1836 he not only added a power loom mill but also one other mill to his *Waterloo* site.[76] But by 1836 he was almost seventy years old and his mill building days were over. Wilson may well have been voicing more than platitude when he wrote that Haley's 'services to the town deserve to be held in grateful remembrance'.[77]

None of the mills had closed permanently by 1831, though fire had caused temporary closures at *Hough* and *Wellington Mills*. Seventy years later *Belle Isle* (or *Westfield*), *Cape, Hough, Waterloo* and *Wellington Mills* were still making woollens. So a long lasting legacy was bequeathed by the early mill builders. In discussing them it has been shown how capital for mill-building partly came from wool-stapler, drysalter, cloth-maker, mason and millwright. To a small degree capital that might have gone to Horsforth, Armley or Farnley was, instead, invested in Bramley. Above all we have seen how Pollard, Rogerson and Haley seized Bramley's potential and made it reality.

Conclusion

Bramley Township's expanding woollen industry led to a growth in population which in turn created a demand for more shops, more servants, and more shoe-makers. As service industries increased so population grew even more. By 1830 Bramley (even allowing for some of the township's inhabitants living in parts of Rodley and Stanningley) had become rather large to be designated a village. More crucially, as its population increased so urban functions, including solicitors, hairdressers and a druggist appeared.[78] It is the presence of these functions that clinches the claim that, by 1830, Bramley had become a small town.

Several years were to elapse before a wide range of urban functions existed but the foundations of urban growth had been laid. Equally it would be some years before power spinning and weaving produced more cloth than the domestic system, but Haley's adoption of power looms had initiated an irreversible change. Moreover it signified the culmination of three critical decades in which the whole economy of Bramley Township had taken off.

Notes and References

1. Thorpe J. *Map of the town of Leeds and the county circumjacent*, 1822.

2. Dobson A. St. Peter's Church, Bramley 1964 p18 Beckwith F. 'The population of Leeds During the Industrial Revolution'. Publication of the Thoresby Society - hereafter Thors. Soc., Vol 1 XLI, part 2, 1948, pp. 118-196. Census of Yorkshire 1801-1911.

3. Census of Yorkshire, 1801 to 1831.

4. Census of Yorkshire. Census of Great Britain, Vol. I, 1851.

5. The figures are derived from a 10% sample of the Census Index of Bramley with Stanningley. Co-ordinated by L A Holmes, 1992.

6. Spurr, R, 'The Autobiography of Robert Spurr, 1867'. *Baptist Quarterly* Vol 26, 1976 pp 282–288.

7. Spurr R. p 283.

8. Spurr R. p 283.

9. Poor relief increased from £1836 in 1802 to £2095 in 1817. These figures are quoted in Dobson A. *The History of Bramley*, unpublished manuscript, 1974. Thors. Soc., MS Box 35, 1 p 265.

10. Census' of Yorkshire.

11. *A Survey and Valuation of all the Mills, Land and Quarries in the Township of Bramley*. Hepworth and Son, 1823. pp 403–412. Hereafter a Survey of Bramley. West Yorkshire Archive Service, hereafter WYAS, Leeds.

12. *Leeds Intelligencer*, 10 June 1777.

13. *A Survey of Bramley*, pp 403–412.

14. Dobson A. *A note on Bramley Enclosure Awards* Thoresby Society, MS Box 1, 32.

15. 1799 Bramley Enclosure Award is located in WYAS Leeds (Ref, 2337); and Thors. Soc., MSS 33E.

16. Census of Yorkshire.

17. Lawrence E 'The Duty of a Steward to his Lord' (1727) quoted in *The Victoria History of the Counties of England*. Yorkshire Vol II, Ed. W. Page 1912r. 1974. p 421.

18. Key and Sources for table 2:

Q	Quarter Sessions Order Books. WYAS, Wakefield.
	Q1 1774, p 16. Q2 1800, p 240. Q3 1810, p 180. Q4 1820, p 188–189.
A	An Assessment made upon all and every owners – in the Township of Bramley, 23 May, 1794. Thors. Soc., MS Box 1, 7 (*l*).
WRRD	West Riding Register of Deeds EF 36 50, Wakefield.
WRRD$_2$	LA 63 56, Wakefield.
j	Jenkins D T, *The West Riding Wool Textile Industry 1770–1835*, 1975 p 218.
R	Rogerson J. *Diaries for 1808–09 and 1811–14*. Entries for 17.02.08, 09.01.09 22.9.09, 20.10.09. Thoresby Society MS Box V, 12.
F	*Factories Inquiry Commission Employment of Children in Factories. Supplementary Report, Part 2*, 1834 (Mill numbers 55, 56, 57, 59, 185).

c   Carr E T, *Industry in Bramley*, 1938 p 46.

M   Taylor J, *Plan of the Township of Bramley, 1811.*

B   Township of Bramley Overseers of the Poor Rate Books (hereafter Overseers of the Poor).

        B1 June 1822 p 32 p 35. WYAS Leeds.

        B2 June 1831 p 30 p 63 p 89. WYAS Leeds.

D1   Baines E. *History, Directory and Gazetteer of the County of York Vol 1 West Riding,* 1822.

D2   Parson W and White W *Directory of the Borough of Leeds*, 1830.

D3   Pigot, *Directory of Yorkshire*, 1830.

S   Survey of Bramley, pp 389–390 and pp 397–398.

        Note M, D1, B1, B2 have been used only when the mill or works were known to exist prior to their respective dates of 1811, 1822, 1822 and 1831.

19. A deed of 23 July, 1669, names Samuel Musgrave as a clothier of Bramley. Thors. Soc., MS Box 1, 32.

20. Report from the Select Committee to consider the state of the Woollen Manufacture of England, III, 1806. Evidence of Mr J Walker p 180 and J Graham Esq., p 444.

21. *Pigot Commercial Directory 1818–20.* 1818 pp 206–8. (A proportion of the people listed in Stanningley has been added to appropriate townships.)

22. Parson and White.

23. *Leeds Mercury*, 25 Nov., 1797. In Crump W B (ed.). *The Leeds Woollen Industry 1780–1820*, XXXII, 1929, p 321. Thors Soc.

24. Sources as reference 18 with the additions following:

    Cudworth W, *Round About Bradford*, c 1870 r. 1968 p 467.

    Horsforth History guides No. 3. *Woodside and its Industries* 1985.

    Parson W and White W *Directory of the Borough of Leeds* 1826.

    Rayner S. *The History and Antiquities of Pudsey*, 1887, p 230–231.

    Strong R. 'Textile Communities in the Making: Pudsey and its neighbourhood, 1700–1840'. *Thoresby Society*, Second Series Vol 5, 1994. p 43 p 47.

25. Wilson B, *Our Village*, 1860 r. 1988 p 46.

Rogerson J, for example, 7.01.09. Factories Inquiry Commission (mills 55 and 57). Survey of Bramley pp 377–402.

26. Rogerson J. Entries for 12.01.08, 8.11.09, 23.3.11. 28.4.12.

Carr E T (ed.), *The Land of Bramley*, 1937, Vestry Entry, 10 June, 1827, p 10.

27. Cary J, *Map of The Turnpike Roads of Yorkshire 1789*, in E Hargrove, *The Yorkshire Gazetteer*, 1806.

28. Richardson C, *A Geography of Bradford*, 1976 p 49 and p 75.

29. Rogerson J, Entry for 4.01.08.

30. Report from the Select Committee, 1806 Evidence of Mr Jo Coope p 33.

31. WRRD EF 36 50.

32. WRRD HP362 329, Wakefield, and WRRD HT 527 498, Wakefield.

33. Shown by a comparison between the sites of the mills and the locations of Commons and Waste as on the map of Tuke J, *A Map of the Parish or Borough of Leeds 1781.*

34. Crump W B, pp 269–270.

35. Carr E T, 1938, p 26.

36. Survey of Bramley, p 377–402, Taylor J.

37. Survey of Bramley, Taylor J.

38. Sources for table 4:

    Cudworth W, p 467.

    Wilson B, p 46.

    Factories Inquiry Commission (Mills 55, 56, 57, 59, 185).

    Jenkins D T, p 217, p 218.

    Laurence A, Histories of Various Old Horsforth Families. Undated typescript, p 31.

    Thors. Soc. MS Box 1 35, 6.

    Overseers of the Poor 1822, p 35 1831 p 89.

    Rogerson J, entries for 01.01.08 and 19.10.13.

    Survey of Bramley, pp 397–398.

    WRRD EF 36 50.

    WRRD EM 311 426, Wakefield.

    WRRD FA 330 446, Wakefield.

    WRRD HT 527 498.

39. Forty names are listed in Bramley Overseers of the Poor Rate Book, 1836, p 106. WYAS Leeds.

40. Lancaster W T, 'The Early History of Horsforth'. *Thors. Soc.*, Volume XV, 1909 p 239.

41. Laurence A.

42. 1799 Enclosure Awards.
43. WRRD DW 264 312 and FU 722 802, Wakefield. *Baines Directory.*
44. WRRD FY 459 579, Wakefield.
45. Cudworth W. p 467.
WRRD FU 724 803, Wakefield and Overseers of the Poor 1822 p 15 and Survey of Bramley pp 381–382.
46. Rogerson J. entry for 30.10.13 and Overseers of the Poor 1822 p 35.
47. Survey of Bramley, p 397–398.
48. WRRD FA 330 446.
49. Rogerson J, entry for 27.07.12 and 09.08.13.
50. Survey of Bramley, pp 189–190.
51. WRRD FA 330 446.
52. Bramley Church Register. In Leeds Chapelries 1763–1812 *Thors Soc.* Volume XXIX, 1928, p 199.
53. Rogerson J. *Diaries* WRRD FA 330 446. *Pigot,* 1818–20.
54. Rogerson J. *Diaries*. Survey of Bramley p 403. Pigot, 1830.
55. Rogerson J, entry of 18.11.13.
56. Survey of Bramley, pp 273–274.
57. Jenkins D T, p 223.
58. WRRD EF 36 50. WRRD FY 635 782, Wakefield.
The Commercial Directory 1814–15 Wardle and Bentham p 84. Parson and White 1830 p 451. Census Index Bramley with Stanningley 1851.
59. Wilson B, p 46.
60. WRRD EF 36 50, and Wilson B. p 46.
61. WRRD EF 36 50, EH 618 752 EH 618 753 FP 40 42 GD 626 709, Wakefield. In contrast to Haley the Rogersons were Church of England.
62. WRRD EL 252 315, Wakefield.
63. WRRD EL 254 310, Wakefield.
64. WRRD EF 36 50.
65. WRRD EM 311 426.
66. Rogerson J, Entry of 19.10.13.
67. WRRD GE 141 145, Wakefield. Survey of Bramley, 1823 p 387.
68. *Factories Inquiry Commission,* mill numbers 11, 12, 55–59, 62, 63, 82, 86, 116, 185, 224, 226–228.
69. *Leeds Intelligencer,* 13 June, 1857.
70. Survey of Bramley, pp 135–136 pp 261–262, pp 273–274.
71. Undated Subscription List in Thors. Soc., MS Box 1, 34.
72. Subscribers for the building of a dwelling house for Methodist Preachers, April, 1811 Thors. Soc., 31 D4. Subscribers to the Wesleyan Centenary Fund, June, 1839. Thors. Soc., 31 D4.
73. Overseers of the Poor 1831, p 30.
74. Factories Inquiry Commission Mill number 56 and 57.
75. Jenkins D T, p 126–127.
76. Overseers of the Poor, 1831 p 30 and 1836 pp 31–34.
77. Wilson B, p 46.
78. Baines E; Parson and White 1830; *Pigot,* 1830.

11. THE BEGINNINGS OF GOTT'S MILL IN LEEDS

by John Goodchild, M. Univ

IN JANUARY 1779, the coach carrying the Royal Mail from Glasgow southwards was stopped and robbed near Morpeth, and a £50 cheque belonging to two leading Leeds cloth merchants was stolen: the names of the two merchants were to survive in the names of Fountaine Street and Wormald's Row, off the Headrow in Leeds. As a result of the robbery, a new cheque had to be issued by the Scottish customers of the Leeds firm, and documents were prepared to cover the possibility of the stolen cheque coming to light. One of these was witnessed by a junior clerk in the Wormald and Fountaine's counting house or office, a sixteen-and-a-half year old boy by the name of Benjamin Gott. He had recently left Bingley Grammar School, and a year after the theft he was to be put apprentice to Wormald and Fountaine for four years. Upon coming out of his apprenticeship his father bought for him a partnership in the business and young Gott had some nine per cent of the capital of 40,000. His father was one of the new profession of consulting engineer; part-time West Riding Surveyor, part-time engineer to the great Aire and Calder Navigation, and living latterly in Butts Court in Leeds: a middle class man of the new breed of engineer.

Young Gott was to be fortunate in the business. He might have expected to be the junior partner in it for many years, but the senior partner died in the year of Gott becoming a formal partner. He did indeed leave a widow and three young sons, but his share of the business had to be divided among these various interests, and although the sons became partners, they were under the influence of the dominating Gott. The other senior partner died in 1791, leaving no son to potentially interfere; there were only a widow and a daughter, both of whom left their money in the business, and who could hardly influence decisions to any marked degree. Thus Ben Gott was left at the helm of what was then only one of the more modest sized Leeds cloth merchanting businesses. There is a list of

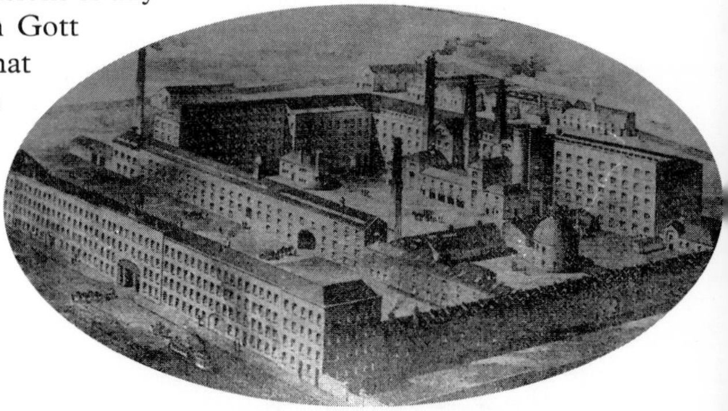

Figure 1. Final complex at Bean Ing. Yorkshire Post Leeds Centenary Supplement 1926.

The John Goodchild Collection, Wakefield.

the turnovers of Leeds merchants of this period.

In 1791, the year in which the last of his older and senior parners died, Gott embarked upon a quite new venture, but in association with the older firm. Surviving documents relate to the firm's new borrowing of additional capital: Gott raised the then substantial sum of some £33,000, nearly all in the form of simple loans secured merely upon the bond or promissory notes. One third of the new capital came from the widow Fountaine, at four-and-a-half per cent, but the rest came in all from ninety-four individuals. Between the firm's establishment in 1758, with a borrowed capital of £600, and 1812, the business raised the sum of £101,000 by loans.

Ben Gott's initial concern was to provide a range of substantial buildings which would house processes for finishing cloth and dyeing it, presumably to avoid the use of independent master dressers and dyers who had hitherto undertaken such work. It was to be on a large scale, but it is significant that Gott deletes from his own instructions (see below) the initial reference to wool-processing. The processes were to be steam-powered, and the text below refers to the consideration of what type of steam engine would be used. Ultimately, Gott himself chose one of the still-under-patent engines manufactured by Boulton & Watt of Birmingham, and a contract with that firm, with the partners' signatures upon it, survives in the writer's Gott papers. Only later was a revision of the process coverage decided upon, with reference to wool cards from the beginning of 1793 and spinning from later that year. Weaving, by hand-loom, was introduced, but at a later stage. So Gott's ambitions were apparently not initially towards an integrated all-process manufactory at Bean Ing, but rather to a mechanised cloth-finishing mill, including dyeing facilities, although he was soon to have further processes in view.

Gott traded in woollen as against worsted cloths, and these ranged in quality from blankets up to the finest costume cloths. For the purposes of his new mill, he bought land on the edge of the town of Leeds, land which was relatively cheap but also lay quite close to the Leeds and Liverpool canal, the motorway equivalent of the period. The site was flat, being on the valley floor, where are now the offices and works of the *Yorkshire Post* in Wellington Street, and the site had indeed to be piled. Gott was to attempt something of a size which had never been tried before, although the principle of multi-process manufacture had been experimented with: he was to combine the latest commercial practice with the latest technology.

Gott was apparently the model business man: innovative but cautious; one who saw others take the first financially dangerous steps in new technology, but who evaluated their experience and was then willing to invest heavily, once the technology was proven. He was also a young man who, as well as possessing the advantages of his character, was in the right position at the right time as a result of the fortuitous deaths of his senior partners without experienced heirs. In fact, he was the right man at the right time, so often the basis for the success of a great capitalist.

The new mill complex at Bean Ing in Leeds was to be built on what a contemporary observer remarked as being 'an unprecedented scale'. Gott wrote down his requirements for the new mill, which at at this stage he intended for cloth finishing, including dressing and dyeing only. The instructions, in his own hand, survive, and are endorsed 'The instructions given to Sutcliffe for Erections in Bean Ing pr Benjamin Gott'; they read as follows:

> *Mr Sutcliffe is desired to state a plan with an Estimate for the under-mentioned works to be erected in such part of Bean Ing as Mr Sutcliffe shall think most eligable –*
>
> *Steam Engine with one or four stocks*
> *Workshops containing Machinery for raising Coatings & Cloth & for dressing Cloth by hand or by Machinery – the power from the Engine*
> *Press Shop – suppose 13 Stang & Six screw presses*
> *Tenters – suppose 1250 Yards say 800 at present & the other added*
> *Dye House containing – Vessels for Dying Wool & Cloth*
> *Scribling [sic] Mill four Engines – or 6 Engines*
> *Dryhouse for lengths of Tenters* ⎤ *These to be included in the Plan*
> *Stoving Room* ⎢ *so as to be erected when found*
> *Frizing Mill – 2 frames 100 each* ⊢ *most convenient & to have*
> ⎢ *every benefit from the*
> ⎦ *Machinery.*
> *A House for the Master Dresser 4 Rooms on a floor*
>   *Do   Do   Dyer   Do   Do*
> *4 Cottages 2 Rooms on a Floor & Pantry*
> *Qu. Scribbling Mill on a small scale* [deleted]
> *these Works are intended to be on a plan for finishing about*
> *76 pairs Broad Cloths Prest of 36 Yards* ⎤
> *long from 5/4 to 7/6 Braod* ⎢
> *114 pairs Coatings 46 Yards* ⊢ *Weekly*
> *each from 6/- to 8/6 Broad)* ⎦
> *76 pairs Yard wide Cloth chiefly fine & Prest Weekly*

Sutcliffe was ultimately to send in an account for his work in connection with the new buildings, and the account forms a useful basis on which to examine the initiation and progress of the building works (Figure 1).

The architect and engineer for the new mill was John Sutcliffe, who described himself as a civil engineer and lived in Halifax; he was possibly the John Sutcliffe who was the eldest son of John (a gentleman) and Elizabeth Sutcliffe of Stansfield Hall near Todmorden, although there were five John Sutcliffe's listed in the *Yorkshire Election Poll Book* of 1807 as resident in the upper Calder valley, and four exercised their vote at the election of a West Riding Registrar of Deeds in 1809; both of these listings include John Sutcliffe of *Stansfield Hall*, gentleman. Little indeed is known of Sutcliffe as an engineer: he reported upon a proposed canal on the south bank of the Tyne upstream to Hexham in the 1790s; he undertook work for the Leeds Water Works at a similar period; and many years later, in 1816, and describing himself on its title page as a civil engineer, he was the author of the sententious but substantial work entitled

> *A Treatise on Canals and reservoirs and the best mode of designing and executing them with observations on the Rochdale, Leeds and Liverpool and Huddersfield Canals and a comparative view of them; and also on the Bridgewater, the Lancaster and the Kennett and Avon Canals. Likewise observations on the best mode of Carding, Roving, Drawing and Spinning any kind of Cotton Twist also instructions for designing and building a corn mill and how to grind upon the best principle: with a new and simple mode of preserving grain from the consequences of a wet or soft Harvest, and rendering useful grain that has become foul or fusty together with important directions on public drains.*

Described as an engineer, he agrees to buy four fields at Wellhead, close to the centre of Halifax, in December 1793.

How Gott came to know of Sutcliffe is not known, but in December 1791 Sutcliffe examined 'the Bean Ing for the new works' and subsequently consulted with Gott as to the possible sale of the lower part of the land which adjoined the river Aire. It was not in fact until March 1792 that the formal conveyance of the land was made to Benjamin Gott and Harry Wormald. The new mill was to contain the most modern machinery, and in January 1792 Sutcliffe visited Matthew Bryan of Netherton Hall near Wakefield to examine the cloth shears he had at work, presumably in his nearby Coxley Mill, opened in 1787. He later, in June 1792 visited Mr Beard's mill in Derbyshire and consulted with him as to shearing cloth by water power; with Gott he examined the dimensions of the dyehouse vessels in the various dyehouses in Leeds and went himself to Hollings Mill at Bradford to obtain details of the dimensions of their dyehouse vessels.

The drawing of the plans for Gott's new mills took forty-seven-and-a-half days. Initially drawings and two sets of plans were made, one of the latter shaded and one not so; Sutcliffe charged £88 15s for the work plus ten guineas for the 'Designing of the Plans'. Sutcliffe explained that

> *The reason why so much time was spent upon them was because Mr Gott desired that they might be drawn two or three times over that no improvements might be omitted.*

In February 1792 the building was set out on the ground and in April 1792 the workmen, masons and bricklayers, presumably the contractors for such works, were given their instructions by Sutcliffe. The digging of the foundations began in May 1792, and a decision had to be reached as to whether to pile or to dig deeper in one corner of this low-lying site. By 10 June, 1792, the foundations were laid; upon average they were five feet below ground level, although for the enginehouse and at the side of the dyehouse where there were to be coal cellars, they were to be of a greater but unspecified depth. The one hundred yard long foundations were to be of undressed stone, and some two hundred yards of such stones, three to three foot six inches broad and five to seven inches in thickness, would be required for the foundations of the dyehouse, enginehouse, warehouses etc [sic], while a similar quantity and size of stones would be required 'as a kind of String Course' to top a three foot thick stone-built foundation wall; the whole of these walls would be below ground level, and on the string course would be built the brick walls of the mill. These were to be two bricks lengths in thickness, a total of some twenty to twenty-one inches. The windows were apparently to be four feet four inches wide and the intervening piers five feet nine inches, the windows to have stone mullions; the stone window cills (five feet four inches long) were to be like those on Mr Cookson's new cotton mill in Leeds. The masons were to be provided with lime and sand, presumably to secure quality. The clerk of works appears to have been one Robert Wear of Leeds, whose name appears occasionally in Sutcliffe's correspondence as manager of the actual building process; he was described in a *Leeds Intelligencer* advertisement in connection with the levelling of the hills on a part of the Leeds and Tadcaster turnpike, as a 'carpenter in Leeds'.

In March 1792 Sutcliffe had examined a number of patented steam engines in and around London, at Gott's request, and he personally favoured one of the steam engines built by Sturges & Co of the Bowling Iron Works near Bradford, probably one of their engines using a separate condenser band based (illegally) on James Watt's patented invention. Sutcliffe arranged for one of Sturges's men to come across from Bowling, after which, he wrote to Gott in June 1792 that he would 'settle with' Sturges and 'get it forward as fast as possible'. This did not quite coincide with Gott's intentions: he was already negotiating with Boulton & Watt's local agent, and a man came down from their Soho Works at Birmingham to view the site and what was required, Gott wishing to take his advice on the necessary foundations, on the supply of engine water and 'which way the power of the Engine could be supplied to most effect'.

Sutcliffe was not at all pleased: he had not been asked to the meeting, although Gott was to point out that on account of the nature of the enquiry, being made of a specific firm

> '... there was nothing improper in our Conduct in following the opinion of a Millwright (Who had lived with Bolton & Watt & was accustomed to their machinery) on the most eligable plan.'

In consequence, on 4 August 1792, Sutcliffe wrote resigning his position ' you will excuse me for declining to have anything more to do with . . . your works.' In December 1792 Sutcliffe sent in his account from Halifax, totalling £163 12s 0d. Gott thought this exorbitant, although Sutcliffe pointed out that Wyatt of London or John Carr of York would have charged forty guineas for designing the plans alone, above the cost of drawing them, rather than his own ten guineas. Gott suggested arbitration by Carr of York, William Jessop, the famous Newark engineer, Gardener, a 'considerable' millwright of Liverpool, or John Rennie of London who was both a millwright and engineer. Carr ultimately suggested allowing twenty-six days for drawing the plans, at two guineas a day, plus ten guineas 'for designing', plus an allowance for the time engaged on that work.

Sutcliffe had little cause to admire Gott, and a letter of December 1792 from Sutcliffe cuttingly alludes to Gott's 'high but momentary Elevation in life.' A letter of pained explanation to Gott from Halifax in August 1792 is worthy of a full transliteration.

Halifax 13th Augt 1792

Sir

When I got home on Tuesday Evening I met with your Letter of the 6 past which would have been answer'd by Wednesday's post but I was called from home all the week. You say having concluded upon on of B & W. Engines there was nothing improper in your conduct for following the opinion of a Mill Wright that was Employed under B & W. Here Sir I must beg leave to differ with you that so far from there being nothing improper in your Conduct on this Occasion there was every thing that could be improper in the Conduct of a man and for the following reasons. Before I ever drew a line for you you Promised me again and again that if I undertake to give you a Design for the works you intend to Erect no one would interfere with them and whatever Engine I concluded upon it would be right with you. It was on these terms and these terms only that I undertook your works and I never would have undertaken them on any other terms. The Conditions on my part was these I was to finish your works and they were to be tried by you for three or four months before I received one Shilling of you for them. After the works were finished if you could point out any Money that had been badly laid out by my direction I Promised to be answerable for that Money and at the same time I tould you I undertook all my works on these Conditions. You have mentioned these as the Conditions I had undertaken your works upon in two or three different Public Companies since I begun of them – Now Sir how does your late Conduct and of these Promises Square together. Before I went to London last March you desired me to Examine all the Steam Engines In London and it that I could get to see which Accordingley I did and in doing this I spent several Days and as many Pounds in Money. On my return home I tould you what I had done and what was my opinion of the different Steam Engines I had seen as well as what was the opinion of the People that had the different Patent Engines. After this you desired me to order your Engine that it might be ready with the rest of the works. I then tould you as I have often done since that I wished to have time to consider of the subject and at the same time I desired you well to consider what power you wished the Engine to have. After some weeks you asked me again if I had made up my mind about the Engine the answer I gave you was that after having Examined a great Number of Engines both in London and in the Country I examine one on the same Principle as that of Mr Sturges'es being fully convinced that it would be the Cheapest Engine and the best Calulated for your business and time will never alter my opinion on this. You then said if that Engine met my approbation it was right to you and you desired it might be ordered immediately. Two or three days after my return from Leeds (at this time) I Wrote to Mr Sturges word to meet me at your Wharehouse on such a day and added in the letter that you had concluded upon one of his Engines and that you had Ordered me to set about it immediately. Mr S. met me at the time appointed and then you told him and me that you had not made up you mind about having a Patent Engine. This was the first time I ever heard you mention having an Engine of this sort. You then said you would wait until Mr Marshall was at work. I do not Blame you for taking the opinion of any Engineer or of all the Engineers in the Kingdom about Sundry Patent Engines as well as common ones but after having taken all the Different opinions you could get you had no right to give Orders for making any alterations or authorising anyone else to make any alterations in any one thing I had done without my approbation and for the reasons I have before given. After you had concluded upon a Patent Engine If you had either sent for me or Wrote me word that you requested my attendence as it was thought necessary to make some alterations in the works you would have found me the rediest man in the world to have attended and assisted in any necessary alterations. If you had done this you acted like a man that paid due regard to your Promises and at the same time had a Respect for the Reputation and the Peace of mind of a man that had taken uncommon pains to serve you and had given up other People's works to the amount of some Thousands of Pounds to be more a liberty to wait upon yours. But so far was this from being the Case that first one alteration and then another was concluded upon without me knowing more or less of the matter and yet in your Esteem there was nothing improper in all this. There are some men in this World that are so full of Pride and Vanity that they think they can never do any improper thing and you appear to me to be one of that happy Number. There is one invariable Rule I always go upon in all my works and it is this I never do nor I never will permit any one to make alterations in my designs without I am first consulted. I will neither permit B & W not any of their agents nor you nor a man of ten times your consequence to take such Liberties with my Designs without my approbation. Thus far your Conduct has relation to breaking a great Number of Promises made to me and trampling upon the agreement I had made with you. Should you have the Fontry to deny that you ever left the sool management of your works to me I have your own hand Writing to prove it and I Esteem it of no small value to me as things have turned out. I have before said that thus far your Conduct of respects breaking every Engagement you had with me and this is bad enough but there is another part of your Conduct that for Treachery Vllany and its Ingratitude I think scarcely knows a Parallel except in the Conduct of Judas. What I am now going to Charge you with I have the authority of Mr Jno. Cookson and Mr Marshall for so doing. Thes two Gentlemen's Veracity I can depend upon for I have the pleasure of being acquainted with them for some Years and in all my dealings with them I have always found them men of strict honour men that will not break their Promises to serve their own Interest. You tould B & W Agent that you had given me Positive Orders to design an Engine House for B & W Patent Engine for this B & W agent tould Mr Cookson. It would have made no difference with me when I was drawing the Plan for the Engine House whether it had been drawn for a Patent Engine or a Common one if I had known it at the time I was Drawing the Plans. If you will prove that I ever had such instructions given as to Design a House for a Patent Engine I will pay for the alterations if they cost a Hundred Pounds. I will not say this was a mistake in you it draws no such Complimt. but it was a Deliberate Lie which you had forged as a kind of Exercise for your unjustifiable Conduct. Is there a Probability that you ever gave Orders to me to design the Engine House for a Patent Engine. Had not the Plans been Drawn some Months before you gave me Orders to Settle with Mr Sturges for such an Engine as he is now using. How will you Reconcile this with you giving me Orders to make Provision for a Patent Engine. You also tould mr Marshall that I wanted to Cram Mr Sturges's Engine down your throat. This Sir is as great an untruth as the former. Has any part of my Conduct ever given you reason to say that I wanted you to have an Engine contrary to your Interest. For what reason did I refuse to Order your Engine some months ago but to give you time to consider upon it that you might be fully satisfied. This Conduct does not appear as if I wanted to Cram any Particular Engine down your Throat contrary to your own inclination. I am ready to admit that your Throat is an uncommonly wide one by permitting so many Large untruths to pass through it without any apparent sensibility of feeling. But notwithstanding it has been so oftens Stretched upon the Tenter hooks of falsehood and Breaded with the Long Liver of Ingatitude yet with all these Particular advantages to widen it I am inclined to think if but a small part of that Engine was Cram'd down your throat it would Choak you. In this you have attempted to shew that I had designed an Engine House Contrary to an Express Command given to me and in so doing I consulted my own humor more that your Interest and in the next place that I presses an Engine upon you which would never answer the end it was designed for. The man that would be Guilty of such a Piece of Conduct as this in any works but Particularly in works of the Magnitude your are ought not to have a Place in Society for one hour and yet this is the Conduct you have chargin me with to my most intimate Friends. In the representation of this matter you have Acted the part of a Dark Designing Hypocrite and have shewn you self to be a man in whose narrow Shrul'd Contracted Bosom there is no Room for the Virtues of truth Charity Humanity Honour or Integrity to dwell in. Many a good mans reputation (whose Life has been an Ornament to Society) has been Destroyed and all his Comforts in together withat by a far less false representation of his Conduct than you have been Guilty of towards me. It is my happiness that my Character will not be Injured by your treachery and Ingratitude neither does it stand in need of being supported by any recommendation of yours for in either of these Cases was it dependent on you I should consider Existence a curse. Perhaps you may think that I Expostulate too freely with you but upon more mature deliberation I would query whether you may or not. To treat such an Audacious invader of the dearest of the rights of men with tenderness and meekness falsly so called would be like Shooting at a Highway man with a Pot Gun or reflecting the Sword of an Assassin with a Straw. I have only given you a whip when you Deserve a Scorpion. Could I have forseen that you had been Equal to such Conduct as I saw in you when last at Bean Ing setting aside what you have Charged me with to my Friends you should not have had the Plans if you would have given me a Thousand Pounds for them. Neither B & W nor any of their agents nor any of your Family were ever able to design and furnish such a set of Plans as I have Drawn for you. If when you Engaged me to Design your works you Expected that I should betray the Secrets of other People's Mills committ'd to my care and others into which I am occasionally called and communicate them to you I say if you expected this of me you was greatly mistaken with the Person you Engaged or if you Expected that I should enter any Gentlemans works in that shaby Clandestine way you have gone into some of your Neighbours works you was mistaken in this also. You must get some of B & W agents to be the Cat's paws for you to do this kind of dirty work for some of them and you appears to be wonderfully wells calculated for ot.

From yours &c J. Sutcliffe.

Something of the story of the equipment of the new mill is told in W B Crump's *The Leeds Woollen Industry 1780–1820*, although numerous further aspects of the Gott business are illustrated in documents in the writer's Local History Study Centre at Wakefield. The mill complex completed (it was of course added to from time to time, and indeed rebuilt in part after fires there) the business carried on there was most successful. (Figure 2 & 3) A warehouse for the sale of cloths was opened on the corner of Woodhouse Lane and Guildford Street, where cloths could be examined by potential purchasers, although of course Gott had a team of travellers. The site at Bean Ing was supplemented by taking Armley Mills on lease in 1800. These mills were rebuilt, and purchased in 1807. They now house the Leeds Industrial Museum. Burley Mill was built and opened probably in 1801, but only a few walls survive today.

The business obviously experienced booms and depressions, which occurred then as they do today, but the books of Gott's son show that the firm made some 54 per cent on capital in the boom year of 1825, and in the depths of depression in 1826, some 10 per cent, with averages of some 20 per cent. Like many businessmen Ben Gott took an active part in the life of the community in which he mixed and worked, and he looked to the future through the careful training of his sons.

Sources

Crump W B, *The Leeds Woollen Indsutry 1780–1820* (Thoresby Society vol 32 1931)

All other material for this essay is to be found in the Gott manuscripts in the John Goodchild Local History Study Centre in Wakefield.

Figure 2. Gott's Mill during its demolition in 1965. *The John Goodchild Collection, Wakefield.*

Figure 3. Gott's Mill during its demolition in 1965. *The John Goodchild Collection, Wakefield.*

12. LOOKING BACK: MEMORIES OF MILL WORK

by June Walton Pearce

WHEN THE MILL CLOSURES came, the heartbeat of many small communities was lost, along with the vocabulary of a trade that had its roots in the industrial revolution. Unfortunately, many youngsters of today have no idea about the process of making material, or the part it played in many small villages, where the livelihood of whole families depended on it.

It wasn't an easy life. The hooters or bells calling people to work at an early hour; the 'overlookers' standing by the clocking-in machine; or the man in the 'time' office calling you in if you were late. The boss of each department had a desk strategically placed so that they could watch what was going on; and the owner of the mill himself would regularly walk through, to check that everyone was working. And if not, why?

From the school, which was just around the corner, we used to go in turn to watch and learn about the manufacture of worsted material as part of our education. We watched the wool being taken in its raw state from the bale to the combing and carding departments where dust and fluff hung in the air like snowflakes (Figures 1 and 2). Then to the drawing and spinning. Bobbin 'liggers' toting round the wooden spools to each machine. On to winding; cones for warp and bobbins for weft. The noise was unbelievable. Back bending, arms reaching, fingers tying endless knots. Dust was everywhere. They tried to keep it

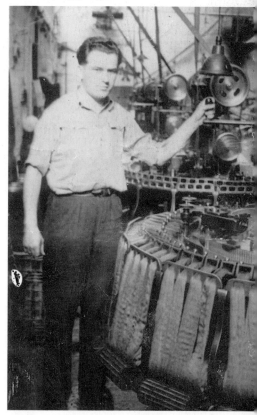

Figure 1. A combing department circa. late 1940s showing the 'Noble' combs. *Courtesy Mrs E Tate*

down by sprinkling the floor with water from watering cans, but it would not mix with the grease and oil from the wheels and cogs of the machinery. The weavers were always classed as the clever ones at lip reading, but it applied to all departments where noise was a big factor. On to warping. Reaching in, the warp twisting. Weaving.

Then there was the smelly, steamy scouring department where the material was washed in long tubs. Then it was passed to tentering, to be stretched and dried (hence that saying 'To be on tenter hooks'). Lastly the material was passed up to the mending department, there to have all the knots and bits removed that had been left in through all the manufacturing processes. Here broken ends were sewn back in, and the threads that were either too thick or too thin were replaced.

Figure 2. Girls from a combing department with 'Noble' combs, late 1940s. *Photograph used courtesy of Mrs E Tate*

Figure 3. Staff from a burling and mending department, c1950. *Author's Collection*

Figure 4. King George VI's Coronation Day celebrations, 12 May, 1937.*Courtesy of Mrs E Tate*

I remember standing to watch this process with, what seemed to me, an old lady. Her glasses were perched on her nose, and she wore a black cotton apron. All the material of the piece was draped around her. She chirpily told me it was a good job, and 'it was only the lucky ones' that were able to get in, whilst at the same time she sewed tiny stitches. She asked if I would like to work there too. I replied with an emphatic 'Definitely not! It looks boring' (Figure 3).

From this very quiet, very clean environment with its plants standing on the sills of huge windows, the pieces, as they were now called, were returned again to the clatter and bang of machinery to be cut and faced, finished, mended, steamed and pressed before ending up in the warehouse to be packed and dispatched to Europe and the Middle East.

It was part of our education and also a taste of the life that lay ahead for many of us who could not choose, but were told by our parents where our future lay (Figures 4,5 and 6).

Figure 5. Coronation day 1953 *Courtesy of Mrs E Tate*

Looking Back

I remember my mother sending
Me to work in the department of mending.
I also vividly recall
Not wanting to go and work there at all.
Confectionry was my intent,
But being no opening I was sent
To work among all these faces;
Who stared at me from their mending places

Which were at an upright board.
They had names of Fanny, Ethel, Minny or Maud.
I was part of a group of fifteen year olds
Fresh from school and waiting to be told
of the in's and out's of this occupation
That took two years before elevation
To full status of acclamation
Of being a burler and mender.

"This is weft and that is warp
We cuttle, flipe or fold.
This is canvas; this is twill. Sit up strait" we're told.
"Look for broken ends and picks, traps and stitching places.
Always mend on the back, making perfect faces.
Learn the pattern of each piece. Hold your needle just like so.
That's Barathea, Fancy, Plain. Lock your ends as you go".

Figure 6. Getting to work during a bus workers strike in 1950s. *Author's Collection.*

We had to learn to sew at speed to get the pieces out.
And if they were bad we worked as a team with the bosses hanging
    about.
"Come on, this piece is wanted. Work through your lunch.
It's wanted down in finishing with the rest of all this bunch.
It's part of an order for the Middle East."
Stretched out over six flat boards,
Twelve of us working, fast as we can.
Cramped fingers; sore heads lowered.
Two years later I went on full pay.
"Best job in the mill" they used to say.
"It's clean and you work all dressed up.
While the rest of us are in dust and muck."
The years passed on, and changes wrought.
Firm's weren't as fussy as when we were taught.
Picks and ends and threads let go;
I couldn't adjust to new ways, and so
I wasn't sorry my notice to tender.
I never wanted to be a burler and mender.

13. THE LEEDS JEWISH COMMUNITY:
A SKETCH OF ITS HISTORY AND DEVELOPMENT

by Murray Freedman

WHEN WILLIAM THE CONQUEROR invaded this country, in 1066, some Jews came over from his Dukedom of Normandy to England where they were encouraged to act as traders and money-lenders – to provide financial lubrication to the feudal economy.[1] At that time moneylending was denied to Christians by Canon Law, but often it was the only occupation open to Jews, so that it is not too surprising that they became quite adept at it. Medieval Anglo-Jewry lived in small communities mostly in London and the cathedral towns, such as Lincoln, Gloucester and York, in the latter of which they were subjected to a horrible massacre in Clifford's Tower in 1190.[2] Having outlived their usefulness after a couple of hundred years, the Jews, in total numbering only some 4,000, were expelled from the whole of the kingdom in 1290. From that date to 1656, when they were re-admitted at the time of Cromwell, the country was officially devoid of Jews. When William Shakespeare introduced the Jewish character of Shylock into his play *The Merchant of Venice* he had probably never even met a Jew.

The Jews living in England in the seventeenth and eighteenth centuries were made up of Spanish and Portuguese refugees from the Inquisition but, thereafter, British Jewry was built up by continental immigrants, first from Central Europe, and subsequently Eastern Europe. At the beginning of the nineteenth century there were about 20–25,000 Jews in the country, resident mostly in London, and strangely enough, in the naval ports such as Chatham and Portsmouth, where many acted as official chandlers to the Royal Navy, providing its ships with provisions. There was a continuous trickle of immigration going on and many of the newcomers began to make their way to the expanding industrial towns where they gradually established embryo communities. Although a few of the immigrants, particularly from Germany, were quite prosperous and came for purposes of trade, the vast majority of the immigrants hailing from Eastern Europe were very poor. Many of them could only make a meagre living by occupations such as hawking and selling old clothes, trudging from an established base in a large town like Birmingham or Sheffield, to the villages in the surrounding countryside.[3]

The Jewish communities in Manchester and Bradford were established mainly by German Jews who had come to this country to trade in cottons and woollens respectively. There is a district in Bradford called Little Germany, which houses the restored mills and offices that the German woollen traders set up in the town. Many of these German traders, who contributed much to the civic and cultural life of that city, were of Jewish origin.[4]

The first reference to the presence of a Jew in Leeds is probably the entry for Israel Benjamin, of Vicar Lane, in the burial register of Leeds Parish Church in 1735. He was stated to have been 'Born of Jewish Parentage at Breslaw in Germany, became a Christian and was Baptized at Dublin in Ireland in the 45th year of his age'.[5] His age at death is not recorded, nor do we know how long he had been living in Leeds (Figure 1). Although there are records of individual Jews and Jewish families from then onwards, a community as such can only be dated from about 1840. It was in that year that a Jewish cemetery was opened (which is still in use), and it is known that about that time religious services were being held in a small loft in a house in Bridge Street. It was a very tiny community however, and the 1841 census reveals that it comprised only nine identifiably Jewish families together with a number of single male lodgers – a total of 56 persons (Figure 2).[6]

Numbers increased only very slowly so that even twenty years later, in 1861, there were still only 200 Jews present in the town. Most of

Figure 1. Burial register entry in the Leeds Parish Register in June 1735 for Israel Benjamin

BURIALS.   401

June. 1735

Elisabeth, daughter of Will. Wormall,	2.
Israel Benjamin, Vicar-lane,	3.

he was Born of Jewish Parentage at Breslaw in Germany, became a Christian and was Baptized at Dublin in Ireland in the 45th year of his Age.

Mary, daughter of Robt Lambertson,	4.
Martha, daughter of Richard Bateson,	5.
Grace Atkinson, Woodhouse,	5.
Elisabeth, wife of John Taylor,	10.
Joseph, son of George Hudson,	11.
Mary, daughter of John Oddy,	11.
Thomas Brown, Call-lane,	14.
Mary, daughter of George Clark,	15.
William, son of Tho. Sawer, Esq.,	16.
Ruth, daughter of James Jackson,	18.
Martin, son of William Newton,	21.
Anthony, son of Anthony Wood,	21.
Robert, son of Robert Whitaker,	22.
Matthew Watson, South part, Drowned,	23.
Mary, daughter of Joseph Flockton,	24.
Mary, daughter of Joseph Lofthouse,	28.

Table 1
LEEDS JEWISH COMMUNITY
Families and Population Totals for each Census year

	1841	1851	1861	1871	1881	1891
No. of families	9	21	44	195	558	1404
Total in families	28	82	189	853	2692	7012
Approx. family size	3	4	4	4	5	5
Families in Leylands	1	10	23	130	457	1002
Leylands families as percentage of all families	11	48	52	66	82	70
Single lodgers	28	62	30	135	245	844
Community Total	56	144	219	988	2937	7856

There was a quickening pace to the growth of the community so that it grew as much in the third decade, quadrupling, as it had in the previous two. Bill Williams has suggested that this increase in immigrant settlement in the 1860s may have been due to the American Civil War which made America temporarily less attractive as a destination. Growth was caused chiefly by immigration and it appears that the majority of the new arrivals settled in the Leylands which by 1871 was housing more than two thirds of the whole community - and by 1881 more than 80% - with many more living literally just yards away in adjoining streets.

From the ages of the first born British children of foreign born parents the time of their immigration can be deduced and analysed as in the next table. At the same time the number and percentage of foreign born members of the community is noted.

Table 2
LEEDS JEWISH COMMUNITY
Immigrants - Periods of Arrival & Proportion of Community: Numbers & Percentages

	1841	1851	1861	1871	1881	1891
Less than 10 years	39	70	95	547	1322	4032
10 to 20 years	4	6	15	58	200	556
20 to 30 years	1	1	2	2	53	109
Over 30 years		1	1	1	1	85
Total No. of immigrants	44	78	113	608	1576	4782
Community Total	56	144	219	988	2937	7856
Percentage of immigrants	79	54	52	62	54	61

The earliest recorded immigrant arrived in this country in the 1810's. The total number of immigrants at each census was cumulative but the figures for those arriving in the previous 10 years is the real indication of the rate of immigration which quickened markedly in pace in the 1860's and 1880's.

Figure 2. Census Statistics on Leeds Jews taken from the author's book *Leeds Jewry: The First Hundred Years* 1992.

this early community was made up of German born immigrants – some of whom were woollen merchants. They were quite well-to-do and had been attracted to Leeds because it was then the leading cloth manufacturing centre. However, nearby Bradford gradually overtook Leeds in importance in the industry, and many of these Jewish German merchants subsequently moved there to be closer to the woollen mills, and joined the larger number of their countrymen who had previously gone directly to Bradford. They included Martin Hertz, a relative of the scientist who gave his name to electro-magnetic waves and Jacob Arnold Unna, who helped found both the first Bradford Synagogue and the Bradford Chamber of Commerce, who was the great-grandfather of famous actress, the late Dame Peggy Ashcroft.[7]

One of the notable landmarks of the early years of the Leeds Jewish community was the very first Jewish marriage in 1842, which took place in the couple's home in Commercial Court, off Lower Briggate.[8] The house has long since been demolished, but the rather shabby entrance to the Court still exists, next to the railway bridge that crosses Lower Briggate. We know quite a lot about this marriage, and the bridegroom worked as manager of the Leeds branch of a Jewish owned chain of tailors and outfitters, Samuel Hyam & Co., at no 9 Briggate – on the site that is today directly under the railway bridge. That firm, incidentally, anticipated much of Marks and Spencer's sales practice in that it regularly advertised its policy of exchanging unsatisfactory goods (Figure 3).[9]

The first real synagogue in Leeds was a converted house in Back Rockingham Street, on the site of what is now the Merrion Centre. It was opened in 1846, and we know from a religious census taken in 1851 that it had 70 seats and that its average Sabbath morning attendance was 35 (Figure 4).[10] Its 150th anniversary was celebrated in 1996 when a Civic Trust plaque was placed near its site in what is today the Merrion Centre. The first purpose-built synagogue was erected in 1860 in Belgrave Street on a site which was to serve the

Figure 3. First Jewish marriage between James Cohen Pirani and Abigail Davis in Leeds on 1 June, 1842.

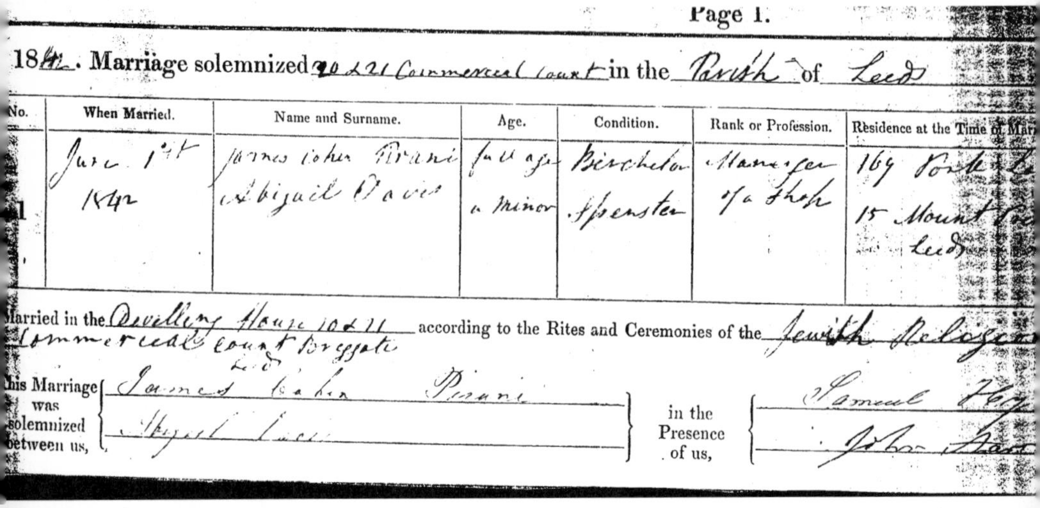

Page 1.

1842. Marriage solemnized 10 & 11 Commercial Court in the Parish of Leeds

No.	When Married.	Name and Surname.	Age.	Condition.	Rank or Profession.	Residence at the Time of Mar
1	June 1st 1842	James Cohen Pirani Abigail Davis	full age a minor	Bachelor Spinster	Manager of a Shop	169 York ... 15 Mount ... Leeds

Married in the Dwelling House 10 & 11 Commercial Court Briggate Leeds according to the Rites and Ceremonies of the Jewish Religion

This Marriage was solemnized between us, James Cohen Pirani, Abigail Davis — in the Presence of us, Samuel Hy... John ...

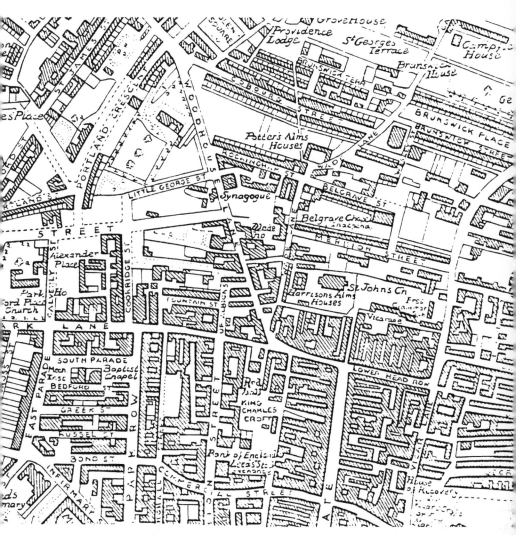

Figure 4. Section of first Ordnance Survey map of Leeds in 1847 showing the synagogue in Back Rockingham Street.

community's religious and welfare needs for the next 123 years.[11] All these locations are in what is now the centre of the city, where no Jews currently reside (Figure 5).

As time went on the flow of immigrants increased, but more and more of them were coming from Eastern Europe – chiefly from the Russian controlled territories and, in particular, from the area that is now Lithuania and north east Poland. That was a time before the introduction of passports, and restriction on immigration was unheard of. The Jews were fleeing from poverty and persecution, and for the vast majority of them the destination was America. The route to the New World for most of them, however, lay through England, passing from Hull, where they would land from Hamburg and the Baltic ports, to Liverpool, there to embark on a ship to New York. There were many tales of immigrants being tricked by unscrupulous shipping agents and being led to believe they had landed in America when they had actually only landed in Hull or Grimsby! In the Maritime Museum in Liverpool there is an excellent display of how the immigrants, not all of whom were Jewish of course, flocked to the port to get on the transatlantic ships, and one is able to get some idea of the hardships they had to endure on their voyage to the New World.

Leeds was on this route from Hull to Liverpool, and many of these U.S.A.-bound Jews would stop there temporarily – often because they had run out of money to continue their journey. But Leeds also specifically attracted Jews because of its growing clothing industry. This was started in 1856 by John Barran (who later went on to become Lord Mayor and a great benefactor to the city), and he was assisted by an immigrant Jew from Russia named Herman Friend.[12] Friend started as an outworker for Barran, for no Jews were allowed to work in

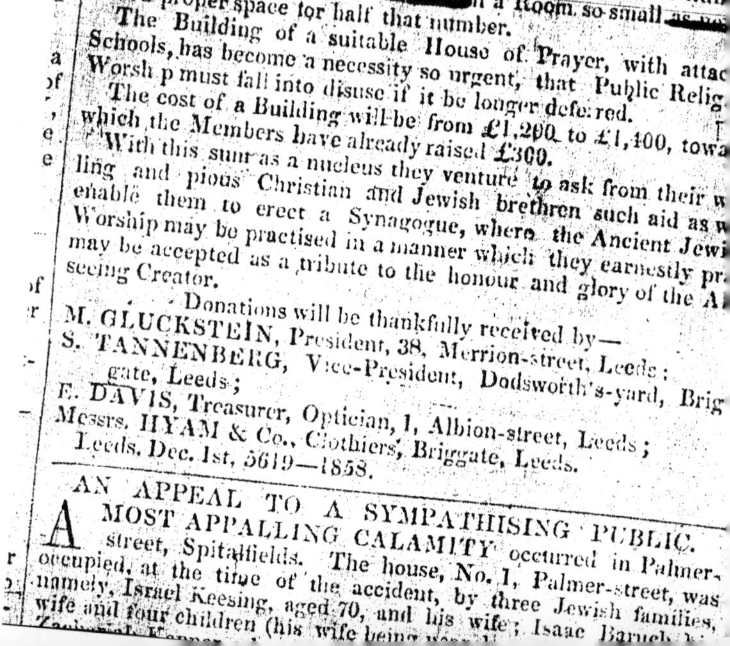

INTENDED NEW JEWISH SYNAGOGUE IN LE

THE HEBREW CONGREGATION of LEEDS, com chiefly of Persons in humble circumstances, and fe number, is on Festival Days augmented by strangers from great Manufacturing Towns, to such an extent that three hun persons are obliged to assem[illegible]n a Room. so small [illegible] afford proper space for half that number.

The Building of a suitable House of Prayer, with attac Schools, has become a necessity so urgent, that Public Relig Worship must fall into disuse if it be longer deferred.

The cost of a Building will be from £1,200 to £1,400, towa which the Members have already raised £300.

With this sum as a nucleus they venture to ask from their w ling and pious Christian and Jewish brethren such aid as w enable them to erect a Synagogue, where the Ancient Jewi Worship may be practised in a manner which they earnestly pr may be accepted as a tribute to the honour and glory of the A seeing Creator.

Donations will be thankfully received by—
M. GLUCKSTEIN, President, 38, Merrion-street, Leeds;
S. TANNENBERG, Vice-President, Dodsworth's-yard, Brig gate, Leeds;
E. DAVIS, Treasurer, Optician, 1, Albion-street, Leeds;
Messrs. HYAM & Co., Clothiers, Briggate, Leeds.
Leeds, Dec. 1st, 5619—1858.

AN APPEAL TO A SYMPATHISING PUBLIC.

A MOST APPALLING CALAMITY occurred in Palmer-street, Spitalfields. The house, No. 1, Palmer-street, was occupied, at the time of the accident, by three Jewish families, namely, Israel Keesing, aged 70, and his wife; Isaac Baruch [illegible] wife and four children (his wife being [illegible]

Figure 5. Article from the *Jewish Chronicle* in December 1858 asking for donations towards the building of a new, purpose built synagogue in Leeds

Barran's factory, and he developed the divisional system of working in tailoring in his workshop at the corner of Vicar Lane and Lady Lane, previously the site of the old Leeds Workhouse.[13] His system allowed unskilled people to learn quickly just one aspect of making a garment – like pressing, buttonhole sewing or machining. One of the early Jewish immigrants to Leeds, Samuel Manham, in an interview to a local newspaper in 1918 when he was an old man, recalled the wonder and excitement that the newly invented sewing machine caused when it was first introduced into Friend's workshop in the 1850s.[14] The industry quickly expanded with an ever growing demand for workers, and Herman Friend actively encouraged his co-religionists to come to Leeds for work.

By the 1891 census there were 8,000 Jews in Leeds.[15] The community had grown, not only by immigration, but by a very high birth rate. Of their listed occupations in that census as many as 72 per cent were involved in tailoring, usually working in the so called 'sweat shops' under conditions that were often very poor. Other favoured occupations included glaziers, slipper makers and cabinet makers. The community grew to some 20,000 by 1905 when immigration to this country was severely curtailed by the *Aliens' Act of 1905* – the first legislation restricting immigration passed by a British Parliament.

Most of the immigrants were penniless when they arrived here and were unable to speak English. Their everyday language was Yiddish – a mixture of medieval German and Hebrew that was hundreds of years old and had a rich literature of its own – though prayer, both in synagogue and the home, was always in Hebrew.[16] The newcomers to Leeds settled in or near to the Leylands, adjoining the city centre, a very badly run down area comprising hardly more than fifty acres, but where property was cheap to rent. There they established their synagogues, often named after the town or region in Eastern Europe from which the founders hailed. They also set up a network of self-help organisations, such as the Leeds Jewish Board of Guardians established in 1878, necessary at a time when there was much poverty and overcrowding, and when there was no Welfare State or government grants.[17] Surprisingly, in spite of the extremely poor quality of the housing and unhygenic conditions, the health of the Jewish children was found to be better than non-Jewish children of the same class.[18] Maybe it was the chicken soup – often called the Jewish penicillin – which promoted this!

The Leeds Jewish community was, at first, overwhelmingly working class, and there were few intellectuals amongst the immigrants who came to the city. There were early attempts to organise themselves into trade unions and, in 1893, the Leeds Jewish Tailors', Pressers' and Machinists' Union was established.[19] This grew into probably the largest specifically Jewish trade union in the country and, perhaps uniquely, it was able to erect its own purpose-built offices in 1910 – a building which still survives and which, though of little architectural merit, may well be listed because of its historical association.[20]

The Jews often faced hostility from their non-Jewish neighbours at all levels, with, of course, no anti-racial legislation in those days to protect them. Some cafés in the centre of town, for example, would refuse to serve them.[21] On one occasion, when a Jew was being tried for some minor offence before a jury, the magistrate caused an outcry by summarily dismissing the jury during the case because he claimed there were too many Jews on it to effect a fair trial. Sometimes violence would flare up culminating in the infamous riots in 1917 when a mob attacked the Leylands, destroying property and looting Jewish shops (Figure 6).[22] Later on, particularly after the First World War, anti-semitism took the form of job discrimination. In an effort to counter this many Jews changed their foreign sounding surnames, and thus the name of Cohen might be transformed to Collins or Cowen, Levi changed to Lawrence, and Goldberg to Grant.[23] One example of job discrimination, well known to the community, was the attitude of the Leeds Medical School and General Infirmary which was very reluctant to employ Jewish doctors on its staff. It was only as recently as 1969 that a Jewish consultant was first appointed – and that was because no one realised he was Jewish! Many Jewish doctors whose ability merited advancement to senior posts had to leave Leeds to further their careers. Social discrimination went without saying and, to give another example, Jews later found it almost impossible to join local golf clubs (a situation that still exists) – with the result that they had, in 1923, to set up their own, Moor Allerton.[24] This club still flourishes but does not restrict membership solely to Jews, for about a third of its members today are gentiles.

In 1881, in what came to be considered a most significant event in modern Jewish history because of its consequences, the Russian Czar, Alexander II, was assassinated. In the backlash that followed, persecution of Jews, endemic in the country, intensified. Frequent bloody pogroms ensued, so that the flow of emigration from Russia became a flood. It is estimated that between that year and 1914 some two million Jews left, mostly for America, but approximately 100,000 settled in this country with a fair proportion of them coming to Leeds.[25] We know, from comparing the 1891 census with that of ten years previously, that 2,700 settled in the city in the 1880s alone. It is from these post-1881 immigrants that most of today's Leeds Jews are descended, and this immigration, together with natural growth, combined to produce a Leeds Jewish population which peaked at some 22–25,000 by the late 1920's.[26]

One of these immigrants, Michael Marks, became famous for founding one of the most celebrated British retailing firms, *Marks and Spencer*, in Leeds Kirkgate Market in 1884. He married in Leeds in 1886 and lived for a short time in Trafalgar Street in the Leylands, before moving to Manchester. A plaque denoting this used to be attached by the side of the main entrance of the Briggate store. The firm's famous trademark of *St Michael* is derived from his first name.

The burgeoning of the community after 1881 was fortunate from the point of view of education. The *Education Act of 1870* had authorised the establishment of local School Boards which were required to provide, for the first time, universal compulsory free education, and the four Board schools that were built in the Leylands area became almost wholly Jewish. Attendances at the schools, encouraged by parents appreciative of the value of education, eager-to-learn children, and a most enlightened approach by the non-Jewish teaching staff, were the highest in the country, and they had remarkable success in gaining the scholarships to high school on offer by the city in numbers

Figure 6. Typical Leylands back-to-back dwellings. Little Templar Street in 1933, prior to demolition. *Leeds City Library*

far out of proportion to their numbers in the total population.[27,28] At one period it was reported that Jewish children were winning as many as a quarter of all these free scholarships – though they then hardly constituted 5% of the total population of Leeds.[29] Unfortunately, some parents could not afford to let their children take advantage of high school education. They had to leave school as soon as possible (at that time the school leaving age was thirteen) to boost the family income – for many of the families were large and poverty stricken. Nevertheless, it is crucial to appreciate and understand this strong desire for education, and the seizing, where possible, of all the educational opportunities open to the Jewish children, for it largely explains the relatively easy integration and rapid socio-economic rise of the community that eventually took place.[30]

In spite of many difficulties the community, as a whole, prospered, and this was reflected in the gradual change, over the years, in the types of occupations, and the gradual, but relentless, drift northwards of the population to better housing in more salubrious districts. It spread from the Leylands to Camp Road and Sheepscar, and then, since the last war, via Chapeltown, to Moortown, Roundhay and Alwoodley. All these are adjoining suburbs on the northern edge of the city. Today all the functioning synagogues and most of the communal organisations can be found within about one square mile. It is remarkable how the community has remained so geographically cohesive since its movement away from the initial area of settlement in the Leylands, though the need to be reasonably near to Jewish facilities like schools, shops and synagogues would seem, in some measure, to explain this (Figure 7 and 8).[31]

Today the community numbers less than 9,000 (recent figures show that there may now be more Chinese living in the Leeds area than Jews) and, as already mentioned, it lives within a comparatively small area of north Leeds with perhaps 90 per cent residing in the postal district of Leeds 17.[32] It is now chiefly middle class in character with numerous professional people within its ranks – although the very large proportion of old people mostly have a working class background.[33] The birth rate is stable but low, mainly because of continuous net emigration of young people from Leeds, to which the lack of a specific Jewish high school may be a contributory factor.

An illustration of the change that has taken place in the economy of the community is the decline in the fortunes of the tailoring industry with which, as has been mentioned, a great many of the Leeds Jews were once closely connected. Even in the 1920s the Jewish marriage registers reveal that as many as 62 per cent of bridegrooms were still

Figure 7. The Beth Hamedrash Hagodel Synagogue opened in 1908. Back Nile Street. *Leeds City Library*

involved in the industry and, by 1935, a majority of the 200 tailoring firms were owned by Jews – including the largest in the world, *Montague Burton and Co.*[34] That firm, started by Russian immigrant Montague Burton, enjoyed a phenomenal growth so that in a matter of only twenty years after his reaching this country with little money and no knowledge of English, it occupied a huge tailoring factory in Leeds, and had shops in almost every British high street.[35] The firm of Burtons still exists, but its success no longer depends on manufacturing clothes. Today there are hardly any Jewish tailoring companies and hardly any Jewish tailors, and the industry as a whole has dramatically contracted in Leeds since the last war. Apparently the 60,000 workers it employed as recently as the 1950s has now been reduced to less than a tenth of that number.[36]

Perhaps a word or two about the structure and organisation of the community is in order here. As can be imagined, there is a multiplicity of different communal bodies which cater for its various needs – be they religious, welfare, cultural, or educational. Most are affiliated to the Leeds Jewish Representative Council which, though it has no real power over its constituent organisations, can act by persuasion.[37] It performs a very useful service in co-ordination and preventing duplication of efforts. Moreover, when the need arises, it can speak with one voice on behalf of the Leeds Jewish community to the outside world.

The many communal institutions include the Jewish Welfare Board which, amongst a varied range of services, runs four day centres, two hostels for the mentally and physically handicapped, and meals on wheels. There is a Jewish Housing Association which has a stock of 400 dwellings, and Donisthorpe Hall, the communal home for the elderly, has approaching 200 residents. Apart from some state and local authority help the latter organisations are funded by the community itself. There is a fine school campus which houses a nursery and primary school, and, of course there are the synagogues – four large ones and a similar number of smaller ones.[38] The main synagogues not only provide regular religious services but their buildings are the venues for many different social groups and gatherings.

From its earliest days members of the community have been involved in the wider general life of the city. There have been three Jewish Lord Mayors and a Jewish High Sheriff of Yorkshire, and the number of city councillors, since the first one was elected in 1904, has usually been larger, pro rata, than the community size would suggest.[39]

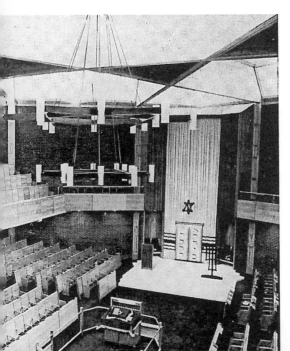

Even in the early years there was Jewish involvement in bodies like the Trades' Union Movement, the Friendly Society Movement, the Leeds Workpeoples' Hospital Fund and the British Legion.[40]

Today Jews are even more widely involved in the general life of the city of Leeds, with many judges, magistrates, leaders and members of profes-

Figure 8. The interior of the present Beth Hamedrash Hagodel Synagogue in Street Lane Gardens. *Author's Collection*

sional organisations, chambers of commerce, voluntary and chari-
table groups, music and cultural societies, sporting bodies and the
like. Because they are not always distinguishable by appearance, and
because nowadays they often do not have foreign sounding names,
their contribution, as Jews, in the foregoing ways, is seldom fully
realised.

Practically all the immigrants were strictly Orthodox Jews, but
religious practice has largely diminished amongst their English born
children and grandchildren – it is, for example, very difficult for a
retailer to correctly observe the Sabbath by keeping his shop closed
all day on a Saturday – usually the best day for business. The vast
majority of the community are, however, still members of synagogues
and in recent times there has been a small but significant religious
revival, with a number of young families becoming as fully observant
as their pious immigrant forebears.[41] The coming years should, therefore, continue to see a vibrant Jewish community that will continue to
play its full part in the general welfare of the city of Leeds, whilst still
contributing to its rich tapestry of life by maintaining and fostering
its own proud heritage and distinctiveness.

Notes and References

1. See Cecil Roth, *History of the Jews in England*, Oxford 1941.
2. For a detailed account see R. B. Dobson: *The Jews of Medieval York and the Massacre of March 1190*, University of York, 1974.
3. Roth, *op. cit.*
4. N. Grizzard, L Oldfield, *Follow Bradford's Jewish Heritage Trail*, Interfaith Education Centre, Bradford 1991.
5. Leeds Parish Church register *Thoresby Society*, Leeds.
6. See Appendix in Murray Freedman, *Leeds Jewry, The First Hundred Years*, Leeds branch of the Jewish Historical Society (JHSE), 1992.
7. *Ibid.*
8. See Murray Freedman: (unpublished) paper *The First Jewish Wedding in Leeds*,1992.
9. See advertisements for S Hyam & Co. in *Leeds Mercury* and *Leeds Times* 28 March, 1841.
10. See V. D. Lipman, A Survey of Anglo-Jewry in 1851 in *Transactions of JHSE* Vol. XVII.
11. Murray Freedman: '*Leeds Jewry, The First Hundred Years*', Leeds branch JHSE, op. cit.
12. Sir John Barran, *inter alia*, was responsible for the purchase of Roundhay Park by the city.
13. The present site of the (disused) West Yorkshire Bus Station.
14. *Yorkshire Evening Post (YEP)* article 8 March, 1918.
15. Murray Freedman: *1891 Census Leeds, List of Jewish Residents*, Leeds 1994.
16. Though now largely died out except in academia (e.g. Oxford), Yiddish is still very much alive amongst certain groups of very religious Jews. Many Yiddish words have come into English in recent years via the US.
17. It was renamed Leeds Jewish Welfare Board in the 1970s.
18. See letter in the *Times* by Dr William Hall, 18 January, 1904.
19. Before the Union was founded there were strikes in 1885 and 1888.
20. Situated in Cross Stamford Street. The inscription of the name of the Union is clearly marked on the outside of the building though there has been an attempt to erase the word 'Jewish'.
21. See Professor Selig Brodetsky, *Memoirs- from Ghetto to Israel*, 1960, for an example of discrim-ination against him shown by a Leeds city centre café in 1920.
22. See Abraham Gilam: 'The Leeds Anti-Jewish Riots in 1917' in the *Jewish Quarterly* Vol XXIX 1981.
23. A process known in the trade as 'ethnic name erosion'.

24. See Ted Hyman, *A History of Moor Allerton Golf Club 1923–1993*, Leeds, 1994. The club was the first Jewish golf club in Europe.
25. See article Lloyd Gartner: 'Jewish Settlement in Victorian England' in the *Jewish Journal of Sociology*, Vol 23.
26. For many years the community size was estimated as 25,000 in editions of the *Jewish Year Book*. For most of that time the figure was patently an exaggeration.
27. See a remarkable article Two Hours with the Jewish Children of Leeds in *Yorkshire Post* 21 May 1903.
28. Leeds School Board Report for year ending 30 September, 1901.
29. *Jewish Chronicle*, 9 July 1909.
30. For more details about these Board Schools and Jewish children see M. J. Dickenson: 'Education for a Multicultural Society, The Historical Perspective; The Jewish Community in Leeds 1885–1920' in *Journal of Educational Administration and History*, XXI January 1988.
31. Dr Peter Bell, in a paper on the ethnic communities in Leeds, presented to a meeting of the British Council of Churches in 1982, comments on this point.
32. See Murray Freedman: 'Annual reports on Demographic Trends in Leeds Jewish Community. 1988–1996 inclusive.'
33. Murray Freedman, *Leeds Jewry, A Demographic and Sociological Profile*, Leeds 1988.
34. See A. Rivlin in Appendix to Ernest Sterne: *Leeds Jewry 1919–1929*, Leeds branch of JHSE, 1990.
35. E. M. Sigsworth, *Montague Burton, The Tailor of Taste*, 1990.
36. Article in *YEP*, 17 April, 1990.
37. See the Council's latest Year Book for current list of associated communal organisations.
38. All but one are Orthodox.
39. Aldermen Hyman Morris (1941) and J. S. Walsh (1966), and Councillor R. D. Feldman (1991).
40. The Rev. Simon Manson, Reader of the New Briggate Synagogue, was for many years the Fund's Secretary.
41. The available evidence points to a religious affiliation rate as high as 95 per cent.

14. GYPSIES IN LEEDS LOCAL HISTORY

by Freda Matthews

SINCE MANY PEOPLE CONSIDER THAT GYPSIES are outsiders, at most passing through the area briefly, the idea of them as being part of our local history in Leeds might seem to be a contradiction in terms. Indeed one or two of the events described in this account concern strangers who appeared briefly and then disappeared for good. However, the main aim in compiling this brief history is to show that traveller Gypsies have been part of Leeds history from the earliest days of the Gypsy presence in this country. It is difficult to prove with regard to a mainly non-literate and mobile population the same families resorted to the same stopping places for many years. Oral evidence is at last being collected, but of course this can only go back a few generations and is virtually impossible to verify from records as can be done with the settled population. The account is made up of a series of historical incidents because in many cases the Gypsies are invisible in the usual records, It is often only by chance that some information appears. The main link between the events described here, has to be that they concern people of the Gypsy race. In view of the present day close knit Gypsy community this is not as tenuous a connection as it may seem initially.

My own interest in Gypsy history began when I was appointed as early years teacher with the Leeds Travellers Education Service in 1987. While preparing for my job, which was to take a mobile nursery on to the Gypsy sites in Leeds, I found an extensive literature about Gypsies and their culture already existed. Many academics both here, on the continent and in the United States, had become interested and involved in Gypsy affairs in the 1960s and 1970s when Gypsy pressure groups had emerged as part of the world wide civil rights movement. The earlier history of the Gypsies had been widely researched as part of this campaign[1]

As a keen local historian, I found myself looking out, both in conversation with the Gypsy families and in my other historical reading, for clues to where the Gypsies had been in the past. For although the Gypsies travelled and appeared to have relatives all over the country, most families considered themselves Leeds Travellers. Although at first their choice of stopping place appeared to be by chance in view of the shortage of almost any place to camp, it soon became apparent

2 LEEDS PARISH REGISTERS.

1572

June 1. Agnes, child of Laurence Farrowe, Holbecke.
,, 2. William, child of Rauf (*Ralph*) Chelders, Hunscelett.
,, 2. Agnes, child of Ralph Chelders, Hunscelett.
,, 5. Edmond, child of John Fletcher,[1] Medow layne.
,, 7. John, child of Robert Langecaster, Holbecke.
,, 8. Usselye (*Ursula*), child of George Deane, Chappeltowne.
,, 8. Elizabeth, child of Robert Brygdewatter, Farnley.
,, 8. John, child of Thomas Tate, Bore Lane.
,, 14. Alice, child of Gregory Fremane, Kyrckegatt.
,, 14. John, child of John Rodlaye, the kydstacke.
,, (15?) John, child of John Nayler, Beeston.
(Date worn out) } Agnes, child of Robert Fearnlaye, Farnelaye.
,, 19. Margery, child of John Ambler, Kyrkegate.
,, 19. Joan, child of Thomas Dycksonne, Brygdegat.
,, 28. John, child of Henry Atkingsonne, Houldebecke.
,, 28. Elizabeth, child of Robert Hindle, Kyrckegat.
,, 29. Elizabeth, child of Anthony Smawleye, the egypsion.[2]
July 1. Suesanne (*Susan*), child of William Jenkingesone, Bridggayte.
,, 1. Elynge (*Ellen*), child of Roger Thornton, Houldbecke.
,, 6. Agnes, child of George Dowverse, the Mayrch lane.
,, 6. Agnes,[3] child of Robert Kyllingbecke, Knawstrope.
,, 13. George, child of Richard Gyll, the Mylhill.
,, 13. Thomas, base-begotten child of Janet Launde, Chrystall (*Kirkstall*).
,, 13. Alice, child of [*blank*], Farnleye.
,, 20. Elizabeth, child of William Broke, beyond the brydge.
,, 25. William, base-begotten child of Jenet Rylay & Robt. Blackburne.
,, 25. Mary, child of Thomas Hurste,[4] the calstele.
,, 27. Robert, child of Thomas Cawdraye, Hearmleye (*Armley*).
Aug. 3. George, child of Thomas Sunderland, the Marche Lone.
,, 3. George, child of William Gerlyke (*Garlick*), Christall.
,, 3. Henry, child of William Iles, yonner, Kyrkgat.
,, 10. William, child of George Fawkener, the Quarrel Hill.
,, 17. Richard, child of Richard Gybson, the Whitcote.[5]
,, 24. Isabel, child of Thomas Killingbecke,[6] Knowstrope.
,, 24. Isabel, child of William Adcocke, the Callsteale.
,, 24. Robert, child of Thomas Broune, the Chapletoune.
,, 24. William, base-begotten ch. of Agnes Yngelande (*England*), the Quarell Hyll.
,, 24, Ellen, child of William Thornton, Holebecke.
,, 31. Christopher, child of Lawrence Newall, Wortley.
,, 31. Ellen, child of Edward Robart,[7] Farnley.
,, 31. Richard, child of Thomas Kyrke, Buslyngthrope.
,, 31. Katherine, child of Lawrence Mydelton, the Chapletowne.
Sept. 7. Agnes, child of Robert Fawsset, Mylngrene.
,, 15. Richard, child of Richard Harabye, Tymble Bredge.

---

(1) John Fletcher, of Leeds Mainriding, was taxed in the Subsidy Roll of 1596 for lands of the value of 20s.—W. W.

(2) Egyptian, now corrupted to Gipsy.—S. M.

(3) Not mentioned in Thoresby's pedigree.—S. M.

(4) The Hirsts were of consequence in the Lancastrian days. Robert Hirste, of Ledes (and brother, as he tells us, of Richard Hirste, "lord" prior of Nostell), by will, dated 13th March, 1498-9, orders his body "to be buried in the parish church of Ledes, under the littill bell stringe." See *Test. Ebor.*, vol. iv. See also *Record Series*, Yorks. Arch. Assoc., vi., 85.

(5) In Bramley; still known by the name. On the 20th Jan., 1500-1, one Thomas Gybson, chaplain, by will orders his body to be buried in the church of Ledes, in the choir of St. Katherine, virgin and martyr, between the tomb of that venerable man, Thomas Clarell, formerly vicar, and the wall. There are other interesting directions, for which see *Test. Ebor.*, vol. iv. William Gybson and his wife, and John Gibson, were resident in Potternewton in 1379.—W. W.

(6) In the Subsidy Roll of 1596, Thomas Killingbecke is assessed for 20s. in lands.

(7) In the Subsidy Roll of 1596, Edward Robert is assessed for goods at £3.

Figure 1. Extract from the Leeds Parish Register. Transcript Thoresby Society Publication vol. 1. *Thoresby Society*

that certain locations were regular camping grounds and were significant. Comments from older Gypsies about how they had stayed from
childhood in certain places, or that older relatives had been born
there, aroused my curiosity and led me to look for references to
Gypsies in local history sources.

The first recorded Gypsy presence in Leeds is at the beginning of
one of the earliest existing records of the ordinary people of Leeds,
the Leeds Parish Register, which began in May 1572. The baptism of
'Elizabeth, child of Anthony Smawleye the egypsion' is entered in the
Register on 29 June 1572.[2] The footnote in the nineteenth century
transcript published by the Thoresby Society reads 'Egyptian now
corrupted to Gipsy'[3] (Figure 1).

This Leeds reference is also relatively early in the history of the
Gypsy people in England. It is widely accepted through linguistic
studies of the Romany language from as early as the end of the eighteenth century that the Gypsies originated in India.[4] It is thought they
left around the tenth century, passed through Europe in the four-
teenth century and arrived in England calling themselves the followers
of the Princes and Dukes of Little Egypt around 1514. It is postulated
that 'Little Egypt' is a translation of the German 'Klein Egypten' as
the Turkish Middle East was then known.[5] Whether the name was a
reference to their past or was to promote a favourable image of fleeing
from pagan persecution is not clear, but it is the source of the name
Gypsy in English and 'Gitano' in Spanish.[6]

Within a short time of the Gypsies' arrival in England strict laws
were passed against them. By 1530 the *Egyptians Act* banned their
entry into the country and gave notice to all Egyptians in the country
to leave.[7] Gypsies were seen as spies, heathens, and perhaps racially
unacceptable since they were universally described as black. A law of
1554 forbade them to enter the country and threatened capital
punishment for Egyptians if they stayed for more than one month.[8]
By 1562 anyone who associated with them could also suffer death,
probably because by now many Gypsies had been born in England
and could not be considered as 'Egyptians' or foreigners.[9] It also
explains why Egyptians such as Anthony Smawleye were ensuring that
their offspring were baptized and had documents to prove their place
of birth. They also suffered from the Tudor repression against
vagrancy, which was widespread due to economic reasons and the
closure of the monasteries who had provided a safety net for the poor
and homeless. The severe 1562 act, although obviously not fully
implemented, was not repealed until 1783.[10]

The Poor Law legislation from the time of Edward VI to Victorian times made it virtually impossible for Gypsies to continue their way of life without breaking the law.[11] It is therefore difficult for the local historian to trace the history of Gypsies other than through details of their transgressions of the law. One such incident concerning a Gypsy woman's 'scam' was reported in the *Leeds Intelligencer* of 1761, as a 'humourous affair', was later mentioned in J B Place's *Woodhouse in the Manor of Leeds* as an example of the 'rural simplicity and rustic credulity' of the village and appeared again in *Criminal Leeds* by Steven Burt as an example of the history of criminal activity in Leeds.[12, 13]

> *On the 19th ultimo, the following humorous affair happened at Woodhouse in this Parish; a Gipsey Woman went to the House of John Geldard, a Journeyman Stuff-Weaver in that Village and offered to tell him his Fortune, which he consenting to, she order'd to put 50s into her Hand, which she said, he should hold fast, while she repeated the Charm etc., when, on opening her Hand, she had but 1s 6d left, which she likewise said, he wou'd not refuse to give her for her Trouble, when he was inform'd of approaching good Fortune, which was, That on the Thursday following he wou'd find, in digging up a Mole-hill in a Close adjoining to the House, a Silver Tankard full of Gold; That he must not on any account, mention the affair 'till the Day appointed, if he did, the whole Charm would be broke; but the Youth was so flush'd with the Hope of receiving his Money with such exorbitant Interest, that the next Day he disclosed the secret; and tho' since then, he has dug up all the Mole-hills in the Neighbourhood, he can neither find the Tankard nor the Money.[14]*

Leeds Intelligencer 1 December 1761.

Evidence of Gypsy presence can be found in other more positive ways. Apart from details in parish registers which are few, place names often give proof of regular Gypsy stopping places over a long period.

One of the earliest references is in the Surveys of the Manor and Borough of Leeds of 1612 and 1628 which refer to a furlong called Tinklers Leas at Knowestrop. Joan Kirby's Edition of these Documents has a footnote which identifies its position as near to Pontefract Lane.[15] The Gypsy Travellers stay to this day on the Cross Green Industrial Estate through which Pontefract Lane runs. Pontefract Lane is now a dead end, but was long ago the main route to York, making it likely that Gypsies stopped there on their travels. Was this an early camp site of Gypsy metal workers?

The Leeds Census for 1871 records 'Gypsy Corner' near Stonegate Farm and Moor Allerton – a tantalising reference not mentioned in

Figure 2. Gypsy, stopping place. Gypsy Lane, Middleton. *Author's Collection*

either the preceding or following census.[16] It is not marked on any local map of the period. Blackman Lane off Woodhouse Lane was also probably so-called because it had been a Gypsy stopping place. A field near there was called Blackman Close in the 1612 Survey of Leeds and Blackman Lane is mentioned in the 1687 Lease of the Tithe of Hay.[17] The Gypsies were known as 'black men' at that time because of their swarthy appearance.

Other places in the Leeds area are: Gypsy Lane near Middleton Woods, Gypsy Hill and Gypsy Mead off Holmesley Lane near Rothwell, Gypsy Wood Close at Colton and Gypsy Street at Thornbury near Bradford. Some of these are modern developments which continue an old local name for the area (Figures 2 and 3).

Edmund Bogg, in his self confessed romantic books of historical memories of Leeds and district, never fails to mention old Gypsy

Figure 3. Gypsy stopping place. Gypsy Lane, Woodlesford. *Author's Collection*

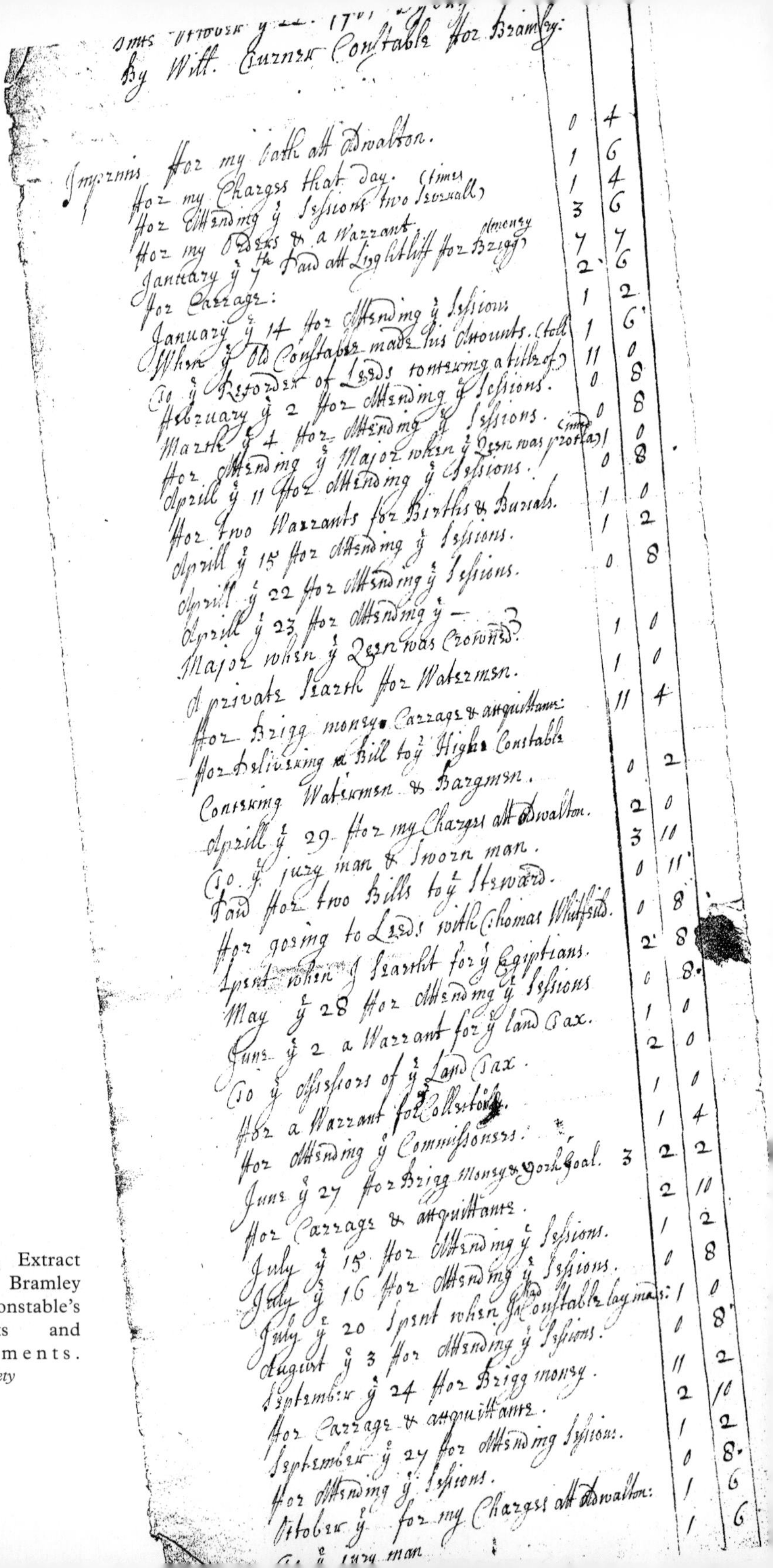

By Witt. Turner Constable for Bramley.

Imprimis For my bath att Edwalton.
For my Charges that day. (times
For attending y Sessions two severall)
For my Oathes & a Warrant.
January y 7 paid att Lightcliff for Brigg
for Carriage:
January y 14 for attending y Sessions.
When y Old Constable made his Accounts. (toll
To y Recorder of Leeds concerning a tithe
February y 2 for attending y Sessions.
March y 4 for attending y Sessions.
For attending y Major when y Queen was proclaimed
Aprill y 11 for attending y Sessions.
For two Warrants for Births & Burials.
Aprill y 15 for attending y Sessions.
Aprill y 22 for attending y Sessions.
Aprill y 23 for attending y —
Major when y Queen was Crowned.
A private Hearth for Watermen.
For Brigg money Carrage & acquittance.
For delivering a Bill to y High Constable
Concerning Watermen & Bargmen.
Aprill y 29 for my Charges att Edwalton.
To y jury man & Sworn man.
Paid for two Bills to y Steward.
For going to Leeds with Thomas Whitfield.
Spent when y Hearth for y Egyptians.
May y 28 for attending y Sessions.
June y 2 a Warrant for y land Tax.
To y officers of y land Tax.
For a Warrant for Collection.
For attending y Commissioners.
June y 27 for Brigg money & York Goal.
For Carrage & acquittance.
July y 15 for attending y Sessions.
July y 16 for attending y Sessions.
July y 20 spent when y Constable lay masse
August y 3 for attending y Sessions.
September y 24 for Brigg money.
For Carrage & acquittance.
September y 27 for attending y Sessions.
For attending y Sessions.
October y for my Charges att Edwalton.
To y jury man

Figure 4. Extract from the Bramley Parish Constable's Assessments and Disbursements.
Thoresby Society

stopping places. There are no fewer than eleven references to their 'abodes' in his book *Lower Wharfedale*.[18] Since he was writing at the turn of the century his memories must go back well into the nineteenth century. Bogg writes:

> *The Rommany tribes, formerly to be seen in large roving bands, sometimes reaching out with their horses and donkeys for a mile or more along the highway, formed another picturesque feature in the landscape; and in the fifties and sixties of the last century were to be found encamped in the wide green by-lanes of this district. Even the half-caste gipsies of the present with their up-to date caravans are less picturesque than of old.*[19]

'The Romany tribes', as Bogg writes, continue to stretch along the B road from Wetherby to York at strawberry picking time.

Gypsies are still to be found camping at the boundaries of old parishes and townships, boundaries which are now irrelevant regarding prosecution, but which were once important when the local constable had powers to move Gypsies on. It was easy to move over the boundary into the next parish where he had no jurisdiction. In 1701 William Turner, Constable of the Parish of Bramley, claimed 2s 8d

> *spent when I searcht for ye Egyptians*[20]

Obviously this was not a straightforward task for him to incur such expense (Figure 4).

The present day campsite at Walton is in fact on the border between the present Leeds authority and North Yorkshire, which was no doubt the line of an earlier township boundary. while the Leeds City Council Traveller site at Cottingley Springs is on the old Morley Leeds border and was another old stopping place according to local Gypsies.

Favourite camp sites are often near the oldest roads between towns, on small patches of land left over after road widening has encroached on old commons. One such place is the long strip of land which is all that remains of Hook Moor near Aberford on the old Ermyne Street near the A1 between York and Castleford. Such stopping places are now too obscure and inconvenient to be found by chance. Knowledge of them must be passed on by oral tradition in a mainly illiterate society. Gypsy camps near the most ancient roads ie Roman roads like Rudgate and Ermyne Street, suggest that Gypsies must have used these places since the times when they were the main routes between important towns.

Figure 5. *The Gypsy Mother* by J N Rhodes. *Thoresby Society*

To see the Gypsies before the age of photography we must turn to drawings and paintings. Whereas in general only the rich and famous among the settled population were portrayed, Gypsies were often painted as romantic or exotic subjects by artists. The almost forgotten Leeds artist, John N Rhodes, who lived from 1809 to 1842, was interested in painting rural scenes. According to his biographer W H Thorp, who wrote about him in 1904, this included 'groups of Gypsies with the picturesque accompaniments of their encampments'.[21] This sounds reminiscent of the later Victorian romanticism that we heard from Edmund Bogg and others, but what is impressive about Rhodes' portrayal of the Gypsies, unfortunately reproduced in black and white in Thorp's biography, is his realism and thus his respect for his subjects. His paintings seems to be a true portrayal of the Gypsies he met around Leeds (no doubt the ancestors of today's Gypsy travellers)

Figure 6. *Gypsy Beggars* by Julius Caesar Ibbotson (1759–1817). *Leeds City Art Gallery*

before photography became common (Figures 5 and 6).

Not all Gypsies stayed in the countryside. Particularly since the late nineteenth century they have moved, like the settled population, to seek their living in the towns. David Mayall states that Gypsies managed to find a role in nineteenth century industrial society without entering wage-labour employment or settling permanently. He mentions the growth of van towns in the large cities and Leeds was no exception.[22]

The *Armley Album* a collection of personal memories of life in Armley in the early twentieth century, has reminiscences of the Gypsy settlement on the 'Brickfields', in Buxtons Yard and Luptons Fold near Winker Green at Armley. Here is part of one reminiscence:

> *It were a Gypsy caravan site, Brickfield. They were bow-top caravans, old Romany ones. Me oldest brother, he used to be a 'bookies runner' for all t'gypsies . . . he used to be friendly with one gypsy and they called her Tilly. 'Er caravan were in Buxtons Yard where they had pigs, scrap iron, all sorts and 'er caravan were a beauty You 've never seen so much brass and silver, coral in all your life. Us gorgios you weren't allowed on t'Brickfield but I used to go running errands for 'em . . .*[23]

There is an interesting entry in the log book of nearby Armley Park School for 19 November 1902, in which the Headmaster writes:

> *Admitted two children today Eliza and Lily Smith aged 12 and 9 respectively. Neither can read or write which I take to be due to the fact that they are the children of itinerant tinkers.*[24]

Were they staying at Brickfields?

These affectionate memories in the *Armley Album* contrast sharply with the accounts in the local newspapers early in 1934 when the Brickfields Gypsy settlement made the headlines after a dispute between two of the inhabitants (Figure 7).[25]

In 1934 the encampment of around 150 vans tents and huts, many of which were reported to have been there for more than fifteen years 'on a large level expanse of cindered ground between Armley Town Street and Stanningley Road, almost opposite to Armley Park' was declared a 'disgrace to the city' and a 'blot on civilisation' by the local magistrates. Although the land was private, the tenants paid rent and sanitary arrangements were provided, Leeds Corporation Health Committee ordered the tenants to leave under the *Corporation Act of 1930*, as they did not have Council permission to be on the land. The Gypsies had become victims of the *Public Health Acts*.[26] By April 1934 the notices to leave came into effect and there were photographs and accounts in local newspapers of the departures from the Brickfield colony.[27] Although it was claimed that some were former house-dwellers and some fairground workers and that Brickfields 'had none of the romance of a gypsy encampment' the majority were probably

E YORKSHIRE EVENING POST, SATURDAY, JANUARY 6, 1934

A Corner of Armley's Caravan Colony.

...er of the Brickfields, Stanningley Road, Leeds, where a number of people live in caravans and tents. ...eeds police court case yesterday the presiding magistrate, Mrs. Leonora Cohen, said, with reference Brickfields: " Having regard to the number of tents, the number of people who occupy them and

Figure 7. A Corner of Armley's Caravan Colony. Saturday 6 January 1934. *Courtesy of Yorkshire Post Newspapers Ltd.*

Gypsies either living there or visiting periodically on their travels. As one of the residents remarked, they did not know where they would go next winter. Many moved to Doncaster and Darlington. Families from these towns regularly visit Leeds today and are probably their descendants.

A different view of Gypsy life-style is revealed in the account of Mrs Maggie Doyle who worked in Doyle's China Shop in Albion Street Leeds between 1937 and 1963. She speaks of her Gypsy women customers who used to call carrying baskets of pegs, bringing their children with them, to place orders of between £50 and £100 for Crown Derby or Worcester plates and ornaments. These had to be ordered and sent on so the Gypsies deposited jewellery in her safe until they came round again and had saved enough money to pay. So

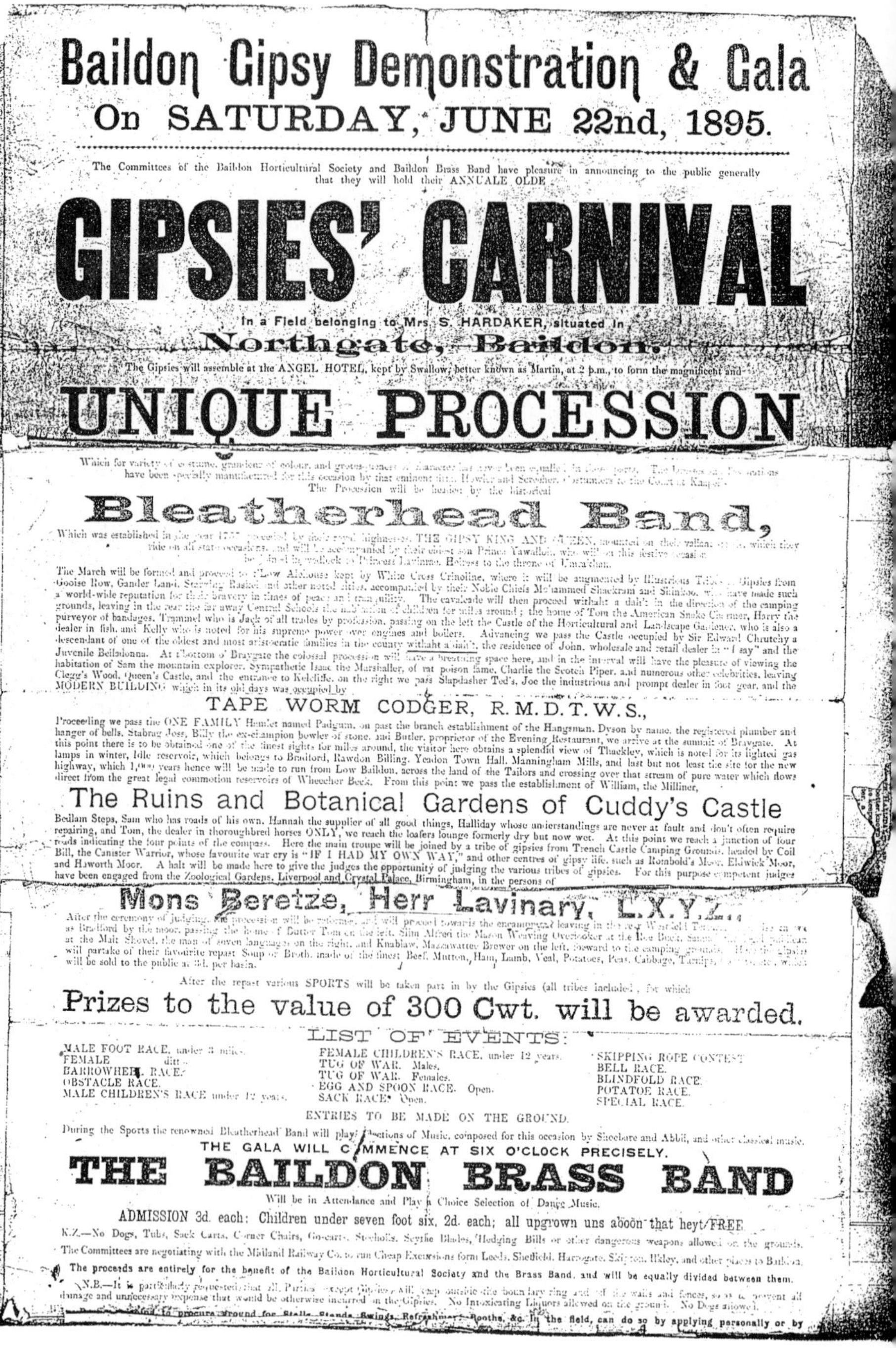

Baildon Gipsy Demonstration & Gala

On SATURDAY, JUNE 22nd, 1895.

The Committees of the Baildon Horticultural Society and Baildon Brass Band have pleasure in announcing to the public generally that they will hold their ANNUALE OLDE

GIPSIES' CARNIVAL

In a Field belonging to Mrs. S. HARDAKER, situated in

Northgate, Baildon.

The Gipsies will assemble at the ANGEL HOTEL, kept by Swallow, better known as Martin, at 2 p.m., to form the magnificent and

UNIQUE PROCESSION

Which for variety of costume, grandeur of colour, and grotesqueness of character has never been equalled in these parts. The [illegible] have been specially manufactured for this occasion by that eminent firm, Howler and Screecher, Costumiers to the Court at Kampel. The Procession will be headed by the historical

Bleatherhead Band,

Which was established in the year 17[illegible] preceded by their royal highnesses, THE GIPSY KING AND QUEEN, mounted on their valiant steeds, which they ride on all state occasions, and will be accompanied by their eldest son Prince Yawalloh, who will on this festive occasion be joined in wedlock to Princess Lavinnie, Heiress to the throne of Uncra'than.

The March will be formed and proceed to t'Low Alehouse kept by White Cross Crinoline, where it will be augmented by Illustrious Tribes of Gipsies from Goose Row, Gander Land, Starving Rasket and other noted cities, accompanied by their Noble Chiefs Mohammed Shackram and Shinkoo, who have made such a world-wide reputation for their bravery in times of peace and tranquility. The cavalcade will then proceed withaht a dah't in the direction of the camping grounds, leaving in the rear the far away Central Schools the habitation of children for miles around; the home of Tom the American Snake Charmer, Harry the purveyor of bandages, Trammel who is Jack of all trades by profession, passing on the left the Castle of the Horticultural and Landscape Gardener, who is also a dealer in fish, and Kelly who is noted for his supreme power over engines and boilers. Advancing we pass the Castle occupied by Sir Edward Chrutchy a descendant of one of the oldest and most aristocratic families in the county withaht a dah't, the residence of John, wholesale and retail dealer in "I say" and the Juvenile Belladonna. At t'bottom o' Braygate the colossal procession will have a breathing space here, and in the interval will have the pleasure of viewing the habitation of Sam the mountain explorer, Sympathetic Isaac the Marshaller, of rat poison fame, Charlie the Scotch Piper, and numerous other celebrities, leaving Clegg's Wood, Queen's Castle, and the entrance to Kelcliffe, on the right we pass Slapdasher Ted's, Joe the industrious and prompt dealer in foot gear, and the MODERN BUILDING which in its old days was occupied by

TAPE WORM CODGER, R. M. D. T. W. S.,

Proceeding we pass the ONE FAMILY Hamlet named Padgum, on past the branch establishment of the Hangsman, Dyson by name, the registered plumber and hanger of bells, Stabrag Joss, Billy the ex-champion bowler of stone, and Butler, proprietor of the Evening Restaurant, we arrive at the summit of Braygate. At this point there is to be obtained one of the finest sights for miles around, the visitor here obtains a splendid view of Thackley, which is noted for its lighted gas lamps in winter, Idle reservoir, which belongs to Bradford, Rawdon Billing, Yeadon Town Hall, Manningham Mills, and last but not least the site for the new highway, which 1,000 years hence will be made to run from Low Baildon, across the land of the Tailors and crossing over that stream of pure water which flows direct from the great legal commotion reservoirs of Wheecher Beck. From this point we pass the establishment of William, the Milliner,

The Ruins and Botanical Gardens of Cuddy's Castle

Bedlam Steps, Sam who has roads of his own, Hannah the supplier of all good things, Halliday whose understandings are never at fault and don't often require repairing, and Tom, the dealer in thoroughbred horses ONLY, we reach the loafers lounge formerly dry but now wet. At this point we reach a junction of four roads indicating the four points of the compass. Here the main troupe will be joined by a tribe of gipsies from Trench Castle Camping Grounds, headed by Coil Bill, the Canister Warrior, whose favourite war cry is "IF I HAD MY OWN WAY," and other centres of gipsy life, such as Rombold's Moor, Eldwick Moor, and Haworth Moor. A halt will be made here to give the judges the opportunity of judging the various tribes of gipsies. For this purpose competent judges have been engaged from the Zoological Gardens, Liverpool and Crystal Palace, Birmingham, in the persons of

Mons Beretze, Herr Lavinary, L.X.Y.Z.

After the ceremony of judging, the procession will be reformed, and will proceed towards the encampment leaving in the rear W[illegible] T[illegible] as Bradford by the moor, passing the home of Butter Tom on the left, Slim Alfred the Mason Weaving Overlooker at the Ree Beck, [illegible] at the Malt Shovel, the man of seven languages on the right, and Knablaw, Mazawattee Brewer on the left, forward to the camping grounds. [illegible] will partake of their favourite repast Soup or Broth, made of the finest Beef, Mutton, Ham, Lamb, Veal, Potatoes, Peas, Cabbage, Turnips, [illegible] which will be sold to the public at 3d. per basin.

After the repast various SPORTS will be taken part in by the Gipsies (all tribes included), for which

Prizes to the value of 300 Cwt. will be awarded.

LIST OF EVENTS:

MALE FOOT RACE, under 3 miles.
FEMALE ditto.
BARROWHEEL RACE.
OBSTACLE RACE.
MALE CHILDREN'S RACE under 12 years.
FEMALE CHILDREN'S RACE, under 12 years.
TUG OF WAR. Males.
TUG OF WAR. Females.
EGG AND SPOON RACE. Open.
SACK RACE. Open.
SKIPPING ROPE CONTEST
BELL RACE.
BLINDFOLD RACE.
POTATOE RACE.
SPECIAL RACE.

ENTRIES TO BE MADE ON THE GROUND.

During the Sports the renowned Bleatherhead Band will play Selections of Music, composed for this occasion by Sheelare and Abbil, and other classical music.

THE GALA WILL COMMENCE AT SIX O'CLOCK PRECISELY.

THE BAILDON BRASS BAND

Will be in Attendance and Play a Choice Selection of Dance Music.

ADMISSION 3d. each: Children under seven foot six, 2d. each; all upgrown uns aboon that heyt FREE.

K.Z.—No Dogs, Tubs, Sack Carts, Corner Chairs, Go-carts, Stechoils, Scythe Blades, Hedging Bills or other dangerous weapons allowed on the grounds.

The Committees are negotiating with the Midland Railway Co. to run Cheap Excursions form Leeds, Sheffield, Harrogate, Skipton, Ilkley, and other places to Baildon.

The proceeds are entirely for the benefit of the Baildon Horticultural Society and the Brass Band, and will be equally divided between them.

N.B.—It is particularly requested that all Parties except Gipsies, will keep outside the boundary ring and off the walls and fences, so as to prevent all damage and unnecessary expense that would be otherwise incurred on the Gipsies. No Intoxicating Liquors allowed on the ground. No Dogs allowed.

[illegible] to procure Ground for Stalls, Stands, Swings, Refreshment Booths, &c. in the field, can do so by applying personally or by

Figure 8. Poster advertising Baildon Gypsy Carnival 1895. *WYAS Bradford*

many of the china heirlooms, carefully treasured and displayed with pride in Gypsy caravans, were bought at Doyle's in Leeds.[28]

One place where Gypsies gathered every year in June was Baildon. It seems to have been a gathering of families and no doubt weddings took place as a result. There is a photograph of a Gypsy bride riding side-saddle to the church in Towngate at the turn of the century.[29] However, nothing in the church records indentifies any marriages as specifically those of Gypsy couples.

The annual events were called 'Gypsy Parties' and a report of 1929 says they had been taking place for two or three hundred years, records were said to go back to 1770 when even then it was an ancient custom.[30] So far these records remain unidentified if they still exist.

In 1881 up to 5000 people are said to have paid for admission and 200 gallons of 'Gypsy broth' had been sold! Obviously by this time the encampment had been enclosed and a charge made for admission. Gradually the event seems to have been taken over by local residents who dressed up as Gypsies and formed 'tribes' presumably following the romantic Victorian custom of wearing fancy dress.

Figure 9. Gypsy Petulengro on his horse

Advertised in 1895 as a Gypsy Carnival with proceeds going to the Horticultural Society, after 1897 the tradition seems to have died out.[31] It was assumed from later local accounts that the 'real Gypsies' who had inspired it all had also died out (Figure 8)!

In 1929 the 'Party' was revived, held in September instead of June, to raise funds for Baildon Hospital and Charities Week. John Kerr, one of those who wished to revive the parties in the 1930s, told the story as an old man how they went to Leeds to find Gypsy Smith and being unable to find him, enlisted the help of Xavier Petulengro, a Romany Gypsy, who was then

A CIRCASSIAN COLONY.

OJOURN OF A STRANGE RACE OF GYPSIES IN LEEDS.

9-12-11

THEIR TEMPORARY HOME IN THE CITY.

LE WHO EAT, WASH, COOK, SLEEP, AND HAVE THEIR BEING ON THE FLOOR.

To-day, writes a correspondent of "The Yorkshire Evening Post," I witnessed a scene almost in the centre of the city which surely has no parallel in its history. It was nothing less than a colony of Circassian gypsies, which has been established in two houses in Coburg Street.

For over a week now there has been great curiosity and excitement in the neighbourhood over the appearance of the gaudily bedecked women in the street, but few appear to know who they are or the why and wherefore of their sudden descent upon the city. And it is not easy to ascertain much about them, for they speak in Russian, and none can converse in English, although nearly all of them can ejaculate one or two English words—sufficient to make you understand it is money they want.

There are about 20 of them, all belonging to one family, and including grandfather, father, and grandchildren, sisters, cousins, and aunts. They have only been in England about a fortnight, and after being in London a day or two they came straight to Leeds because they were told there were a large number of Jews here who understood Russian.

The two houses in Coburg Street have been taken for a period of three months, and here these strange people have settled down—to live just as they would were they in the great province to the north of Mount Caucasus, except that they are housed within brick walls instead of a tent. Most of the time they spend in the back-yard, of which more will be mentioned hereafter.

There is no furniture, such modern day Western luxuries are entirely dispensed with. Everything is done on the floor. They prepare their meals on the floor, and eat them on the floor; they wash up on the floor and sit on the floor; and they sleep on the floor, but they have beds on which to lie.

First of all I went into the back room, and there saw the beauty of the party with her two little children. The Circassian females are renowned for their bewitching appearance, and this one—she spelt her name for me, but I got no further than "Volga"—certainly has a most charming and fascinating physiognomy, although she is the only one of the party I saw that can be so remarked upon.

DELICATELY FEATURED FACE.

Slightly built, with jet black hair, a delicately featured round face, dark flashing eyes that seemed to search you through and through, two rows of perfectly formed pearly white teeth, and a complexion darkened by a life in the open, she is a typical daughter of Circassia.

The costume she wore lent charm to her figure. With all the gipsy love for colour and brightness she had a loose fitting bodice, over which was fastened a handkerchief of brilliant red hue fastened with gaudy jewellery, and a short skirt, much of the fancy pattern of which was hidden for want of soap and water.

Round her neck she wore several large silver and gold coins, and when she got a tambourine in her hands threw a sort of mantilla of cardinal over her hands, and seemed to have her photograph taken.

The room in which I saw her was gaudily with turkey red and vari-coloured prints, couple of twopenny Coronation Union Jacks tures of the King and Queen in the middle curtains. In the corner were piled the b wrapped in chintz, looking the worse for w the floor was stretched a length of coloure canvas, on which were squatted the two bright and healthy looking, but scantily clad a cold morning.

Water was boiling on the fire, not in a pan, large metal bowl such as ordinary persons ma themselves in. Here you have a slight pictu back room and its occupants. The front r very similar, but cleaner, the beds there al piled in the corner out of the way until nightf

THE SCENE IN THE BACKYARD

remarkable yard, though that presented a branches of a tree or tree of stunted grow suspended a big piece of canvas, evidently me wind shield, and in front the male members of assian troupe had constructed an open-air smit were manufacturing copper pans with amazing rap

Their implements were of the most primitiv but it was truly remarkable to see what fine wo ship they turned out. There are at least half men in the party, who all bear a hand in the b and what time they are working they are la laughing, and jabbering one to another, and a n the highest state of happiness and contentm pite of their none too pleasant surroundings.

HOLE DUG IN THE EARTH.

These pans are properly brazed together, necessary heat is gained by a simple, but ingenio rivance. A small hole has been dug in the ear illed with coke, a small piece of iron-piping underneath, and a heavy bar of iron placed or keep it in position. Into this iron-piping is pla nozzle of a remarkable pair of bellows, which be likened to a pair of men's cycling knickers di he top.

One of the men squats on his haunches and each "leg" of the bellows alternately, opening a let the air in as he pulls them up, and squeezin and so forcing the air into the fire as he push down.

A powerful current of air is thus obtained, ar s much coal as one would put into both hal slower engendered an intense heat which brou opper pans to a white heat in a few seconds. I hot these men are equally dexterous in makin rticles, such as knives and forks.

TWO YEARS' TRAVELLING.

Some of the party are actors, singers and dancers, and they make their first appearance in England to-night in a Circassian performance at the Leeds Jewish Institute. It appears they left their native country two years ago to travel over Europe, and already they have been to Moscow, St. Petersburg, Paris, Rome, Milan, and Berlin. They are hoping to get some engagements at the music-halls in the district.

The men, it should be mentioned, are not gaudily dressed, but their costume, though poor, is none the less picturesque, and strangely unfamiliar to English surroundings. Most of them wear very baggy trousers and sport top boots. Smoking seems to be quite a serious business with them; and the women and youngsters puff their cigarettes as vigorously as the men. They know the value of English money, and not until they made a bargain for reward would they stand to be photographed, and even then they would not be satisfied without "more monish."

Figure 10. Opposite Left and Above: A Circassian Colony: from the *Yorkshire Evening Post*, 9 December 1911.

living in a caravan in Manchester.[32] This was the beginning of the involvement of Petulengro, culminating in the Carnivals of 1937 and 1938 which were reported in the national press and appeared on cinema newsreels.[33] Petulengro became a famous broadcaster, it is said, as a result of the publicity (Figure 9).

The Gypsy Parties ended with the start of the Second World War and were never revived. Old local Gypsy Travellers confirm that 'real' Gypsies did attend the parties alongside the locals dressed up as Gypsies and can be identified in the newspaper photos.[34]

Xavier Petulengro was, according to his life story, from Eastern Europe on the Danube.[35] His family seems to have arrived in England at the turn of the century when many foreign Gypsies seem to have visited England, often fleeing from persecution which affected them as it did the Jews of Eastern Europe, and sometimes seeking to emigrate to the Americas.[36]

There are two incidents involving Eastern European Gypsies which were reported in the Leeds newspapers at that time. In 1904 a group of sixty Russian Gypsies were said to have settled temporarily in the Leylands in four houses. There seems to have been some disorderly conduct and summonses were taken out against them. It was said that they had been refused permission to enter the United States. However much to the relief of the police they decided to leave Leeds by train for Manchester. They were watched by a large crowd as they went along Commercial Street and Albion Street with the women and children with their luggage on two large drays followed by the men in their square cut long coats, long scarves and round felt hats. Their departure from the station was attended by such crowds that it reminded the newspaper reporter of the departure of the Volunteers for the South African War and the platform was barricaded off.[37]

In 1911 another group of Russian 'Circassian' Gypsies were living in Cobourg St in Leeds. The men were apparently tinsmiths, making copper pans in the backyards, whilst others were singers and dancers. They had been travelling in Europe for two years, and had come to Leeds because they had heard that there were Russian speaking Jews living here. They were engaged to appear at the Jewish Institute to give a display of Gypsy dancing and singing during their stay. The newspaper report and the photographs were by Charles Howdill, a Leeds architect and keen amateur photographer, who had travelled widely in Bosnia and Serbia. His photographs and the description suggest that both groups were Kalderash Gypsies who spoke Romany as well as Eastern European languages.[38] They had begun to migrate round Europe in the 19th century, partly as a result of the abolition of Gypsy slavery in Romania in 1856 and moved to Western Europe and Britain in the twentieth century (Figure 10).

A recent book by Angus Fraser puts these two incidents into context.[39] Apparently the Eastern European Gypsies drew crowds all over Europe, and were able to charge admission to their camps! They discarded their wagons in France, travelled round Britain by train and camped all over the British Isles in the huge tents they had brought with them. Eventually a few stayed in Britain, some returned to the Continent and others emigrated to America. No doubt many of those families who returned to Europe were among the thousands of Gypsies who died alongside the Jews in the Holocaust during the Second World War.[40]

Between the two wars, Thomas Acton suggests that the Gypsies lived in fairly 'stable symbiosis', with the settled (gaujo) society, (each depending upon the other for mutual services) as the Armley Album suggests.[41] Apart from incidents such as the Armley eviction, due to

Figure 11. Leeds City Council Cottingley Springs Caravan site (Site A) soon after opening in 1988 with the nursery bus (Leeds City Council Travellers Education Service). *Author's Collection*

public health concerns, Gypsies found yards and small plots to live in. They were not yet motorised, so could not travel as swiftly between towns and were able to stop along roads which were not yet crowded with traffic.

After the Second World War land shortage due to expanding housing and industrial needs and later road developments, left no room for the Gypsies. Caravan dwelling was regarded generally as an unacceptable way of life. The *Caravan Sites Act* of 1960 made it impossible to stay on private sites even when owners were willing or if Gypsies owned their own land.[42] All this led to the rise of Gypsy pressure groups and civil rights groups.

In Leeds, as in most cities, there was pressure from Gypsy Travellers and their supporters for the City to set up an official site in accordance with the *Caravan Sites Act* of 1968.[43] Newspaper articles of the time chronicle the stages of the campaign and its results.[44] This act was to be the answer to the lack of stopping places for the Gypsies, but unfortunately also gave authorities the right to move on anyone not on a legal site. A site was built at Cottingley Springs in response to the Act and the pressure groups, but as it only provided sixteen pitches to serve the two hundred or so families frequenting Leeds, it created further problems (Figure 11).

Eventually Leeds City Council built the two present sites at Cottingley in 1987 and 1990 accommodating fifty-six families but still not providing places for every Leeds Traveller family. The ending of local councils' duties to provide sites and the passing into law of the *Criminal Justice Act* in 1994 means that Gypsy families are once again on the wrong side of the law if they follow their nomadic life-style as they were when they first appeared in Leeds over four centuries ago.[45]

A Postscript

There may seem little connection between Leeds University and the Gypsy caravans at the roadside. However the Brotherton Library at Leeds University is the home of the Romany Collection, an important collection of printed works and other items related to Gypsy life and culture which continues to receive contemporary contributions.[46] One of only two such collections in the country[47], it was established in 1950 by Dorothy McGrigor Phillips (better known as Dorothy Una Ratcliffe, the writer) niece-in-law of Lord Brotherton founder of the Brotherton Library. In 1913–14 she acted as Lady Mayoress of Leeds when Lord Brotherton was Lord Mayor.

According to her biography, Dorothy Una Ratcliffe believed that a drop of Gypsy blood ran in her veins through some liaison of her great great grandfathers with a Gypsy at Brough Fair.[48] Whether this story was just due to the romanticism of the times and the fact that she was a writer and poet, or was the real source of her interest in Gypsies is not clear. However her affection for Gypsies led her to found and maintain the Romany Collection. It is surely fitting that this unique resource for scholars and all those interested in Gypsy culture and affairs should have its home in Leeds where Gypsies have been so long a part of its history.

Appendix 1

The Gypsy Mother by John N. Rhodes

The Gypsy Mother, painted by J N Rhodes in 1840 and first exhibited in Leeds at the Music Hall in 1843, was considered by experts to be one of Rhodes' materpieces.

W H Thorp, his biographer, describes it as representing

> . . . *a gipsy woman seated on a mossy stone, nursing a child. A handkerchief thrown over her head partially conceals her raven black hair, her eyes are dark and lustrous, and her cheeks are flushed with the glow of health; her skirt is of bluish green cloth, and a crimson shawl of opulent colour is wrapped round her shoulders. . . . A donkey is eating herbage in the middle distance; beyond is the silvery glimmer of water, and further still, the distant landscape is faithfully rendered with true atmospheric effect. . . . The sky is luminous and is excellently painted. Blue overhead, it is gradually obscured by a filmy pinkish grey haze or cloud, merging into a pale amber glow, which extends to the horizon. . . . The gipsy's hands are well modelled and are painted in slight shadow with reflected lights, and the pearly shadows which veil her neck and bosom are the work of no novice. In colour, the work leaves nothing to be desired. The greens are of fine quality without a suspicion of crudity, and are juicy and mellow in effect, looking as if they might afterwards have been toned down with a glaze of raw sienna . .*

W H Thorp, *John N. Rhodes A Yorkshire Painter 1809–1842*, Leeds, 1904, text p.60–61, illustration plate XVIII facing p.62

Notes and References

1. See D Kenrick & G Puxon, *The Destiny of Europe's Gypsies*, Sussex 1972, T Acton, *Gypsy Politics and Social Change*, 1974.
2. Leeds Parish Register, original manuscript in Leeds District Archive Office, West Yorkshire Archive Service.
3. S Margerison, (ed) *Leeds Parish Registers First and Second Books 1572–1612*, Thoresby Society Vol 1, 1891 p 2 and note.
4. T Acton, *Gypsy Politics and Social Change*, 1974, p 88, mentions earliest hypothesis of the Indian origin of the Gypsies and their language which appeared in H M G Grellmann, *Die Zigeuner*, Dessau and Leipzig 1783 (English translation M Raper 1787 and E Wilson 1807)
5. *See Ibid.* p 61 for discussion of origin of word 'Gypsy', reference to F. de V. de Foletier, *Mille Ans d'Histoire des Tsiganes*, Parish 1970, pp 20–21.
6. D Kenrick and G Puxon, *Gypsies under the Swastika*, University of Hertfordshire 1995, p 9.
7. D Mayall, *Gypsy-travellers in nineteenth-century society*, 1988, Cambridge pp 189–192, Appendix 1: Major Legislation relating to Gypsies 1530–1908. Egyptians Act, Statute Reference: 22 Henry VIII, c. 10, 1530.
8. *Ibid.* Egyptians Act, Statute Reference: 1 & 2 Philip and Mary c. 4, 1554.
9. *Ibid.* Egyptians Act, Statute Reference: 5 Eliz., c. 20, 1562.
10. *Ibid.* Egyptians Act, Statute Reference: 23 Geo.III, c. 51, 1783, repealed all previous laws re Gypsies.
11. See *Ibid.* and D Hawes and B Perez, *The Gypsy and the State*, Oxford 1995, pp 10–16 for overview of legal measures affecting Gypsies 1530–1945.
12. J B Place, *Woodhouse in the Manor of Leeds*, Thoresby Society XXXVII 1945 p 361.
13. S Burt *Criminal Leeds : From Earliest Records to 1879*, Leeds 1985 p 2.
14. G D Lumb, *Extracts from the Leeds Intelligencer 1755–63*, Thoresby Society XXVII 1928, p 155.
15. J W Kirby, *The Manor and Borough of Leeds 1425–1662: an Edition of Documents*, Thoresby Society LVII 1983, p xliii and note, pp 148 and 184.
16. Census Records for Leeds 1871 in Leeds Central Reference Library.
17. Kirby, *op.cit.* p 79 and G D Lumb (ed.), *Lease, dated 1687, of the Tithe of Hay in Leeds*, Miscellanea Thoresby Society XXIV 1919, pp 403–406.
18. E Bogg, *Lower Wharfedale* 1904, (facsimile Smith Settle 1988).
19. *Ibid.* p 275.
20. The Bramley Parish Constable's Assessments and Disbursements for October 22 1701, an original document in the Thoresby Society Library.
21. W H Thorp, *John Rhodes, A Yorkshire Painter 1809–1842*, (limited edition) Leeds 1904, p 25. Description and illustration of the painting *The Gypsy Mother* pp 60 and 62.
22. D Mayall, *Gypsy-travellers in nineteenth-century society*, 1988, discusses Gypsy role in industrial society pp 1–3, and van-town settlements, p 17 (mentions Leeds specifically), 21, 35–39, 181.
23. *The Armley Album, Leeds 1980* p 9.
24. Armley Park School Log Book, Leeds District Archive Office WYAS. Ref. 2D 86/3 2D 86/40.
25. *Yorkshire Evening Post*, Friday 5 January 1934, Sat January 6 1934: photograph of Armley Brickfields 'Caravan Colony', *Yorkshire Post*, Saturday January 6 1934, *Yorkshire Evening Post*: Old Yorkshire Diary, February 9 1988.
26. *Yorkshire Evening Post*, Friday February 2 1934. Leeds Corporation Act 1930 was local legislation, and similar to later national legislation, The Public Health Act of 1936, essentially directed at overcrowding in slum dwellings. However these acts introduced camp site licensing by local authorities, which aimed to distinguish between use by vagrants and holiday caravanners. R J F Gordon, *Caravans and the Law*, London 1978. See also Hawes and Perez p 14 and Acton p 123 *op.cit.*
27. *Yorkshire Evening Post*, Wednesday April 4 1934: article and photograph.
28. See M Hartley and J Ingleby, *Life and Tradition in West Yorkshire*, Otley 1976, p 120.
29. Baildon Public Library: photographs and references about Baildon Gypsy Parties.
30. *Ibid.* (Official Programme Baildon Hospital and Charities Week, Sept 7th–14th 1929).
31. Poster for the 1895 and 1897 'Gipsies Carnival' in Baildon Public Library and Bradford District Archive Office WYAS. See also M Taylor, *A Short History of Baildon*, 1987. pp 31,41,42.
32. L. Gill, *Baildon Memories*, 1986,. pp 66–68.
33. Bradford Archive Office WYAS, Baildon Gypsy Fairs; miscellaneous references include cuttings and photographs from local and national newspapers for 1937 and 1938.
34. *Ibid.*
35. X Petulengro, *A Romany Life*, London 1935.
36. A Fraser, *The Gypsies*, Oxford 1992, pp 226. Gypsy emancipation from slavery in Romania 1856 began migration but did not prevent persecution in Europe.

37. Leeds Central Library Local History Library, 'Gypsy' references in cuttings from Leeds newspapers dated 'Leeds D.News 6.12.04' and 'Leeds & Yorks Mercury 7.12.04'

38. *Ibid.* (Photograph (by C B Howdill) and account headed *A Circassian Colony, Sojourn of a strange race of Gypsies in Leeds*, dated "Yorks. E. Post, 9.12.11')

39. A Fraser, *op.cit.* pp 231–233 with a photograph of Kalderash women in England in 1911.

40. See D Kenrick and G Puxon, *Gypsies under the Swastika*, 1995 for the account of the Nazi persecution of the Gypsies, which also belongs to the story of the Holocaust. Also C Supple, *From Prejudice to Genocide, learning about the Holocaust*, 1993.

41. T Acton, *op.cit.* p 131.

42. Gordon, *op.cit. The Caravan Sites and Control of Development Act*, 1960 introduced caravan site licences and prohibited caravanning on commons

43. *Ibid (The Caravan Sites Act* 1968 made the provision of caravan sites for Gypsies a duty for local authorities, but also enabled them to control unauthorised camping. Once authorities had provided some caravan pitches [which need not be related to the number of Gypsies in their area] they were allowed to apply for designation, which allowed them to move on Gypsies and Travellers not on the official site).

44. Private collection of newspaper articles cuttings etc. relating to the struggle for sites in the 1960s and 1970s.

45. *The Criminal Juctice Act and Public Order Act 1994,* aimed principally at New Age Travellers, removed the duty for local authorities to provide sites, gave them extended powers to evict unauthorised campers with extra police powers.

46. Catalogue of The Romany Collection, Brotherton Library, University of Leeds, Edinburgh 1962.

47. The Scott Macfie Gypsy Collection in the University of Liverpool is the other.

48. W J Halliday, *D.U.R. (Dorothy Una McGrigor Phillips) A Memoir*, 1969, p 2.

Sources

West Yorkshire Archive Service
Leeds District Office:
    Leeds Parish Registers
    Armley Park School Log Book ref. 2D 86/3 2D 86/40
Bradford District Office:
    'Itinerant' References
    Baildon Gypsy Fairs, miscellaneous references
Baildon Public Library:
    Posters etc of Baildon Gypsy Fairs
Leeds Central Reference Library:
    Leeds newspapers (on Microfilm)
Leeds Central Local History Library:
    'Gypsy' Newspaper cuttings
    Census Records, 1871
The Thoresby Society Library, Leeds:
    Bramley Parish Constable's Assessments and Disbursements for 1701

Select Bibliography

Acton, T *Gypsy Politics and Social Change*, 1974
Bogg, E *Lower Wharfedale*, 1904 (facsimile 1988 Smith Settle)
Burt, S *Criminal Leeds: from earliest records to 1879*, Leeds, 1985
Fraser, A The Gypsies, Oxford, 1992
Gill, L *Baildon Memories*, Otley, 1986
Gordon, R J F *Caravans and the Law*, London, 1978
Halliday, W J *D.U.R. (Dorothy Una McGrigor Phillips) A memoir*, 1969
Hartley, M and Ingilby, J *Life and Tradition in West Yorkshire* Otley, 1976
Hawes, D and Perez, B *The Gypsy and the State*, Oxford, 1995
Kenrick, D and Puxon, G *The Destiny of Europe's Gypsies*, Sussex, 1972

Kenrick, D and Puxon, G *Gypsies under the Swastika*, Gypsy Research Centre, University of Hertfordshire Press, 1995

Kirby, J W *The Manor and Borough of Leeds 1425–1662: An Edition of Documents* Thoresby Society LVII, 1983

Liégeois, J P *Gypsies: An Illustrated History*, 1983

Lumb G D *Extracts from The Leeds Intelligencer 1755–63* Thoresby Society XXVIII, 1928.

Margerison, S (ed) *Leeds Parish Church Register, First and Second Books 1572–1612* Thoresby Society Vol I, 1891.

Mayall, D *Gypsy-travellers in nineteenth-century society* Cambridge, 1987

Petulengro X *A Romany Life by Gypsy Petulengro*, London, 1935

Place, J B '*Woodhouse in the Manor of Leeds*' Thoresby Society, XXXVII 1945.

Supple, C *From Prejudice to Genocide, learning about the Holocaust*, Stoke-on-Trent 1993

Taylor, M *A Short History of Baildon,* 1987

Thorp, W H *John Rhodes, A Yorkshire Painter 1809–1842*, Leeds, 1904

The Armley Album, Leeds, 1980.

The Catalogue of the Romany Collection, University of Leeds, Edinburgh, 1962

CONTRIBUTORS

1: BRIGGATE AND ITS PUBS
AND
9: THE MOSAICS OF ST AIDANS

Barrie Pepper is a journalist who specialises in the pub and brewing scene, particularly of Yorkshire and Ireland. He writes a weekly column for *Pubspeak*, is the North-East correspondent for *What's Brewing?* and he contributes to several other magazines and newspapers. Barrie has written ten books, all but one of which are about pubs and beer. They include *The Old Inns and Pubs of Leeds* and *A Haunt of Rare Souls – the Old Inns of Yorkshire*. The odd one out was *A Goodly Heritage*, the history of St Aidan's parish church in Leeds. His latest publication was *The International Book of Beer* and his next one will be *Irish Pubs*, an illustrated almanac of the best pubs in Ireland. Barrie Pepper is the Chairman of the British Guild of Beer Writers and the founder Chairman of the International Federation of Beer Writers; and a member of the Brewery History Society and the Campaign for Real Ale. He is also an experienced travel writer and a former news producer with BBC Radio Leeds.

---

2. AT THE FLICKS

Robert Preedy has had a lifelong fascination with films and cinema buildings, and this led to Robert's first book *Leeds Cinemas Remembered* in 1980. Now ten books later he has recorded cinema history in all three Ridings. More recently another passion, riding roller coasters has led to his pioneering books on the subject. Away from writing he has also operated two cinemas. The first, the *Castle* cinema in Pickering, from 1984 to 1992 and now the Wetherby Film Theatre which reopened in 1994. His broadcasting career started with BBC TV in London, and then from 1976 at Yorkshire Television as a cameraman, sound technician, researcher, promotions producer and currently continuity announcer. He also broadcasts on local radio, including one show of his favourite music, *American Country*. Robert has a ten year old son.

---

3. A VISIT TO THE PALACE
AND
12. LOOKING BACK

June Walton Pearce was born in Stanningley, which joins Farsley village where she has lived most of her life, attending local schools and working at various jobs in the area. Her first job was as a 'burler and mender' at Woodhouse Sunnybank Mills. She is married with two children and two grandchildren. June enjoys many hobbies, mostly craft work dealing with flowers, embroidery, painting and sketching. She enjoys the privilege of singing in the church choir. Poetry has long been a love affair arising from schooldays; the flow and rhythm of words, and being  able to get inside the subject, particularly when writing about nature, giving her great pleasure and satisfaction. Some of June's poetry and prose has been published over the years. Many of her poems are written in response to friends' special requests for poems to commemorate particular special occasions.

---

4. A LETTER TO THE EDITOR: READERS LETTERS
TO THE LEEDS PRESS 1795–1850

David Thornton is a retired headmaster who regularly lectures on local history to adult groups and has written over thirty educational books for children, many on a local history theme. For ten years he has contributed weekly to the *Yorkshire Post*. Since retirement, he has

concentrated on writing articles for adults, producing political articles for *Issues in Focus,* and both scripting and presenting a fifty-five minute documentary video of the life of photographer Frank Meadow Sutcliffe. In 1990 his production, for visually handicapped people, of John Constable's painting of *The Haywain* won the Talking Newspaper of the United Kingdom national prize for the most original contribution to a talking newspaper. He edited *Leeds Cassette* talking newspaper for the blind from its establishment in 1975 until 1996. He holds a degree of Master of Philosophy from the University of Leeds where he is currently engaged in research for a doctorate on a local history theme.

5. THE HEATONS OF *CLAREMONT*

Dorothy Payne with her husband Brian, has produced several books of photographs of old Leeds, published by the Leeds Civic Trust. A long standing member of the Yorkshire Archaeological Society, she was their Publicity Officer for thirteen years. For the past twenty-eight years she has made a detailed study of the Society's headquarters, *Claremont,* and many of the neighbouring houses in Little Woodhouse. It was this interest in *Claremont* which started her research into the Heaton family and its descendants and her long search for their family records.

6. ST CHAD'S, A HOME FOR WAIFS AND STRAYS: A HISTORY OF HOLLIN HALL 1895–1996

Samantha Fisher was born at St Luke's Hospital, Bradford on 15 May 1961. She moved to Leeds with her family when she was three and grew up in Roundhay. She went to Talbot Road Primary school, Allerton Grange Middle School and Roundhay High school, completing her 'O' and 'A' levels. Samantha left school and started work at Austicks Bookshop in Leeds city centre, where she worked for nine years. Whilst working there she attended night school, taking classes in maths, computing and business studies. Her interests are many and varied. She

loves walking and wildlife, swimming, riding and archery. More sedentary interests include reading, writing, cake decorating, piano and crafts in general. Samantha now lives in Weetwood, Far Headingley with her husband and five children, Calico cat Haida and Alsation-cross Holly. She is currently working on a science fantasy novel.

7. NOTHING BETTER: A SHORT HISTORY OF THE CITY SCHOOL OF COMMERCE

Lynne Stevenson Tate was born in Bradford, brought up in Pudsey, has lived in Farsley since 1970 and worked in Leeds since 1971. A life long interest in history resulted in her gaining a BA Honours, concentrating mainly in English and History, from the Open University in 1995, while continuing to work full-time as an assistant manager at Austicks Bookshops in Leeds. She is married to Michael and they are both active in their local church. Lynne is in the process of collecting and transcribing a series of women's oral histories from the residents of the area where she

lives. These she hopes one day to turn into a book in their own right. Lynne is also the editor of *Aspects of Leeds*.

8. WOODHOUSE MOOR

Edna Bews was born in January 1916, and went to Blenheim School  in Leeds. She left at the age of fourteen and eventually got a job in Hitchen's department store in Briggate, where she stayed until conscripted to A V Roe in Yeadon in January 1941. Edna stayed there until March 1947 and then left to work in the claims department of an insurance company that had been evacuated from London due to the war. The company returned to London in 1948 and Edna was asked to join them at the Head Office. She stayed in London until 1965 when she came back to Leeds and worked for a short time at the Ministry of Pensions. In 1966 she returned to work for her old insurance firm at their Leeds branch until she retired in 1980. She now lives in Farsley.

10. BRAMLEY TAKES OFF

Anthony Silson has always lived in Bramley, although he crossed the  Pennines to study at Liverpool University. His interest in Bramley's history heightened as a result of redevelopment, and led him to write a book *Bramley: Half a Century of Change*. From St Peter's School Bramley he went to West Leeds High School where regrettably he had to choose between history and geography. He became a geographer and subsequently taught in Barnsley, Bradford and Leeds and has had several geographical articles published. His recent retirement has enabled him to devote more time to his historical interests. In 1996 he contributed a chapter to *Railways Around Whitby vol 2*, an area which interests him almost as much as Bramley

11. THE BEGINNINGS OF GOTT'S MILL IN LEEDS

John Goodchild, M Univ, is a native of Wakefield and was educated at the Grammar School there. He has been active in local historical research since about the age of thirteen, and is the author of some 140 books and published essays on aspects of history of the West Riding. He was the founder-Curator of Cusworth Hall Museum near Doncaster, and subsequently Archivist to Wakefield MDC; in his retirement, he runs a Local History Study Centre at Wakefield which houses his immense collection of manuscripts and research materials, and which is open to all  to use, free of charge by appointment. Mr Goodchild holds an honorary Master's degree from the Open University, awarded for academic and scholarly distinction and for public services. Outside historical research, his interests lie in Freemasonry and in Unitarianism – and in his dog.

13. THE LEEDS JEWISH COMMUNITY: A SKETCH OF ITS HISTORY AND DEVELOPMENT

Murray Freedman is Leeds born and bred and was educated at Roundhay School and the University of Leeds. He is married with three daughters and a grandson. Since retirement from dentistry some eight years age, he has devoted much of his time to research into local Jewish history and demography. He has produced a number of books and articles on these and allied subjects (he jokingly refers to them as products of a misspent retirement!) and his work on national census returns has, by chance, lately involved him increasingly in genealogy. He now  regularly deals with enquiries from all over the world from people with

Jewish roots in Leeds. Finding he still has some time on his hands he has gone back to university and is currently studying for an MA in Modern Jewish Studies.

14. GYPSIES IN LEEDS LOCAL HISTORY

Freda Matthews worked as a teacher in primary and special education in Leeds for forty years. She joined the Leeds City Council Travellers' Education team in 1987, visiting Gypsy sites with her mobile nursery bus until her retirement in 1992. A keen local historian, she has continued her research of Gypsy history, as well as the history of the Little Woodhouse area of Leeds where she lives. She would like to dedicate this article to all the Travelling families she met during her happy time as a teacher on the *Leeds Nursery Bus*.

ENERAL INDEX

Valorum 1947 30
el Reformatory Band 85
ens Act 1905 167
hambra Orchestra 23
ied Breweries 12
RP- (Air Raid Precautions) 90
GC Students Magazine 102
mbi 36
BC TV 30
ckett & Co 82
ue Angel 36
ue Diligence 14
ulton & Watt 144,148
adford Chamber of Commerce 4
adford Girls Secretarial College ,102
itish Archaeological Institute 65
itish Association 65
itish Legion 172
itish Lion 26
itish Medical Association 65
rnham Scale 100
rton's previously Montague rton & co 171
aravan Sites Act 1968 192
mbridge Local Examination 65
entrakaylian 102
artists 39
hildren's Union 82, 85
ristus Consolator 85
holera 47, 50
urch of England Society 77-92
nemascope 30
nematograph Act 1938 28
nerama 26,30
rcassian Gypsies 188, 190
olumbia 26
ommercity 102
ok's Tours 71
orn Laws 42
orporation Act 1930 184
ouncil for the Yorkshire College
imean War 115-6
riminal Justice Act 1994 192
addy Long Legs 26
efiance 16
bb Lupton 63
rcks & co - Manchester 49
sease 50
ducation 50-1
ducation Act 1870 169-170
18 98
gyptians 176-7,180-1
gyptians Act 1530 177
ntertainment Tax 1939 27,29
os 26
xclusive 26
aculty of Teachers in Commerce ,100
enton - Manufacturer 49
estival of Britain 117-8
x & Butchers 26
eemasons 102
iendly Society 172

Fry's chocolate 26
GCE examinations 106
Gone with the Wind 36
Good Old Days 21
Granada ITV 30
Grand National 21,26
Great War see World War I
Gypsy 175-195
Gypsy Carnival 186-190
Harrogate Technical Institute 104
Highflyer 14
Holocaust 191
Huddersfield Examiner 103
Huddefield Technical College 95
Hyam & Co - Samuel 166
Ideal Homes Exhibition 118
Income Tax 41
Ind Coope 18
Inquisition - Spanish 161
Invitation to a Gunfighter 26
Jackson's Guide to Leeds 18
Jackson - Manufacturer 49
Jane Eyre 15
Jewish Chronicle 166
Jewish Housing Association 173
Jewish Institute 189-190
Jewish Welfare Board 172
Johnson & Crawford Hick Messrs - Architects 119
Kalderash Gypsies 190
Keep an Eye on Amelia 30
Knights Templar 21
Lady of Woodbank 59
Leeds and Wakefield Brewery 12
Leeds Astronomical Society 114
Leeds City Council 90
Leeds City Fire Brigade 14
Leeds Civic Trust 164
Leeds Civil Service Institute 94
Leeds Conservative Journal 41
Leeds Corporation Health Committee 184
Leeds Gazette 41
Leeds Hunt 113
Leeds Independent & York County Advertiser 41
Leeds Intelligencer 7, 39-41,44,46,49,53,147,178
Leeds Jewish Board of Guardians 167
Leeds Jewish Representatives Council 172
Leeds Jewish Tailors', Pressers' & Machinists' Union 168
Leeds Literary Society 58
Leeds Magazine 41
Leeds Mercury 7,14,37-46,49- 51,53,54,57,85
Leeds Models' Prize Band 114
Leeds Motor Club 116
Leeds Patriot 42-3, 52
Leeds Philosophical & Literary Society 51,58
Leed Rotary Club 103
Leeds Savage Club 20
Leeds Temperance Herald 41
Leeds Times 39-42,46,53

Leeds Travellers Education Service 175,191
Leeds Wednesday Journal 41
Leeds Workpeople's Hospital Fund 173
Let's Switch Off and Talk 32
Life of Christ 23
Local School Boards 169
London Chamber of Commerce 97
London Corporation 109
Luddism 42,53
MGM 26
McQuat & co 13
Marks & Spencers 164,169
Marlbeck Tailors 99
Melbourne Brewery 12
Merchant of Venice 161
Murray - Manufacturer 49
Musgrave & co 136
New Century Pictures 28
New Realm 26
Northern Music Hall 33
Northern Tutorial Services Ltd 103
Opera North 22
Order of St John of Jerusalem 21
Our Gang 36
Paramount 26
Parliamentary Reform 42
Paton & son 80
Pease & Heaton 59
People's Charter 39
Peterloo 42
Peveril of the Peak 14
Pola Maid 26
Prostitution 42-5
Public Health Acts 184
Quakers- Society of Friends 16
Quota System 1927 27
RKO Radio 26
Rank 26
Rebel Without a Cause 30
Red Rover 14
Renown 26
Republic 26
Riot Act 14
Rock Around the Clock 30
Royal Academy 68,74,123
Royal Commission for Schools 65
R.S.A - Royal Society of Arts 97
Rust Henry 120
School Certificate 106
School of Accountancy 94
  Banking 94
  Insurance 94
Self-Help 7
Smith Samuel -Brewery 13
Speakers' Stones 113-4
Sturges & Co - Bowling Iron Works 148
Swarthmore Adult Education Centre 60
Tetley & co Joshua 22
3-D 30
Thoresby Society 7,21,177

Thing The 24
Three Stooges 36
Trade Unions 172
True Blue 14
True Briton 14
United Artists 26
University Extension Lectures 62
University Middle Class Examination 65
Victorian Society 7
Walt Disney 26
Warner Brothers 26,34
Weslyan Centenary Fund 139
West Leeds Amusements 25,29
Woolworth 15
Woodhouse -Feast 7,111-2
Workhouse 78,167
Worlds Fair - Chicago 80
World War I 93-4,115-6
World War II 94,100,102,104,192
Wormald & Fountaine 143
X Certificate 23,30
Yiddish 169
Yorkshire Archaeological Society 7,58,69
Yorkshire College of Housecraft 90
Yorkshire Evening Post 7,32
Yorkshire Ladies Council of Education 62
Yorkshire Post 7,85,102-3,144

INDEX OF PEOPLE

Ackroyd Joseph 136
Acton Thomas 191
Adams John 13
Alexander II 168
Ashcroft Dame Peggy 165
Astaire Fred 36
Atkinson John William 62-63,70
Atkinson Marion (nee Heaton) 59,62-3,70
Austick brothers 107
Baines Edward 39,41-42,53
Baker Mr 21
Balfour Lady 78
Barker John 134
Barker Samuel Snr 134,138
  Samuel Jnr 138
Barran John 166-7
Barrett Rev HD 78
Barter Miss 89
Beard Mr 146
Beatrice HRH Princess 61
Beckett Earnest William MP 78,82-85
  Lucille 82,84-85
  Lucy (ne Lee) 78,82-84
  Muriel 82,84
  Ralph 82,84
Bellhouse Alfred 11-12
Benjamin Israel 162,164
Bentley Ann 101-102
Betjeman Sir John 18,123
Bogg Edmund 18,179,182
Brangwyn Sir Frank 8,119-123
  Rodney 120

Bronte Charlotte 15
   Patrick 39,53
Brotherton Lord 192
Browning Elizabeth Barrett 61-62
Bryan Matthew 146
Burn Henry 48
Burt Steven 178
Burton Montague 172
Butler Hon. Henry 85
' C Mary ' 98
Calverley Sir Walter 15
Capewell Miss 103
Carr John 148
Carey Most Rev George 123
Chaplin Charlie 21
Charles James 69
   John William 69
Chartres & Honeyman 94
Clues Arthur 103
   Muriel (nee Wood) 104-107
Colehan Barney 21,33
Cook HE 'Bert' 103
Cook Thomas 65-71
Cookson Jonathan 146,150-1
Cromwell Oliver 161
Crump WB 152
Cudworth John William 16
Cudworth William John 16
Darrieux Danielle 30
Davies Bette 36
Defoe Daniel 9
Dibb Mr 63,76
Dors Diana 118
Doyle Maggie 185
Edward VI 177
Edward VII 114
Elizabeth II 123
Fairburn Andrew 59
   Sir Peter 59,64-5
Fairfax Sir Thomas 109
Farrar William 138
Fiennes Celia 9,15
Fitch Mr 65
Fountaine Widow 144
Fraser Angus 190
Friend Herman 166-7
Freeborough Jessie 96,100
Gable Clark 36
Garbo Greta 36
Gardener Mr 148
Gascoigne Mr 75
Geldard John 178
Geneste Rev Mr 14
George III 16
Gibb Mildred 122
Goldman William 34
Gott Benjamin 8,49,139,143-8,152-3
Graham James 133
Haddock Joseph 44,48
Hainsworth Abimelech 136
   Joseph 136
Halstead Jack 97,100,104
Haley John 135,138-140
Hardwick Rev FN 85
Hare Dr & Mrs 74
Haxby John 50

Hazel Margaret 'Peg' 95
Healey of Riddlesden Lord Dennis 123
Heaton Alan Baldwin 69-70
   Anne 70
   Bereford Rimington 70
   Ellen 59-62,65,69-70
   Fanny 59,62-3,65-74
   Helen Francis 62,64-5,70,73
   Dr John Deakin 7,57-9,61,63,65-73
   John 58-9,70
   John -Stuff Merchant 59,64,69,70
   John Aldam 59-60,62,64,70
   John Arthur Dekeyne 65,68-9,70
   Lucy 70
   Marian 59,62,64,69,71-3
   Marian 'May' 64-5,70-73
Henry VIII 14,135
Hertz Martin 164
Hobson Mr 84
Holt Miss 75
Horsfall William 53
Howard Mr 90
Howdill Charles 190
Hoyle Rev JF 85
Hughes Arthur 62
Hume Joseph 39
Ibbotson JC 183
Jenner Edward 50
Jessop William 148
Johnston Mr A 89
' K Peter ' 103
Kaye John 53
   Leonard 95-7,100,102-3
   Norman 95,103
Kerr John 187
Kirkby Joan 178
Kitson Sir James 119
   Robert Hawthorn 119-20
Lancaster Joseph 50
Landon Miss 75
Lanza Mario 36
Leake Lawrence 100
Lee Joe 95,96,103-4
   Malcolm 104
   Mrs 84
   Thomas 46
   William P 82
Lintott Mr 73
Lister John 134,38
Lord Charles 134, 136-7
   Dennis 95
MacConnachie E 102
Manham Samuel 167
Marks Michael 169
Mary HRH The Princess Royal 118
Marsden Sir Henry 116
Marshall Mr 149-151
Mason Rev William 120
   William 136
Mayall David 183
Mellor - Luddite 53
Metcalfe Dorothy 102

Molyneaux Mr 18
Morley Ellen 59
Moxon Thomas 14
Myers Frederick 12
   Robert 130
Napoleon 42
Nimmo Derek 32
Oastler Richard 7,38
Oddie James 136
Oldham Irene 96,104
Pawson Thomas 134,138
Pease Mr 71
Peel Sir Robert 116
Pemberton Herbert 23
Perring Robert 41
Petulengro Xavier 187,189-190
Philip HRH The Duke of Edinburgh 123
Pickard Mr 128
Pickford Mary 26
Pickles Wilfred 33
Pitman Joseph 39
Place Francis 38
   JB 178
Plint The Misses 60
Pollard John 134,135,137-140
   Richard 135
Pritchard William 49
Ramsden Sir Walter 15
Rank J Arthur 30
Ratcliffe Dorothy Una (Dorothy McGrigor Phillips) 192
Reid Sir Thomas Wemyss 57-58
Rennie John 148
Rhodes John N 182,193
Richardson HE 96
Richmond Bishop of 85,119
Rimington Miss 64,70
   Roberts Janie 75
Rodgers Ginger 36
Rodgers Roy (& Trigger) 36
Rogerson John 128,133,137
   Joseph 136-7
   Thomas 134-140
Rossetti Dante Gabriel 59,61-2
Rudolph Edward de Montjoie 77
Rushforth Joyce 102
Ruskin John 59,61-2
Saville Sir William 109
Shakespeare William 161
Shaw Norman 60
Shylock 161
Simpson Mrs 16
Sinclair Mr 71
Smawleye Anthony 176-7
   Elizabeth 176-7
Smiles Samuel 7,39
Smith - Luddite 53
Smith Eliza 184
   Gypsy 187
   Lily 184
   Mark 138
Smyth Rev Dr 78,80,87
Southcott Joanna 40
Sparrow Sylvester 120
Spurr Robert 127-8
Stansfield Miss 78,84

Stead Thomas 134,138
Sturges Mr 148-9,151
Susman Herr 73
Sutcliffe Elixabeth 146
   John 145-8
Tait Archibald Campbell 78
Talbot Dr 85
Talford Field 62
Taylor Rev Samuel Munford 119
Tetley Charles Francis 20
   Joshua 20
Thorpe WH 182,193
Thorpe - Luddite 53
Thoresby Ralph 9,17
Thorwaldson Bertel 85
Turner George 40
   Joseph 62
   William 181
Unna Jacob Arnold 164
Varley Mr 139
Vaughan Frankie (Abelson) 21
Vernon Di 51
Vickers John 136
Victoria Queen 57,61,64,115-6
Wakefield Bishop of 85
Walshaw Rebecca 43
Waltham The Misses 60
Ward Sykes 64
Waterhouse Keith 21
Watt James 148
Wear Robert 146
Wellington Arthur Duke of 116
Whincup Lakeland 21
Whitelock family 18
Whitley Mr 138
William I 161
   IV 10
Wilson William 14
Wolfe Mr & Mrs 71
Wood Frank 95,100,103-4
Wormald Harry 146
Wren Alfred 22
Wright Griffith 41
Wyatt Mr 148
York Archbishop of 119
Young Mr H 90
   Sir Arthur 13

INDEX OF PLACES

Abbey Cinema 31
ABC Cinema 25,31
ABC Minors Club 23
ABC Shaftesbury Club 23
Aberford 181
Adam and Eve Gardens 114-5
Adel 84
Adelphi 10-13
Adwalton 131
Aire & Calder Navigation 143
Albion 10
Albion Street 26,116,185,190
Alhambra Picture Palace 23
Allenbrigg Mill 132-5
Alloa 80
Almshouses 111
Alwoodley 170

merica 29,166,168,175,191
ngel 10
mley 125,127,130,139,140,184,191
rmley Mills 152
mley Park 184
mley Town Street 184
ssembly Rooms 28,51
ustick's University Bookshop 108
ustralia 93,103
uthorpe Road 90
ack Nile Street 171
ack Rockingham Street 164-5
agley Beck 136
aildon 186-7
aildon Hospital 187
all's Hotel - Penzance 71
altic Ports 167
arnsley 6
asinghall Street 26
ath 72
attersea 120
attersea Park 117
ay Horse 10,16-8
ean Ing 8,143-6,152
eckett's Home 78,85
eckett's Park 117
eckett's Park Training College ,89
ede's Home for Boys 78,85,89
eeston 13,29
elgium 48
elgrave Street 164
elle Isle Mill (Westfield) 131-4,136-7,139
elle Vue Road 113
eth Hamedrash Hagodel rnagogue 171-2
erley 132
ngley 59,143
rmingham 144,148,161
ack Bull 111
ackman Close 179
ackman Lane 179
ackwell Ox 10
enheim Terrace 96,100
oomsbury -London 59
ue Angel 36
oar Lane 10,14,30,44
snia 190
oulogne 14
ay & Barrell 10
owling Iron Works - Bradford147
adford 14,50,59,96-0,109,133,162-5
adford Synagogue 165
amley 8,125-142,181
amley Baptist Sunday School *5
amley Fall 128
amley School 135
amley Swimming Baths 125
amley Town Street 137
eslaw 162
ckfields 184-5
idge Street 164
dgewater 71
idgewater Canal 143

Bridlington 68
Briggate 69,10-1,15,17-8,21,44,58-9,68,94,164,166,170
Bristol 71-2
Broad Yate 18
Brooke Street - London 73
Brotherton Library 192
Brudenell Road 113,117
Bruges 123
Buck 10
Bull & Bell 10,15
Bull & Mouth 10,14-5
Burley Mills 152
Butts Court 143
Buxton 14
Buxtons Yard 184
Calais 95
Calls The 10
Call Lane 15
Calverley 125,130
Calverley Bridge 129
Camp Road 170
Cape Mills 132-6,139
Capitol Cinema 31
Carlton Cinema 31
Castleford 181
Cathcart Street 109
Central Kaye's College - Huddersfield 94-5,102
Chapel Allerton 33
Chapeltown 50,170
Chapeltown Moor 17
Chatham 161
Chicago 80
Church of England Society for the Providing of Homes for Waifs & Strays 77-78
City School of Commerce 8,93-108
City Sqaure 25-7
City Varieties 21
Claremont 7,57-8,61-5,68-71,73-5
Claremont Nursing Home 69
Clarendon Road 63-4,114
Clarkes College 96,100
Classic Cinema 27
Clifford's Tower 161
Clifton Cinema 31
Clock Cinema 25,27,31-2
Cobourg Street 188,190
College Road 111,114
Colton 179
Commercial Court 164
Commercial Evening School 94
Commercial Street 10,190
Company Mill 132
Corn Exchange Hotel 10
Cornwall 71
Cottage Road Cinema 23
Cottingley Springs 181,191-2
Coxley Mill 146
Crescent Cinema 31
Cross Green Industrial Estate 178
Crown Cinema 23,31
Darlington 185

Dallas 36
Danube 190
Darlington 185
Dawlish 71
De Grey College 96-7,100
Denison Hall 63
Derbyshire 146
Devonshire 71
Devonshire House - Harrogate 68
Dominion Cinema 31-3
Doncaster 6,185
Donisthorpe Hall 172
Doyle's China Shop 185-6
Duke of Leeds 14
Dublin 162
Duncan Street 10,22
Eagle Tavern 13
East Parade 26,57,64
Edinburgh 14,73
Electra Cinema 31
Eldon Terrace 96
Elland 34
Empire Theatre 32
Ermyne Street 181
Eton 82
Exeter 71
Fairburn House 65
Far Headingley 78,81
Farnley 125,130-3,139
Farsley 125,130
Fiddler's Elbow 22
Fleet Street 18
Forum Cinema 31
Fountaine Street 143
France 11,37,42,48,191
Gaiety Cinema 25
Gainsborough Cinema 31
Gaumont Cinema 31
George & Dragon 10,15
George Inn 14
Germany 161,162,168
Gildersome 127
Glasgow 143
Glebe House 77-81,88-9
Globe Foundry 132
Gloucester 72,161
Golden Cock 10
Golden Fleece 10
Golden Lion 10,13
Grand Central Hotel 15
Grand Hotel - Scarborough 68
Grand Theatre 21
Gregg's 94
Griffen 13
Grimsby 166
Guilford Street 152
Gypsy Corner 178
Gypsy Hill 179
Gypsy Lane 179
Gypsy Mead 179
Gypsy Street - Bradford 179
Gypsy Wood Close 179
Haddon Hall Cinema 31
Half Mile Lane 135
Halifax 14,133,146,148
Hamburg 166
Hampstead-London 60

Hanover Street 60
Harehills 8,32,119
Harewood 13
Harrison's Arms 21
Harrison Street 21
Harrogate 68,75,104-5
Havre 38
Howarth 53
Headingley 21,34,90,103,125,127,130,133
Headrow 143
Hexham 146
Hillary Place 96
Hillcrest Cinema 31
Hirst Mill 49
Holbeck 48-9
Hole in the Wall 10
Hollin Hall 7,77-91
Hollin Lane 81,88
Hollin Mount 90
Hollings Mill - Bradford 146
Holmesley Lane 179
Holland 49
Hollywood 24,27-30,32
Hook Moor 181
Horse & Trumpet 10
Horsforth 125,130,132-5,139
Hotel Inn 15
Hotel Tap Room 15
Hough House - Bramley 139
Hough Mill (aka Hough End) 131-4,138-9
House of Lords 45
House of Recovery 58
Howarth 53
Hudson Road 99
Huddersfield 94,98-100,143
Huddersfield Canal 146
Hull 14,16,166
Hunslet 15,23,127
Hunslet Lane 16
Hunslet Road 11
Hyde Park 109,114,117
Hyde Park Corner 111
Hyde Park Road
Ireland 162
Keighley 34
Kendal 14
Kennett & Avon Canal 146
King Street 26
Kingston Upon Thames 119
Kingsway Cinema 25,29,31
Kirkstall Road Multiplex Cinema 34
Kippax 75
Kirkgate 10,50
Kirkgate Market 169
Kirkstall 133
Kirkstall Abbey 133,135
Kirkstall Grange 82,84-5
Kirkstall Road 34
Lad Lane - London 14
Lady Lane 167
Lancaster Canal 146
Lands Lane 21
Langham Place 73
Leeds & Liverpool Canal 128,133,144,146

Leeds Bridge 9,13
Leeds Cloth Hall 133
Leeds Court House 45-6,48
Leeds General Infirmary 50,58,169
Leeds Grammar School 94
Leeds Industrial Museum 152
Leeds Lock Hospital 45
Leeds Medical School 169
Leeds Metropolitan University 86,90-1
Leeds Music Hall 73,193
Leeds Polytechnic 90
Leeds Rugby League Football Club 103
Leeds Town Hall 64,77,116
Leeds University 2,8,58,95,109,114,192
Leeds Water Works 146
Leopard 10
Leylands 167-171,190
Lido Cinema 31
Lincoln 161
Lithuania 167
Little Horton Lane - Bradford 96
Little Germany-Bradford 162
Little Templar Street 169
Little Woodhouse 7,59,61,76
Liverpool 127,143,148,166
London 13,15,21,46,59,61,73-4,77,117,120,147-149,161
Long Preston 37
Lounge Cinema 23
Low Road 23
Lower Briggate 15,44,164-6
Lower Headrow 10,41
Lupton's Fold 184
Lyceum Cinema 31
Lyric Cinema 25,29,31
Lyon 48
Majestic Cinema 31
Malvern 65
Malvern Cinema 31
Manchester 14,49,162,170,189-199
Mansion House - Bramley 137,139
Market Street 18
Marshall's Mill 43,49
Meadow Lane 13
Meanwood 127
Merrion Centre 164
Middle East 157
Middleton 179
Middleton Colliery 53
Middleton Railway 53
Mirfield 60
Monkbridge House 79,81
Monkbridge Road 81,90
Moor Allerton 169,178
Moor Allerton Golf Club 169
Moor Road 81,84
Moorside 79,81,84
Moortown 170
Moot Hall 9
Morley 181
Morley Street - Bradford 96

Morpeth 143
Myrtle Grove 113
Nag's Head 21
National Portrait Gallery - London 62
Netherton Hall - Wakefield 146
New Inn 15
New King's Arms 15
New Mills 132,134,138-9
New Road End 52
New Theatre 16,27
New York 82,166
Newark 73,148
Newcastle 119
Newlay 134,136
Newlay House 135,139
News Theatre 27
Newtown Cinema 31
Normandy 161
North Parade - Bradford 96
North Road-Huddersfield 94-5
North Street 13
Northern Institute 94
Odeon Cinema 25
Odeon Merrion Centre 31
Old Cheshire Cheese - London 18
Old George Hotel 10,15-6
Old Judges Lodgings- Little Woodhouse Hall 62-3,76
Old King's Arms 13-5
Old Red Lion 13
Ossett 127-8
Otley 109
Otley Road 84,89,90
Pack Horse 10, 21
Pack Horse Yard 20
Palace Cinema 31,36
Paris 48,57
Park Lane 53,59
Park Row 14,94
Park Square 60,94
Park Street 14
Pavilion Cinema 26,36
Penzance 71
Pitman's College 94
Plaza Cinema 28,31
Plymouth 71
Poland 61,165
Pollard Lane 135
Pontefract 15,50,178
Pontefract Lane 178
Portland Chambers 95
Portland Crescent 95
Portsmouth 161
Post Office 44
Princess Cinema 31
Prussia 49
Public Dispensary 59
Pudsey 125,127,132-133
Queen's Arcade 16
Queen's Cinema 31
Queen's Hotel 27
Raglan Road 109-111,115-6
Railway Station 76
Red Lion 13
Redcar 68

Regent Cinema 31
Reservoir Street 114,117
Rex Cinema 25,29,31
Riley's Court 47
River Aire 9-10,133-4,146
River Tyne 146
Rochdale Canal 146
Rodley 125,127,135,140
Romania 190
Rome 61
Rooley 131
Rose & Crown (aka Bink's Hotel) 10,16,17,19
Ross Mill 132
Rotherham 6
Rothwell 15,179
Rouen 38
Roundhay 82,170
Royal Hotel 10,15
Rudgate 181
Russia 61,168
St Aidan's Church 8,119-124
St Andre's 123
St Chad's Church 78-80,82,84-5
St Chad's Home for Waifs & Strays 7,78-92
St Chad's Primary School 90
St George's Church 59,70-1
St Helen's Mill 132-4,136
St John's Cottage 64
St John's Dyehouse 136
St Mark's Street 116
St Michael's College 64
St Petersburg 61
Saddle 10
Salamanca 52
Saltash Viaduct 71
Savoy Cinema 31,36
Scala Cinema 31
Scarborough 68
Selby 14,52-3
Serbia 190
Shaftesbury Cinema 31
Sheepscar 170
Sheffield 6,14,75,161
Ship 10,21
Skipton 34
Slipin 21
Slipin Yard 21
Soho Works - Birmingham 148
South Kensington 61
Southwark 119
Sportsmans Row 113
Stanningley 26,125,140
Stanningley Road 184
Star Cinema 31
Station Inn 72
Station Street - Huddersfield 95
Stonegate Farm 178
Strand Cinema 31
Street Lane Gardens 172
Suffolk Place - London 73
Sussex 123
Swan Street 21
Swarthmore Adult Education Centre 60
Tadcaster 13,147

Talbot Inn 10,17-8
Tate Gallery - London 62,70
Tatler Cinema 27,30-1
Taunton 71
Teignmouth 71
Theatre Royal 33
Thornton's Arcade 17
Thornton's New Music Hall 21
Three Legs 10
Tinkers Leas - Knowstrop 178
Tivoli Cinema 31
Tordmorden 146
Torquay 72
Tower Cinema 24
Towngate - Baildon 187
Trafalgar Street 170
Trinity College - Cambridge 82
Turk's Head 10
Turk's Head Yard 18
USA 167,190
Upper Headrow 10
Vicar Lane 162,167
Victory Cinema 31
Victory Hotel 15
Wakefield 14-5,152
Walton 181
Warsaw 61
Waterloo Corn Mill 132,139
Waterloo House 139
Waterloo Mill 131-4,138-9
Waverley House 63
Weatherby 181
Weetwood Primary School 91
Wellhead - Halifax 146
Wellington Bridge 53
Wellington Mill 131-4,138-9
Wellington Street 24-5,94,144
Westgate - Huddersfield 95
West Park 88
West Riding 38,49,105
Wetherby 34,181
Wheatsheaf 10
Whip 10,18,22
Whitby 68,82
White Cross 10
White Hart 10,18
White Horse 14
White Swan - Barney's 10, 21
Whitkirk 20
Whitelock's 17-18
Winker Green 184
Woodbank - Bingley 59
Woodhouse Lane 95,107,109,115-6,118,152,179
Woodhouse Moor 7,109-118
Woodhouse Square 57,60-1,63
Woodhouse Street 109
Woodlesford 179
Woodsley House 64-5
Wool Exchange - Bradford 59
Wormald Row 143
Wortley 23
Wrens 22
Ye Bush 9,15
Yeadon Cinema 31
York 16,148,161,178,181
York Street